"*Border Crossing* Brothas moves us one step closer to breaking down silo-based knowledge regarding the experiences of Black males. For the most part, the empirical evidence we have on Black males in education has been country- and context-specific, with little effort to share knowledge across borders. More recently, we are recognizing the imperative to learn from the collective knowledge generated globally about Black males if we want to move the needle. Ty-Ron M. O. Douglas should be commended as an early subscriber to this new movement."
—*Jerlando F. L. Jackson, Chair of the International Colloquium in Black Males in Education; Vilas Distinguished Professor of Higher Education and Director of Wisconsin's Equity and Inclusion Laboratory, University of Wisconsin-Madison*

"*Border Crossing* Brothas is a valuable resource to the field of education. If you have a real commitment in understanding how Black males globally navigate obstacles to success, you must read and implement the strategies presented so eloquently in this book to assist this population to reach their full potential. I strongly encourage you to pick up your copy today. This book is destined to become a classic."
—*Chance W. Lewis, Carolyn Grotnes Belk Distinguished Professor of Urban Education and Director, The Urban Education Collaborative, The University of North Carolina at Charlotte*

"In this poignant and engaging book, Ty-Ron M. O. Douglas draws upon his nuanced and in-depth research of the educational and social development of Bermudian men to theorize about Black masculinity in ways that honor the fullness of black males' humanity, complexity, standpoint, resiliency, and diversity. His work is relevant to the identity formation, learning, and success of Black males in various locales and across the African Diaspora. It also serves to help educators of all backgrounds better appreciate the educative value of home and community spaces for youth. This book is a wonderful contribution to scholarship on race, identity, and critical educational studies."
—*Camille M. Wilson, Associate Professor, University of Michigan*

"*Border Crossing* Brothas offers a critical, challenging, and provoking gaze into the 'real' education of Black Bermudian men—through the examination of previously unchartered learning spaces. Ty-Ron M. O. Douglas sets out a canvas for growing the institution and community learning of Black men everywhere beyond the broken schoolhouse."
—*Lou Edward Matthews, Director of Educational Standards and Accountability, Bermuda Public Schools*

D0860975

"This text crosses traditional scholarship borders in order to celebrate non-traditional spaces for gathering data in conducting research. The Bermudian context of this work asks the reader to embrace the study's findings in a specific geopolitical space while simultaneously asking how this text can be applied to the border crossing experiences in which African American men also engage. The book honors community-based pedagogical spaces and rightly situates the dynamic of teaching and learning especially for Black Bermudan males in venues that for some would be discredited and devalued for their impact. But it is exactly in those learning and teaching spaces where the finesse to cross borders becomes practiced and perfected. This text broadens, in every way, our perspectives on legitimate spaces for teaching and learning."

–Michael E. Dantley, Dean, College of Education, Health and Society and Professor,
Educational Leadership, Miami University

"*Border Crossing* Brothas is an exceptional scholarly work that utilizes the life experiences of Black Bermudian males to shed light on the ways that young men form identities, define success and utilize a variety of community-based educational spaces such as sports clubs, barber shops, and churches. Ty-Ron M. O. Douglas argues that the interplay of these processes, together with the influence of the aforementioned community-based educational spaces, equip Black males to navigate the borders in their paths to manhood and/or success. By foregrounding the narratives of Black Bermudian males, *Border Crossing* Brothas centralizes the agency of Black males, demonstrating their capability to identify and negotiate tactics to deal with borders such as family conflict, educational achievement, gender expectations, workplace inequalities, and institutional racism. The tactical footprints laid down by these Black Bermudian males during their struggles to overcome a variety of sociopolitical challenges serve as a pattern worthy of emulation for others in the African Diaspora. Consequently, *Border Crossing* Brothas will be welcomed by parents, professors, teachers, mentors, and community members throughout the African Diaspora who are seeking ways to aid young Black males as they traverse the challenging terrain to manhood."

–Theodore Francis, Assistant Professor of History, Huston-Tillotson University

"As a scholar and speaker who has transitioned from homelessness as a teenager, to completing my GED, and now having earned a Ph.D., I know the power of border crossing personally and professionally! In addition to my personal experience, I have dedicated my life to assisting others in border crossing and I am pleased that my friend and colleague, Ty-Ron M. O. Douglas, has made this his life's work. I am excited about [this] book and its capacity to provide access, perspective, and practical possibilities for others who desire to cross borders toward the fulfillment of their destiny!"

–Eric "ET" Thomas, Renowned Speaker, Educator, Author, Activist, and Minister

BORDER CROSSING *BROTHAS*

Rochelle Brock, Richard Greggory Johnson III,
and Cynthia Dillard
Executive Editors

Vol. 101

The Black Studies and Critical Thinking series
is part of the Peter Lang Education list.
Every volume is peer reviewed and meets
the highest quality standards for content and production.

PETER LANG
New York • Bern • Frankfurt • Berlin
Brussels • Vienna • Oxford • Warsaw

TY-RON M. O. DOUGLAS

BORDER CROSSING *BROTHAS*

BLACK MALES NAVIGATING RACE, PLACE, AND COMPLEX SPACE

PETER LANG
New York • Bern • Frankfurt • Berlin
Brussels • Vienna • Oxford • Warsaw

Library of Congress Cataloging-in-Publication Data

Names: Douglas, Ty-Ron M.O., author.
Title: Border crossing *brothas*: black males navigating
race, place, and complex space / Ty-Ron M.O. Douglas.
Other titles: Black males navigating race, place, and complex space
Description: New York: Peter Lang, 2016.
Series: Black studies and critical thinking; vol. 101 | ISSN 1947-5985
Includes bibliographical references and index.
Identifiers: LCCN 2016030613 | ISBN 978-1-4331-3539-2 (hardcover: alk. paper)
ISBN 978-1-4331-3538-5 (paperback: alk. paper) | ISBN 978-1-4539-1922-4 (ebook pdf)
ISBN 978-1-4331-3556-9 (epub) | ISBN 978-1-4331-3557-6 (mobi)
Subjects: LCSH: Blacks—Bermuda Islands—Race identity. | Blacks—Bermuda Islands—
Social conditions. | Blacks—Bermuda Islands—Interviews. | Masculinity—Bermuda Islands.
Men—Bermuda Islands—Attitudes. | Men—Bermuda Islands—Interviews.
Classification: LCC F1640.N4 D68 2017 | DDC 305.38/89607299—dc23
LC record available at https://lccn.loc.gov/2016030613

Bibliographic information published by **Die Deutsche Nationalbibliothek**.
Die Deutsche Nationalbibliothek lists this publication in the "Deutsche
Nationalbibliografie"; detailed bibliographic data are available
on the Internet at http://dnb.d-nb.de/.

The paper in this book meets the guidelines for permanence and durability
of the Committee on Production Guidelines for Book Longevity
of the Council of Library Resources.

© 2016 Peter Lang Publishing, Inc., New York
29 Broadway, 18th floor, New York, NY 10006
www.peterlang.com

Printed in the United States of America

To the memories of Ivy "Ma" Richardson, "Granny Mary" Wilkinson, Henry "Papa" Thomas, Louise "Nana Louise" Jackson, Bernard "Uncle Jack" Jackson, Mandell "Hillside" Hill, Barry Richardson, Mother Burruss, Papa Burruss, Ronald Burruss, and Johnny Barnes—men and women whose lives, legacies, and love inspired me to be a border crosser and bridge across time and space.

To my sons, Jalen and Essien, and my brother, Jeron—border-crossing *brothas* in their own rights; Black males who are learning all they can, serving all they can, and being all they can daily.

To every reader of this book who desires to live beyond narrow colonial identities and oppressive constructs. Your life, your history, your voice … your story matters!

Finally, if you've ever dreamed of *playing Cup Match*, climbed a loquat tree, or *gone fishing off de' rocks*, this book is dedicated to you.

CONTENTS

Appendix B: Methodology   179
Appendix C: A Conceptual Model of FREEsearch,
            FREEach, and FREEdership   185
Appendix D: 30 Keys/Cs to Cracking Community Codes
            and Classrooms   187

            Bibliography   189
            Index   199
            About the Author   209

ACKNOWLEDGMENTS

I have been blessed with a supportive community of mentors, colleagues, and scholars who have contributed to my professional and academic journey. I would like to acknowledge my grade 2 teacher at Paget Primary, Mrs. Rochelle Furbert Bean, who assured me that I was "likeable and capable," and encouraged my love of words by tolerating my declaration—as a precocious 7 year old—that she was "being facetious." I am also grateful to the other formal and informal educators in the various schoolhouses and community-based pedagogical spaces in which I was nurtured: "I am because we are." I am particularly grateful for the educators, colleagues, mentors, and friends at Bermuda College, Oakwood University, the University of Alabama in Huntsville, and the University of North Carolina at Greensboro (UNCG) who helped me foster a love of learning. In particular, I am grateful for Dr. Camille M. Wilson, whose sage counsel, professionalism, and friendship helped create a foundation for me to emerge and blossom as a scholar. Dr. Tyrone C. Howard is more than the contributor of the Foreword to this book—he is an admirable Black male leader who has modeled for me what I hope to be as a mentor to the next generation of scholars. At UNCG, the University of Missouri, and the many organizations with which I am associated, I have encountered numerous colleagues and students who have stretched me as a theoretician, inspired me as a thinker, and embraced me as a friend. Thank you! This project would not exist without each of you.

My sincere gratitude must be extended to the 12 border-crossing *brothas* who participated in this study. From each of you I drew wisdom, strength, and perspective. Your insights and stories inspired me to write and live with greater purpose. Thank you to my prayer line brothers and my accountability partners, inside and outside the academy. I am a reflection of the cadre of amazing men in my circle.

Living with purpose is possible in large part because of my loving and supportive family. I thank *my bride*, Bobbie. You are and will always be "My rib, My love, My Eve." To my *fellas*, Jalen and Essien, I am grateful for the tangible reminders that my first and highest calling is to my role in our home. Thank you for the impromptu football (soccer) games and the crashing sound of drums that draw me from the computer to learn more intimately what fun and fatherhood is all about. I love you both! I am also especially grateful to my dad, Stanley, my mother, Lucy, my sister, Zakiya, and Nana Bean for your love and support. Thank you to my papas, aunts, uncles, friends, and the rest of *the Village*.

Finally, thank you to God for the wisdom, strength, and opportunity to complete this project. With each day, I come to know and experience Proverbs 16:3 with greater clarity: "Commit your works to the Lord, and your thoughts will be established."

CREDITS

Portions of Chapter 2 were previously published as Douglas, T. M. O. (2012). Resisting idol worship at HBCUs: The malignity of materialism, Western masculinity, and spiritual malefaction. *The Urban Review*, 44(3): 378–400, and Douglas, T. M. O. (2016). Black fathers as curriculum: Adopting sons, advancing progressive-regressive black masculinity. In L. Bass (Ed.), *Black mask-ulinity: A framework for black masculine caring*. (pp. 93–107). New York, N.Y.: Peter Lang Publishing. Reprinted with the permission of *The Urban Review and Peter Lang Publishing*.

Portions of Chapter 3 were previously published as Douglas, T. M. O., & Peck, C. M. (2013). Education by any means necessary: An historical exploration of community-based pedagogical spaces for peoples of African descent. *Educational Studies*, 49(1), 67–91 and Douglas, T. M. O. (2014). Conflicting messages, complex leadership: A critical examination of the influence of sports clubs and neighborhoods in leading Black Bermudian males. *Planning & Changing*, 45(3/4): 311–338. Reprinted with the permission of both *Educational Studies* and *Planning & Changing*.

Portions of Chapter 4 were previously published as Douglas, T. M. O. (2013). Confessions of a border crossing *brotha*-scholar: Teaching race with all of me. In D. J. Davis & P. Boyer (Eds.), *Social justice and racism in the college classroom: Perspectives from different voices* (pp. 55–67). Bingley, U.K.: Emerald Publishing Group Ltd. Reprinted with the permission of Emerald Publishing Group Ltd.

Portions of Chapters 4 and 7 were previously published as Douglas, T. M. O., & Witherspoon-Arnold, N. (2016). Exposure in and out of school: A black Bermudian male's successful educational journey. Journal manuscript. *Teachers College Record*. 118(6), 1–36. Reprinted with the permission of *Teachers College Record*.

FOREWORD

DR. TYRONE C. HOWARD

In Gloria Anzaldúa's (1987) important work on the "Borderlands," she offers what she calls an *"autohistoria"* which she refers to as a genre of mixed media, comprised of personal narrative, *testimonio*, factual accounts, *cuento*, and poetry—that repudiates equilibrium just as the *Borderlands* from which Anzaldúa comes. According to Anzaldúa, the Border is an alterative space or a "third country" whose history has been told primarily through an Anglocentric lens, which she attempts to disrupt through a feminist analysis. It is in this prism that Anzaldúa challenges readers to understand the importance of a particular type of consciousness that can be culturally, politically and socially liberating. According to Anzaldúa this consciousness entails a "shift out of habitual formations: form convergent thinking, analytical reasoning that tends to use rationality to move toward a single goal … characterized by movement away from set patterns and goals toward a more whole perspective, one that includes rather than excludes" (p. 101).

It is against this backdrop in search of a greater consciousness that we see Ty-Ron Douglas heeding Anzaldúa's call for crossing borders, interrogating space, place, and race and seeking the creation of a new narrative; but this time for one of the more marginalized populations globally—Black men. This timely work offers its readers a new narrative as told by those who have been historically on the margins socially, economically, politically and

educationally. Douglas offers a new narrative that defies traditional boundaries and categories to elucidate transformative accounts of how populations
affected by the horrors of colonialism, patriarchy, and racism continue to
thrive and resist the vestiges of conquest. In *Border Crossing Brothas: Blacks
Males Navigating Race, Place and Complex Space*, we hear the voices of strength,
resilience, vulnerability, inquisitiveness and resistance of young Black males.
At a time when Black males continue to be over policed, under educated, and
grossly misunderstood, Douglas provides a compelling and inspiring account
of how to humanize these young men. Yet, he offers this insight not from the
perspective of policy makers, political pundits, or social media, but from the
men themselves. This work does not offer simplistic interventions and solutions, but a highly nuanced combination of frameworks and analytic tools
that delve deep historically and contemporarily into the reality of Black men
in Bermuda. The need for humanization of Black males has long been one of
the missing pieces of the project called democracy. At a time when nation-
states continue to make claims of inclusivity, justice, and freedom, listening
to Black males offers a counter-story that disrupts the egalitarian tale as told
by countries across the world. There is need to challenge this reality and only
by capturing the voices, experiences, and hopes of Black males can we capture
authenticity in acceptance and global justice.

Douglas' work is important because it challenges us to think about Black
life, identity, education, and manhood historically, and within a diasporic
context. In the United States, when the emancipation proclamation was
signed in 1865 it formally ended one of the most brutal and inhumane projects in human history—the institution of slavery. Though rejoiced by many
at the time in the United States, the global impact of three and half centuries of enslavement had left its dreadful footprints on countless nations
whose remnants are still felt today. The human costs of slavery have been
well documented, but also critical are the spiritual, political, economic, psychological, cultural and colonial affects that slavery left on millions of people of African descent. Where the dialogues of slavery are concerned in the
US, much of it is on the descendants of enslaved Africans who made it to
North America. Often missing in the larger discussion around slavery is the
African presence throughout the voyage from the continent of Africa to the
Americas. A perusal of the geo historical treks of slavery would show that
the port stops throughout the journey resulted in only 4–5% of enslaved
Africans ever reaching what is now the United States. Understanding the

complete legacy of slavery would entail being mindful that by some accounts as many as a third of stolen Africans ultimately settled in Brazil and northeastern parts of South America. Equally important is that by some estimates half of enslaved Africans found themselves in what is now referred to as the West Indies, and its northern and southern regions. Given that the majority of stolen Africans found themselves situated in Caribbean nations and surrounding territories, the experiences of these populations are germane to the complete story of slavery. To the far north of the West Indies we locate the country of Bermuda. A small island where Douglas situates this masterful work, and challenges us to expand the Black male narrative. Throughout this work he encourages us to understand the long-lasting influences of colonial domination, and how it has, and continues to influence the African diaspora. Moreover, building on the work of Kimberle Crenshaw (1989), Douglas nicely situates the salience of intersectionality in a manner that helps readers to reflect on how race, gender, masculinity, and immigration continue to be a confluence of dynamic social identities that are often under theorized and researched where Black life is concerned. Frantz Fanon (1961) reminds us about the long lasting affects of colonialism and the damage it continues to inflict on its victims. He adequately described the psychological violence against the colonized that has been perpetuated by the settlers. He surmises that colonialism hinges in part on the acceptance by the colonized of their inferior status. It is challenging this inferiority status and deficit based accounts of Black male identities that Douglas seeks to disrupt with the voices of Black males whom he refers to as *border crossers*. This inferiority is economic and social, it is political and educational, and it can have a profound affect on identity formation.

By using the context of being a *border crossing brotha-scholar*, Douglas engages us in his own *mesearch*—the study of his own personal experiences and journey—to extrapolate pedagogical possibilities that can be replicated, altered, or institutionalized toward the healing of others that share in marginal identities. In this way, Douglas provides readers with a glimpse into the effects of postcolonial and border theory and reminds readers that Bermuda as an English colony still suffers from many of the same challenges as Black minds and bodies do in the United States, in that the quest for identity affirmation and confirmation is an ongoing pursuit. For Black males, the formation of a self-sustaining identity is often rooted in a narrowly defined construct of masculinity, which Douglas reminds us is fluid and complex. Moreover, masculinity as a contested notion, must be re-conceptualized and re-imagined in a manner that disrupts singular, reductive forms which ignores the multiple ways that masculin*ities* are embodied, explored, and experienced. The disturbing notions of masculinity held by many Black boys and men are defined in patriarchal, misogynistic, and materially based concepts and are often the source of Black men's inabilities to live, love, learn, and last in self-sustaining ways. These affects reverberate throughout entire Black communities across the globe. Douglas provides us with cogent accounts from young Black men who are challenging these notions in formidable ways that are full of struggle, yet plentiful with possibility and a determination to be difference makers in their homes, schools, and communities.

Douglas explores the essential question of "How do Black Bermudian males form personal identities as they journey from boyhood to manhood?" This question is salient because it is one that continues to defy Black people the world over. In a world steeped in white supremacy, patriarchy, homophobia, and xenophobia, far too many Black males are looking to identify spaces and places for their person hood to be honored, recognized, affirmed and uplifted. Instead of imposing colonial frames on these young men, what Douglas does is compellingly provide the space for these young men to be the authors of their stories, to craft their own narratives, and he does it in safe and sacred spaces that have long been pedagogical stages for Black men to grapple with the realities of life. Black churches, Black barbershops, sports clubs, and neighborhoods in Bermuda are situated as educative spaces for Black males and serve as the locations where Douglas engages this work. This work is sobering, yet hopeful, bold, yet distressing, and it conveys a series of possibilities that can serve as a platform for future research. As the United States continues to witness unprecedented diversity, the increasing influence of immigration is real. This reality will challenge researchers, scholars, and practitioners to rethink old frames, to challenge age-old axioms about various social groups, and to engage in praxis that is informed by our 21st century reality. Our reality is one where culture, race, identity, and global histories matter. To that end, Ty-Ron Douglas offers us a granular analysis and a pedagogic framework for how scholars need to re-imagine the telling of story and the crafting of narrative for marginalized populations. Not only does this work offer its readers a border crossing in the Bermudian context, but it offers us a crossing into the complexities of how we all must think about our work in our rapidly transforming global community.

References

Anzaldúa, G. (1987). *Borderlands: La Frontera. The New Mestiza*. San Francisco: Aunt Lute Books.

Crenshaw, K. (1989). Demarginalizing the intersection of race and sex: A Black feminist critique of antidiscrimination doctrine, feminist theory and anti racist politics. *The University of Chicago Legal Forum* 140: 139–167.

Fanon, F. (1961). *The wretched of the Earth*. New York: Grove Press.

INTRODUCTION

Context Matters

The lyrics to a popular Bermudian song, "Bermuda is another world, 700 miles at sea; and the way that people greet you is like a friendly melody," tagged with images of the beautiful beaches and crystal-clear water, make for a compelling marketing package for tourists looking for an escape into paradise. And yet, while Bermuda is stunningly beautiful, there are some lived realities for Black Bermudian families that ask more nuanced questions about the breadth of White supremacy and barriers of systematic oppression. Mincy, Jethwani-Keyser, and Haldane (2009), in their Bermuda government–sponsored report, "A Study of Employment, Earnings, and Educational Gaps Between Young Black Bermudian Males and Their Same-Age Peers," found that the prevalence of academic underachievement and the overrepresentation of Black Bermudian males in the penal system mirror findings on Black males across the African Diaspora (p. 2). The work of Mincy et al. (2009) is significant to this book project because their work documents key insights on the educational experiences of Black Bermudian males, such as the disturbing finding that over 50% of Black Bermudian males fail to graduate from the public school system.

Notably, the Bermuda Department of Statistics's *Report on the 2000 Census of Population and Housing* (2000) reveals that despite the fact that Black males account for 12,434 (25%) of the 49,465 "population aged 16 years and older," only 2,412 of Black males (19%) hold a technical, vocational, or associates degree, and a mere 1,243 (or 10%) hold a 4-year bachelor's degree or higher. When surveying the global African Diaspora of industrialized nations, similar discrepancies for males of color in educational attainment, employability, and life experiences are revealed. Still, statistics on Black males in tertiary levels of education alone cannot adequately frame the context of schooling in Bermuda (Bermuda Department of Statistics, 2004). Certainly, light must be shed on the precollege systems, institutions, and experiences that influence young males, as well as the larger historical context that influences the status quo. There is a conspicuous divide between public and private education in Bermuda, forged from historical divisions in race, class, and culture. Although Black people in Bermuda account for 54% of the population, Black children make up over 90% of the population in a public school system that has experienced significant challenges and changes in the last 30 years (Bermuda Department of Statistics, 2006, 2010). These dynamics have associated and overt theoretical connections: deficit-based beliefs about the ability, motivation, and parental interest in the public high school; color/culture/*country* blindness in course material and assessment; and divergent reputations and resources that are steeped in White privilege and reinforced by the media outlets (Douglas & Gause, 2009; Iverson, 2007; Villenas & Deyhle, 1999). For instance, there is a perception that historically White private schools in Bermuda are privileged by preferential media coverage which contributes to more favorable reputations when compared to public schools and historically Black private schools. Notably, because Bermuda is a cultural microcosm of North America, the Caribbean, and Europe, research on Bermudian peoples has value and implications for understandings of world cultures and peoples. To this end, Hodgson (2008) asserts that "the black Bermudian experience has frequently shadowed the black American experience" (p. 4). In addition, as Gerald Horne notes in praising Swan's (2009) book *Black Power in Bermuda: The Struggle for Decolonization*, there is a case to be made "for the importance of Bermuda as a laboratory for political developments that reverberated significantly on the U.S. mainland." Drawing on my belief that education must be more broadly defined to consider the impact of spaces outside of the schoolhouse, I believe that Bermuda can be used as a "laboratory" for greater understandings of Western educational constructs and their effects on peoples of African descent—peoples who are consistently required to cross literal and metaphorical borders in order to participate in our global community and the dominant Anglo-centered paradigms that are privileged in our society. The privileging of the *schoolhouse* as the sole educative space for all young people and the lack of attention paid to learning spaces outside schools for Black people is emblematic of the cultural domination that must be considered if discussions of academic divides and achievement gaps are to evolve into more fruitful approaches and outcomes for all students; this includes consideration for how opportunity gaps are significant variables of student success. It is for these reasons that the study that undergirds this book, although conducted outside of the United States, also offers insights into Black masculinity and education in the U.S. and across the African Diaspora.

Amalgamating Lenses, Associating Literature

My conceptual framework for this book is grounded in the belief that amalgamating theoretical traditions can strengthen our capacity to examine the macro and micro operations of power and resistance in ways that illuminate nuanced workings of domination without confining those who are oppressed to victim status. For Black Bermudian males, there are multiple and competing dynamics that can simultaneously serve as sources of oppression and positionalities that can oppress: For example, men can use their gendered positionality to oppress women, even as these same men can be oppressed by the positionality of their *Blackness* and their *Bermudianess* in a Western or Eurocentric paradigm, since Bermuda is still a colonized subject of Britain. The coupling of postcolonial theory with border-crossing theory offers me analytic opportunities to agentically center a marginalized group—namely, Black Bermudian males—while exposing institutional and individual power in ways that resist tendencies to essentialize difference. How I define, amalgamate, and operationalize postcolonial and border theories is later explained in chapter 4. Notably, much like my unique examination of Black Bermudian male success, identity, and the roles of community-based educative spaces, the theoretical amalgamation of postcolonial theory and border-crossing (PCBC) theory in a Bermudian context is unprecedented. In both theory and practice, the conceptual framework of PCBC is a significant contribution to the body of research on Afro-Bermudian culture in general, and Black (Bermudian) masculinity in particular.

There is a limited body of research on Afro-Caribbean males. Studies on African Caribbean males in the United Kingdom highlight patterns of underrepresentation and underachievement similar to the findings of studies on Black males in the United States and Bermuda (Fitzgerald, Finch, & Nove, 2000; Gillborn & Gipps, 1996; Rhamie, 2003; Wrench & Hassan, 1996). Notably, there are distinct differences between my study and an important study conducted by Wrench and Hassan (1996), which sought to provide insight into the absence of Black men on college campuses by focusing on underachievement through the limited lens of 16- to 24-year-old Afro-Caribbean young men "in the years immediately following their schooling [with the hope of better understanding] the relationship between education and postschool experiences" (p. vii). For one thing, Bermudians are not considered "Afro-Caribbean" because of Bermuda's geopolitical positionality as a dependent territory of Britain in the middle of the Atlantic Ocean. Additionally, unlike Wrench and Hassan (1996), I seek to delineate between the narrow confines of schooling and the broad, pervasive concept of education—namely, the classroom of lived experience, which has shown signs of being more influential than traditional constructs of schooling—particularly for Black males (hooks, 2004a, 2004b; Ogbu, 2007). Additionally, it is not my intent to limit or define Black male success based on their presence on a college campus or their ability to "make satisfactory progress in the labour market" (Wrench & Hassan, p. vii). Instead, I have allowed the Black males in my study to define *success* for themselves. In this light, I have attempted to embrace the totality and variability of what my participants see as *education* and *success*—two concepts that are as complex and contextual as the interpretive communities and individuals who define them. If Wrench and Hassan's (1996) assertion that young Afro-Caribbean males have not been adequately represented in educational research is accurate, then this book—which explores the influence of community-based pedagogical spaces on the life journeys of Black Bermudian males—is not only revelatory but highly impactful for educators who want to understand how Black males form identities and define success. Although the body of research on Black males in general is growing, gaps still remain. Few scholars have explored the dynamics of identity formation within the context of their educational and familial experiences, and even fewer utilize qualitative research to investigate the educational experiences of Black males beyond the context of traditional schooling. Research on Bermudian Black men, whether qualitative or quantitative, is even more scarce. Thus, the findings and discussion in this book are germane to understanding how Black males are educated and socialized across the Black Diaspora.

Loaded Language

Understanding that language is loaded and language usage is both political and powerful, I wrestled with an appropriate label to describe the non-school–based educative venues I sought to learn more about through this project.

I have chosen to avoid the terms *nontraditional* and *alternative* to describe the non-school–based venues, in favor of the term *community-based pedagogical spaces*, which is used to describe non-school–based locales, institutions, forces, or methods that are utilized for educational purposes. From my review of the literature, I realized that although non-school–based spaces like the Black church and the Black barbershop may be seen and described as *nontraditional* or *alternative spaces* in mainstream discourse, or from the perspective of those in dominant schoolhouse settings, these spaces are actually *traditional* educative locales for peoples of African descent that continue to buttress and supplement the experiences that Black people have in the schoolhouse. In fact, this book is undergirded by my belief that worse than being minimized as mere social or educational appendages, the power of community-based educative spaces to impact the education of Black youth has been virtually ignored and underutilized. This cannot continue. This book affirms the educational relevancy of community-based spaces that have already been established as socially and culturally relevant for peoples of African descent.

For stylistic variety, I use several phrases interchangeably to describe non-school–based locales, institutions, forces, or methods that serve educational purposes, including *community-based pedagogical spaces*, *learning spaces outside schools*, and *non-school–based educative venues*. While the terms *education* and *community-based pedagogical spaces* have already been defined, it is necessary to clarify other key terms. For example, the labels *people of African descent* and *Black people* will be used interchangeably in this book. At times in this book, specific references may be made to subcultures within and across the Black Diaspora—for example, African American, Bermudian, or Caribbean people—but these references and descriptors are to be considered within the context and understanding of the complexities, similarities, and differences of Black identity development and not as attempts to reify the tendency to oversimplify people and the labels (mis)used to describe them. Additionally, the term *education* is broadly defined—drawing on the legacy and writings of scholars like Lawrence Cremin (1970) and Paulo Freire (1970) who embrace the breadth of what it means to educate.

Ultimately, using qualitative research methods and an amalgamation of border-crossing theory and postcolonial theory within the context of race (e.g., the work of Anzaldúa, 2007; Bhabha, 1994; Giroux, 2005; Hall, 1996; Hickling-Hudson, 1998), this book, *Border-Crossing Brothas: Blacks Males Navigating Race, Place and Complex Space*, explores the educational and socializing experiences of Black males in Bermuda to understand how Black males form identities, define success, and utilize community-based pedagogi-cal spaces (i.e., barbershops, churches, sports/social clubs, neighborhoods) to cross literal and figurative borders. Through the use of an oral history research design, I offer insights into how educational forces inside and outside of the schoolhouse influence their journeys. The book's subtitle alludes to a central theme of the book: the reality that the transitions, trajectories, turbulence, and triumphs of Black males are contextualized and complicated by the inter-secting elements of their racialized, spacialized, and place-based identities.

The book is organized into nine chapters. In the first chapter, I share how a *mesearch–research–wesearch* continuum undergirds my approach to this book. This chapter provides important context for the book by high-lighting aspects of my own journey and positionality as a border-crossing brotha scholar, and the intersections and implications for the work I seek to do through this project and beyond.

In chapter 2, I discuss common characteristics of Westernized masculinity, explore some nuances of Black masculinities, and examine and challenge how these particular brands of masculinity are transmitted in social institutions. Aspects of this chapter were originally published as an article in the *Urban Review*.

In chapter 3, I overview salient literature related to four community-based educative spaces—the Black church, the Black barbershop, the sports club, and the neighborhood—before briefly outlining aspects of Bermuda's educa-tional context. In discussing these *spaces*, I seek to confirm the veracity and complexity of various community-based locales of learning. Portions of this chapter appear in articles I originally published in *Educational Studies* with my colleague Craig Peck and *Planning and Changing*.

In chapter 4, I present the theoretical framework that I used in this study: postcolonial theory and border theory (PCBC). In particular, I discuss key elements and intersections of these theorizations to posit the amalgam-ated framework I used to account for the unique context and study I engaged. Portions of this chapter were previously published in the edited volume *Social Justice and Racism in the College Classroom: Perspectives from Different Voices*.

In chapter 5, the first five narrative portraits are situated within the first of the four main themes: *expectations*. Using a scaffolding approach, each sub-sequent chapter introduces the narratives of other participants to the book while also positioning their narratives within the theme that resonates most prominently with their life stories. For instance, chapter 6 builds on the foun-dation laid in chapter 5 by extending what we learn about *expectations* to consider the intersections between four participants' *experimentation/experiences in community-based pedagogical spaces*. In chapter 7, I introduce the final three participants to explore Black Bermudian male *exposure to life options*, and in chapter 8 I offer analyses and findings drawn from all twelve participants' narratives, including insights on their *expressions of identities*, and a conclusion that incorporates implications and recommendations for educational stakeholders. Of note, chapters 4 and 7 draw on an article I originally published with my colleague Noelle Arnold in *Teachers College Record*. Additionally, readers should know that pseudonyms have been used where appropriate throughout the manuscript.

It is my intent in this introduction to contextualize this book by outlining some of the distinct challenges that Black males face in Bermuda, and to assist you, the reader, in navigating this book. It is my hope that the contents of this book can inspire and incite critical thought, conversation, and action in classrooms, schools, universities, administrative chambers, and community-based settings around the globe. I have sought to avoid language and approaches that would objectify or position Black men as an *endangered species*. I have also sought to do justice to the conditions and contexts that frame significant aspects of the life journeys, personal identities, and educative experiences that Black males encounter, embrace, and endure. Certainly, this is a delicate balance.

· 1 ·

MESEARCH, RESEARCH, WESEARCH

Overlooking the iconic pillars on the University of Missouri campus from my 2nd-floor office window, I can't help but wonder if I ever would have graced this campus had I been raised by my biological father and family in St. Louis. I might easily have attended the same schools as Michael Brown, in the Normandy School District, and I often wonder if I would be a professor at the flagship institution of the state if I had grown up on Natural Bridge Road in St. Louis rather than on Ord Road in Bermuda, with pink sand and blue water nearby. The underrepresentation of Black male faculty on my campus would suggest that the answer is likely "no."

Undoubtedly, the tragic and untimely death of Michael Brown in Ferguson, in addition those of Freddie Gray in Baltimore, Tamir Rice in Cleveland, and the numerous other Black men and women whose lives have been taken prematurely by law enforcement, suggest that negotiating race, place, and complex space can be a matter of life and death for Black males. Certainly, the uprisings in Ferguson, Baltimore, and Bermuda have incited heated debate, reawakened fears, and exposed the naiveté of those who believe(d) we live in a postracial society. In many spaces where I function, racial tensions are as palpable and obvious as the reality that the average citizen has no idea how to reasonably respond. I define a "reasonable response" as thoughtfully urgent, culturally and critically grounded engagement that accounts for and draws on the best of what we know (*research*), the core of who we are (*mesearch*), and the needs and histories of those we serve (*wesearch*).

Sadly, it has become apparent to me that many administrators and leaders in Congress, colleges, churches, classrooms, and community organizations are not only unsure how to respond to the current racial and political climate; most are also unwilling to engage or uncomfortable with engaging in meaningful and healthy conversation about privilege, race, and racism. This means they are unprepared and unable to take meaningful and thoughtful action, in teaching and activism. While I do not claim to have all the answers, I do have a responsibility to respond in word, deed, action, and any other medium that can positively impact those with whom I have influence and access. I also have a responsibility to challenge you to do the same.

I am a *border-crossing brotha scholar*, a Black male academician who has traversed many geopolitical, cultural, and physical borders between Bermuda—my country of birth and rearing—and the U.S. university classroom. But the real story is that my mother was a 19-year-old college freshman standing in the abortion clinic when she felt a flutter in her stomach and *knew* she couldn't do it. Long before the opportunity to earn a Ph.D., I was moments away from being flushed down a toilet ... never to exist, much less write a book! Yet, my mother chose to keep me and face the scorn and disappointment of family and friends in Bermuda. Instead of returning home with a college degree, she returned home with me. Mom was kicked out of the church and scorned by those who had supposedly hoped for so much more for her life. Feeling abandoned but resolute, she did the only thing she knew to do as she gave birth to me alone: Her reasonable response was to lift me up to God and ask for His guidance in my life. And if I'm honest, the urgency in which I seek to live *mesearch* is grounded in my knowledge that [creating a] movement—a flutter—can be the difference between life and death. I've been negotiating race, place, and complex space from my inception in the womb.[1]

I share this vignette because while my resumé notes that I am a researcher, my personal journey challenges the assumption that *academic researcher* is my only salient identity. Beyond Western understandings of academic research, I live and engage in *mesearch*—the study of my personal experiences and journey—to extrapolate pedagogical and leadership possibilities that can be replicated, modified, or systematized toward the healing of others that share my marginal identities. This personal commitment may explain why many teachable moments emerge outside of academic spaces for me.

I am often invited to speak, and as I engage with audiences across the country and around the world, I typically share my *mesearch–research–wesearch* framework. Sharing this paradigm is more than a clever oratorical strategy. It is, instead, part of my authentic efforts to connect with people at the point of identity through the establishment of homophily—a common field of interest with members of the audience. Said differently, *mesearch* is the border-crossing, bridge-building aspect of the model; it's the link between the linear, the sometimes abstractness of scholarship (research), and the call to action and activism that is *wesearch*.

Border-Crossing Brotha Scholar

I am the product of *a village*—a community of people whose actions, advocacy, and love affirmed that I was not going to merely survive. I knew I was created to thrive. This village included a dad who loved me and adopted me as his own, and I proudly carry his last name; the village included a barber whose shop became a safe space for a dark-skinned Black male to feel good about how he looked and who he could become; the village included uncles, cousins, teachers, and mentors who sowed into my life. Because of my experiences, I look at students and people through a lens of hope, grace, and gratitude for the opportunity to have life and to teach toward a more abundant lived experience for others. My history … my story … *mesearch* undergirds my role as a *border-crossing brotha scholar* because it influences how I *know* reality and also influences my approaches to students who often confess that I am their first Black male teacher at any level. As a Black Bermudian/American male who has been afforded the opportunity to prepare future educators and leaders in the United States, I am both an insider and an outsider on multiple levels—a border crosser. Drawing from the work of West (1993), it is clear that for academicians, researchers, and scholar practitioners who see their work as part of a larger emancipatory project and/or a fulfillment of their "prophetic-Socratic" calling, it is essential that they themselves are first emancipated. I see my work in this vein.

To be clear, though I am a professor at a research-intensive institution, I am also a Black man, a husband, and a father of two Black sons, who understands his vulnerability and responsibility in this complex social milieu. I know what it is like to be feared—and to fear—because of the skin I'm in (Flake, 1998). I know what it is like to be both *seen*—hyper-visible because of my dark complexion in an ivory tower—and to be *scenery*—an imperceptibly

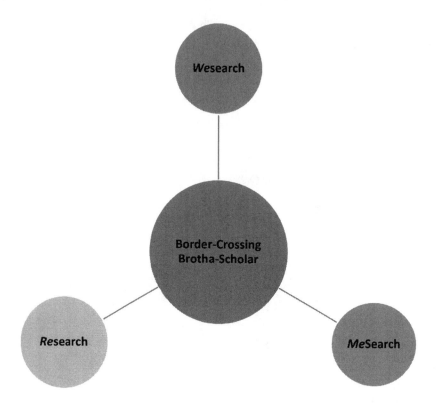

Figure 1. A Conceptual Model of a Border-Crossing Brotha-Scholar.

dark "unknown" in a large crowd on campus or in a corridor. And still, I teach and lead! And I teach and lead with all of me. To do this requires that I negotiate the personal, professional, and pedagogical continuum of *research*, *me*search, and *we*search (see Figure 1).

Research: Contextualizing Disproportionalities

Arguably, Barack Obama's tenure as president of the United States and Craig Cannonier's tenure as former premier and leader of Bermuda have added additional layers of complexity to understandings of the Black male *voice*, Black identity development, and Black masculinities. Specifically, although a Black man has occupied the highest political positions in the United States and Bermuda, the perspectives of Black males continue to be marginalized, and the condition of Black males in both jurisdictions continue to deteriorate: Black males are still disproportionately underrepresented in nearly every statistical category of *success*, and overrepresented in nearly every statistical marker of supposed *failure* (Children's Defense Fund, 2007; Ferguson, 2000; Harper, 2012; Mincy, Jethwani-Keyser, & Haldane, 2009).

Studies have highlighted the disproportionate underrepresentation of Black men on college campuses, the disproportionate overrepresentation of Black men in the prison system, and the disturbing rates of father loss, poor schools, school dropout, and troubled neighborhoods that impact families of color (Ferguson, 2000; Mincy et al., 2009). Similarly, the growing and persistent achievement gap in schools between White students and students of color is well documented (National Assessment of Educational Progress, 2007; Seiler, 2001). There are no simple explanations for these realities. What is clear, however, is that achieving educational equality in Western schooling has been an elusive goal, and the individual and political accomplishments of President Obama and former Premier Cannonier do not account for the systematic and systemic challenges that Black males face. In the United States and Bermuda, the *voice* of Black masculinity teeters on the brink of bedlam, as Black leaders speak for their nations while the voices and experiences of Black male citizens continue to be conspicuously limited in scholarly discourse. Moreover, there is great need for educators to better understand and reconsider the roles that non-school–based settings play in how Black males define success and form identities.

Although race is a social construct that cannot be supported biologically, it has real implications for how history and identities have been experienced and framed in the Western Hemisphere (Bonilla-Silva, 2006; Johnson, 2006; Wright, 2004). Race and Western racism were systematically created, and they are systemically maintained (Bonilla-Silva, 2006; Johnson, 2006; Wright, 2004). These realities have created a hierarchy where "blackness is visible and yet it is invisible, for I see that I cannot see it" (Kincaid, as cited in Wright, 2004). As a subordinate identity within the dominant Eurocentric context, "Black identity has been produced in contradiction" (Wright, 2004, p. 1). As such, Black masculinity is complex and contested. No two individuals, entities, or cultures are exactly alike, nor are the forces, power differentials, or *power-wielders* that influence them (Giroux, 2005; Villaverde, 2008). This reality is particularly poignant for cultures and peoples who have been historically and systematically subjugated and "Otherized." *Otherization*, which Villaverde (2008) describes as "the process of marginalizing difference, most times through negative stigmas and stereotypes" (p. 42), is a method by which those who hold dominant positionalities have sought to silence difference and stultify subordinate groups (Bonilla-Silva, 2006; Johnson, 2006). Since the legacies, vestiges, and *presentness* of institutionalized oppression must be understood as both collective and individualized forces that play out differently from person to person, culture to culture, and country to country, Black identity construction is as unique as it is diverse.

Educators who seek to make sense of the recent uprisings in cities like Baltimore and Ferguson in the United States and in Bermuda must first seek to understand the historical injustices related to educational access, social policy, and economic displacement of Black families. We must remember that every major institution in these countries was created when White supremacy was the overt, explicit national prerogative. Said another way, we currently operate in educational systems that were not created for the healthy development of people of color; legal systems were birthed in the belief that liberty and justice "for all" excluded Black and Brown people. Moreover, educational systems were complicit in slave labor and expanded with profits from chattel slavery (Wilder, 2013). These understandings can be difficult for some educators to consider as such assertions may be perceived as unpatriotic. As such, it is helpful to define key terms like *White supremacy* and *racism* in order to explicate its systematic and systemic nature.

In my work with students and teachers, we define *racism* as *race prejudice + social and institutional power* (Okun & Jones, 2000) and, White supremacy as *White racial domination* (Leonardo, 2004). These definitions push us beyond the narrow constructs of individual prejudices or personal achievements, and instead challenge us to consider how prejudice and privilege can be supported by access to power. We all have prejudices. We all make judgments of others based on previous (mis)information and assumptions. But how our prejudices are created and supported by social and institutional power varies greatly.

Research can help educators understand that race matters and racism persists. But not only that. Research also helps educators to realize that there are global dimensions to issues of White supremacy and racism, and the disparities and inequities we see in Baltimore also transcend the borders of the U.S. to affect countries across the Diaspora, like Bermuda. For example, as a keen follower of Bermudian news, I am aware of recent protests related to the economic disparities that Black Bermudian families face. I share with my students in the U.S. the reality that nearly every victim of gang violence in Bermuda has been a Black male, despite the fact that Black people make up only approximately 54% of the population (Bermuda Department of Statistics, 2010). This information is not shared to reify stereotypes about Black males; instead, I share this context so that students can begin to ask different questions about systems of oppression rather than highlighting the individual accomplishments of some (e.g., my privileged positionality as a professor from Bermuda) and criticizing those who have had trouble navigating the systems or simply have chosen to engage differently in a system they see as oppressive and contradictory.

These considerations have significant implications for our understanding of research and the questions and approaches we utilize as we engage in research. I often share the *fish in a lake* metaphor with my students to illustrate the tensions between individual successes or challenges and institutional issues: If one or two fish are found floating dead in a lake, the most prudent approach is to ask questions about the health of the individual fish. But when over 50% of the fish in the lake are floating dead in the water, it is prudent that we ask questions about the lake: the water, the ecosystem, the environment, and the conditions in which the fish must survive. Asking different questions with sensitivity about how and where oppression is being replicated opens new vistas of opportunity. Certainly, anyone who understands research also understands the significance of the questions we ask and the frameworks of those initiating the research. Rather than employing approaches that frame Black people as the problem, we need to ask questions that appropriately account for the systematic nature of racism and interrogate the deficit lenses that often frame Black males and Black communities as the source of the problem.

Doing *We*Search

Wesearch is where the intersections and disjunctures between *me*search (what you know experientially and epistemologically) and *re*search (what scholars have found, espoused, and written) meet and are activated for pedagogical, social, systematic, and systemic impact. Wesearch occurs when we allow our positionalities to push us to ask new questions about the people, possibilities, and problems that are most pressing for understanding and disrupting impediments to the health of marginalized communities. *Wesearch* is about the people. It's about hearing their voices and learning from their truths. None of the stages of the *mesearch–research–wesearch* continuum are meant to be static or narcissistic in nature. My work as border-crossing brotha scholar is always about the people and working toward personal, family, and community uplift. The study that undergirds this book on the journeys of Black Bermudian males is an example of *we*search.

Note

1. When I finished my master's degree, my mother and I exchanged places. I returned to Bermuda to begin my teaching career. My mother returned to the U.S. and Oakwood University to finish the degree she had to abandon in order to give birth to me. She has since finished her master's degree and she now has her sights on a Ph.D. Additionally, my grandmother returned to Bermuda College to earn a certification during this time. Ironically, my grandmother had also postponed her academic dreams when she became pregnant with my mother at age 19. She was also encouraged to have an abortion but instead chose to persevere and overcome the adversity.

RACE, PLACE, AND SPACE

Transmitting Black Masculinities

Chapter 2 is meant to serve multiple functions. First, I draw on relevant literature to further explain a few key terms and ideas that undergird this study. I highlight common characteristics of Westernized masculinity, explore the contours of Black masculinities, and discuss how these particular brands of masculinity are transmitted in social institutions. By establishing that masculinities are transmitted in social institutions such as schools, I prepared the terrain for my investigation into how social institutions outside of the schoolhouse can also be spaces where educative exchanges take place. Additionally, I challenge some of the historical constructs and literature that privilege particular brands of masculinity and threaten to reinscribe deficit-based models of Black masculinity. I conclude the chapter by overviewing the salient literature on the history of two non-school–based educative spaces, the Black church and the Black barbershop, before providing a succinct outline of Bermuda's educational context.

Defining "Man"

The Concise Oxford Dictionary defines *man* as a "human being" or "the human race," and *male* as "the sex [of humans, animals, and/or plants] that can beget offspring by performing the fertilizing function." In sharing these admittedly concise definitions, I do not seek to establish a unified or universally accepted understanding of these terms, nor do I fully exhaust all of the definitions and contexts of these terms—that undertaking would be beyond the scope of this study. Instead, I share the definitions for the purpose of exposing how power and privilege—which are central to masculinity (Connell, 1987; Edley & Wetherell, 1996; Kaufman, 1994; Kimmel, 1987)—are at work in the language and labels used to describe and understand identity. For example, the definition of *male* is a reflection of the gendering process that orders particular social practices, as these practices relate to the "reproductive arena, [which is] defined by the bodily structures and processes of human reproduction" (Connell, 2005, p. 71). Similarly, the fact that *man* can become an all-encompassing descriptor of the entire human race speaks volumes about who are the chief wielders of power (men) and who are most likely to be oppressed (often, women and children). But power and power differentials are never simplistic, and neither are critiques of power.

Power and Identity

Power, like identity, is much more fluid and contextual than the descriptions and definitions suggest. Power is described as a multifaceted, multilayered construct or force that encompasses the capacity to act or engage in action, the possession of legal, political, or social authority, and the ability to command, control, dominate, and liberate others and ourselves (Gause, 2008; Johnson, 2006). Foucault (1978) asserts that "power is not an institution, and not a structure … it is the name that one attributes to a complex strategical situation in a particular society" (p. 93). In this respect, power is not inherently positive or negative; it is a neutral force that can be employed for both positive and negative ends. Identity can be described as an amalgamation of "fluid and multiple" constructs that rest on and respond to "historical, political, racial, and sociocultural contexts" (Gause, 2008, p. xiv). One's access to power, then, is based on a continuum that is influenced by the multiple identities, roles, and associations that one embodies or is affiliated with—to the extent that men can be both wielders of power and subjects of it. Men can be oppressors even as they are simultaneously oppressed. For example, many men of color who draw on patriarchal traditions to oppress women in the home and the workplace are subjected to and victimized by Eurocentric paradigms in other spaces (Mutua, 2006). These understandings of power and identity must undergird any theory or discussion of masculinity, and must be considered with the understanding that language is complex (Edley & Wetherell, 1996; Hearn & Collinson, 1994). Moreover, language and identities are sociocultural constructs that can function as vehicles for the differential dissemination of power and privilege.

Defining "Masculinity"

Villaverde (2008) defines masculinity as "the character or performance of being male exemplified through different social, political, historical, and cultural practices. It is pluralized ... to capture the various ways one can embody and express one's gender" (p. 73). Said another way, there is no singular, unified, or universally accepted manifestation of masculinity. Whitehead (2002) reveals that masculinity is not a biological or genetic phenomenon, but is, instead, a "mere illusion" that, according to Threadgold and Cranny-Francis (1990), cannot be made biologically real through cultural representation or social construction. Furthermore, Hearn and Collinson (1994) opine:

> Particular masculinities are not fixed formulas but rather they are combinations of actions and signs, part powerful, part arbitrary, performed in reaction and relation to complex material relations and emotional demands; these signify that this is man. Masculinities are thus ideological signs of particular men of the gender class of men, particularly in relation to reproduction broadly defined. For example, 'being macho' (itself a racist turn of phrase) involves a variety of ideological signs of particular men of the gender class of men. (p. 104)

Moreover, masculinities are as diverse as the people who embody them and as varied as the strategies employed by those who perform them. It is significant for my study on the life experiences of Black Bermudian males to note that "[t]he interrelations of masculinities and social divisions are not just a matter of different structural locations of men. ... These forms of masculinities exist and interrelate at the different levels of personal biography" (Hearn & Collinson, 1994, p. 112). Thus, the oral history research I have conducted on Black Bermudian males is significant for understanding how the characteristics of Western masculinity play out in their unique life stories, their communities, and their culture.

Masculinities as Variables of Identity

As a variable of personal and collective identity, *masculinity* is fluid and complex. In fact, masculinity is a contested notion, in part because the term itself, in its singular form, ignores the multiple ways that masculin*ities* are embodied and experienced (Gause, 2008; Whitehead, 2002). Even in Western cultures, where particular brands of masculinity have been normalized, difference exists within and across masculine paradigms and the gendered language used to describe them. For example, men of color experience masculinity differently from Caucasian men, even as other dynamics, such as social class differences and sexuality, form multiple and competing layers of complexity and difference. For this reason, it is necessary to define *masculinity*, and to delineate between other terms like *man* and *male*. Understanding language is an important aspect of any analysis. Similarly, it is necessary to challenge some of the assumptions of Western masculinity in order to better understand how this particular brand of masculinity influences the experiences and understandings of masculinity for Black males in a colony like Bermuda.

Typical Notions of Western Masculinity

According to *The New American Webster Handy College Dictionary*, the West is understood to be synonymous with the economic, social, cultural, and geopolitical positionalities of Europe and the Americas. I cautiously accept this definition, with the understanding that this concept is problematic and symptomatic of capitalistic domination and essentialism; an in-depth interrogation of *Western* is beyond the scope of this discussion. Tangentially, it should be noted that Bermuda—the locale in which I conducted this research—is considered a part of *the West*, based on its status as a dependent territory of England and its geopolitical relationship with the United States.

In spite of the existence of other forms of masculinity, Western masculinity as a destructively aggressive and highly sexualized posture is the dominant and commodified brand of masculinity that many men subscribe to (Kimmel, 2006a, 2006b). Typically, Western masculinity is characterized as violent, domineering, and competitive (Hatty, 2000; Holliday, 1978; Kivel, 1992; Segal, 1990; Whitehead, 2002). The emphasis on the development of large and intimidating male bodies is consistent with the historically ingrained stereotypes of men as noncommunicative brutes (Connell, 2005; Kimmel, 2006a). In this light, it is not surprising that Bowker (1998) declares that 90% of violent acts are committed by men.

Other characteristics of Western masculinity include an emphasis on ownership, money, materialism, and possession of things (e.g, property, cars) and people (particularly women) (Connell, 2005; Whitehead, 2002). The maintenance of distinct roles and gendered biases, as well as an emphasis on control through sexual and physical prowess, are all common characteristics of Western masculinity (Kimmel, 2006a, 2006b; Whitehead, 2002). All of these dynamics frame how men define success and failure—those who do not measure up are often labeled and libeled as effeminate, unsuccessful, or unmanly (Connell, 2005; Gause, 2008). The psychological and physical toll of *not measuring up* according to dominant norms is another way that Western masculinity impairs how men see themselves and those with whom they share the world.

When one speaks of a masculine norm, this language is usually synonymous with Western masculinity, which is implicitly tantamount to *Whiteness* and particular (sometimes destructive) behavioral norms that are seen as fixed and inevitable rather than fabricated and engendered. Men and masculinities have been harmed by the belief that men are unemotional beings who are capable of expressing themselves only through acts of physical aggression and force. Black masculinities, in general, and Bermudian masculinities, in particular, are influenced by these typical constructions. In fact, Black masculinities have been Westernized to the extent that representations of Black masculinities can both subvert and support dominant masculinities. These dynamics are rooted in the way Black masculinity has been historically co-opted and transmitted in Western social institutions like schools.

Exploring Black Masculinities

The masterscript on Black men and Black masculinities in a Western context has a long and disturbing history that has been carefully crafted since the forced arrival of enslaved Africans on this continent. Documents and deficit doctrines, such as Daniel Moynihan's (1965) report *The Negro Family: The Case for National Action*, have served as vehicles for establishing and maintaining Black male stereotypes of abortment, apathy, and abuse (Dodson, 2007). The dominant views about Black men have proved especially problematic and persistent, particularly in social institutions (like schools) where Black men are conspicuously absent. Unlike the Black woman, who in spite of her horrific experiences at the hands of systematic oppression is believed to have maintained her parental instincts, the Black man's instinctual capacities have been misappropriated and his intentions misunderstood: He must not only overcome the dominant ideology that paternal instincts (for any man) are void of the capacity to nurture, but also prove that his instincts (as a Black man) are not animalistic, anarchic, and anti-intellectual (Dodson, 2007; Ogbu, 2007; Perkins, 2000). These dynamics affect the climate in which Black males form personal identities, which is significant to this book and the Black Bermudian males who shared their truths with me. The connections between these dynamics are learnings I sought to extrapolate from the narratives of the Black males you will meet in chapters 5 to 7.

It still must be noted that Black masculinity paradigms are not off the hook, and it would be disingenuous to reduce Black males or Black masculinities to victim status. In fact, Black masculinities paradigms are also complicit in their promotion of damaging ideologies of what it means to be a man. Gause (2008) speaks to the condition of Black masculinity by highlighting society's collective fascination with a narrow, performance-oriented brand of Black masculinity that commodifies the lives and images of Black male rappers and athletes for the sake of capitalistic gain.

A power analysis reminds us that capitalism is also raced as White. Thus, we are challenged to consider the difference between individual gains (by Black males) and institutionalized oppression (of Black communities). Although Black male bodies may be the *center attraction* of many musical and athletic performances, Black communities, in general, are not the beneficiaries of these performances. Butler (1999) speaks to the inscriptive and prescriptive power of performance and "performative" acts as expressions of gendered norms and ideologies that create and reify identities through their repetition on/through a body. By extension, Butler's (1993) point about "performativity" is particularly poignant within the context of a Black male body which has been the subject of dehumanizing, debilitating, and narrow historical, cultural, and ideological inscriptions/ideologies. For example, the deification of a Black male body leaping above a basketball rim to complete a dunk, partnered with the "signifying absences" of other diverse forms of positive Black male expression, create a context where "fabrications [in the form of *performative* acts] manufactured and sustained through corporeal signs" can demarcate limits to Black male dreams and identities (Butler, 1999, p. 173). Even worse, "performativity" as the incessant "reiteration of a norm … conceals or dissimulates the convention of which it is a repetition" (Butler, 1993, p. 283)—in this case, the slavery of Black males to athletic and entertainment systems that exploit their bodies and communities for economic gain. This reality is sadly evident in the way Black student-athletes are often exploited in schools and the media.

The athletic talents of Black students are often put on display in exhibitionist fashion, often with little regard for their academic futures and even less regard for what these narrow constructs of *success* mean for Black communities. These realities give credence to Gause's (2008) appeal for "new and different critiques" of the media; they also support his declaration that "a new public enemy number one, a sadistic and masochistic heterosexist black masculine cyborg [who is] devoid of emotion, thought, and remorse" has been created (p. 10). Plus, as Butler (1993) suggests, these dynamics are promoted in environments where the "theatricality" conceals the "historicity" of oppression so that not only are contrived identities inscribed on and often welcomed by *others*, but "a certain inevitability" becomes culturally ingrained and institutionalized (p. 283). For example, the athletic prowess or "performances" of Black male basketball players can distract and desensitize Black males and those who are entertained by their athleticism to the racist stereotypes and structures which suggest that *all* they can do or want to do is shoot a ball in a hoop. We all have a price to pay for these narrow, commercialized images of what it supposedly means to be a Black man. Moreover, Black masculinities are inextricably linked to hegemonic masculinities in content, creed, and character(istics). In the following section, I discuss hegemonic masculinity in greater detail in order to demonstrate how Western masculinity is normalized and how these constructions may impact the identities that Black Bermudian males construct.

Hegemonic Masculinity

The acknowledgement and emergence of hegemonic masculinity in the literature reflects the evolution of masculinity studies and the influence of feminist discourses, critical race theory, queer theory, and other theoretical and subversive paradigms (Brittan, 1989; Mac an Ghaill, 1996; Villaverde, 2008). Haywood and Mac an Ghaill (1996) describe hegemony as "a social and historical phenomenon, where the constitution of what is defined as 'normal' masculinity is a process of production" (p. 52). Of particular interest to my work on how Black Bermudian males define success is *hegemonic masculinity*, a concept that demarcates the contours of what it means to "be a man" in proximity to time and space, and at the expense or subjugation of other ways of being a man (Beynon, 2002; Connell, 1995; Kimmel, 1994). Connell (1995) is careful to point out that *hegemonic masculinity* "embodies … the legitimacy of patriarchy, which guarantees (or is taken to guarantee) the dominant position of men and *the subordination of women*" (p. 77; emphasis added). Hegemonic *masculinity* is also reflected in the fact that one of the aforementioned definitions of *man* ("the human race") encompasses the entire human species. This language, and the inherent tensions it creates, has already been addressed.

At this point, it is more important to note that the broad definition of *hegemonic masculinity*, coupled with the implicit and explicit norms of dominant people groups, has the capacity to render *Others* invisible; marginalized groups become part of society's null curriculum, as the values, beliefs, and expectations of dominant groups become the standard by which all *Others* are assessed. Still, as Whitehead (2002) warns, we must ensure that "complex gendered power relations are [not] reduced to an 'oppressor-victim' dualism, in which multiple subjectivity and self-identity processes are made invisible by the power of political categories of gender and sexuality and their ideological and material forces" (p. 99). Said differently, oppressor-victim dichotomies, as an extension of discourses of power, are far too simplistic. Essentialism—the tendency to truncate complex constructs, discourses, and identities into narrow, hegemonic monoliths (Anzaldúa, 2007; Keating, 2009)—is never a sufficiently critical tool for dismantling how power is differentially experienced and disseminated. We are often both oppressor and victim at the same time; at varying times and in various contexts, we are all complicit in and co-conspirators of the oppression of others. These dynamics are critical in light of my goal to better understand the various ways that Black Bermudian masculinity is experienced and expressed, particularly if I hope to avoid reducing Black males to a victim status or other narrow constructs of identity.

Transmitting Masculinities in Social Institutions

While this book focuses on the role of community-based educative spaces, it is necessary to establish the broad influence of institutions on masculinities. In so doing, I have provided a context that allows my participants the space to discuss institutions beyond the four non-school–based venues I focus on in this book. Not surprisingly, some participants mentioned other educative spaces, including schools. In addition, the influence of the media on the global community cannot be understated. In fact, through exposure to the global influence of Western media, men around the world are socialized to accept and embrace Western masculinity based on Western societal norms and institutional influences (Bahr, 1976). The influence of these socializing forces varies from nation to nation; still, it is clear that most social institutions around the world are run by men.

The schoolhouse is one such social institution that is controlled by men, even though there are more female teachers in classrooms than male. The structures, practices, and hierarchies in school systems reflect patriarchal ideals, and the individuals making national-, state-, and district-level policy decisions are more likely to be men. Specifically, in schools, Western masculinities are transmitted and oppression is propagated. In social institutions such as schools, typical characteristics of Western masculinity are seen in the competitive language and practices of government policies (e.g., Race to the Top), stereotypes, and gendered expectations (e.g., math, science, and *athletic sports* are for boys; English and the other humanities are for girls). Similarly, schools promote the distinct masculine characteristics of rugged individualism and meritocracy through the de-emphasis on dialogue and collaboration, and through the promotion of the "banking system of education" (hooks, 1994). In many ways, by focusing on standardized testing rather than on the process of thinking and learning, schools reflect and promote Western masculinity's preoccupation with the external features or *bodily* aspects of what it supposedly means to be a man. In this respect, social institutions are gendered male, just like Western masculinity (Connell, 2005; Franzway, Court, & Connell, 1989; Grant & Tancred, 1992). Connell (2005) takes it a step further by declaring that

> [t]he state ... is a masculine institution. ... [S]tate organizational practices are structured in relation to the reproductive arena. The overwhelming majority of top office-holders are men because there is a gender configuring of recruitment and promotion, a gender configuring of the internal division of labour and systems of control, a gender configuring of policymaking, practical routines, and ways of mobilizing pleasure and consent. (p. 73)

Moreover, the results-driven, production-orientated foci of schooling reflect the masculine ethos of competition and conquest. Males, in general, are socialized to place greater emphasis on their physical prowess than on their ability to share their thoughts and communicate their emotions effectively (Balswick, 1988). These characteristics of masculinity are certainly promoted in schools, much like the masculine notions of violence and domination continue to be promoted in school sports. As I sought to understand how Black Bermudian males form personal identities, define success, and utilize spaces outside of the schoolhouse, it was significant to recognize and acknowledge how social institutions like schools promote and transmit particular brands of masculinity.

Transferring Westernized Black Masculinities in School

Western masculinity is always about the domination and subjugation of Others. This Western masculine ethos of domination is evident in schools, where stereotypical ideologies about Black people, in general, and Black men, in particular, go largely unchallenged (Howard, 2000). For example, students are taught about the institution and legacy of slavery in America from a deficit-based lens that detaches the lived realities of Black people today from the generational residue of systematic oppression. In essence, Western masculinity renders the histories of people of color insipid or invisible. The historical existence of women and people of color is marginalized at the expense of *his-story* (Whitehead, 2002): Eurocentric and patriarchal narratives that exclude the contributions of *Others* characterize this masterscript, even as Western masculinity employs this same masterscript to impose and inscribe deficit, self-deprecating ideologies on Black males and the masculinities they embrace.

Significant to the identity formation processes that Black males engage in, Black students are often forced to piece together personal and national identities through history lessons that begin with their people in chains and bonds. Students are rarely challenged to consider what it means to be both African and American or African and Bermudian—for if they did, the rich history of a resilient people would provide a counternarrative to the discourse of textbooks and instructors (both of which are usually reflective of the dominant White power structure in identity or ideology). Schools become a vehicle for the transmission of a deficit-based brand of Black masculinity, which is an extension of Western masculinity (Gause, 2008; Howard, 2000, 2010, 2014). The absence of educators who challenge a defeatist reading of slavery is one way that the system of slavery (as a product of Western masculinity) is transmitted and maintained in schools, since "many if not most scholars working on African American families have argued or assumed that the African family heritage was all but obliterated by the institution of slavery" (Sudarkasa, 2007, p. 31). For Black students, then, resisting the debilitating features of Western masculinity becomes highly problematic without the tangible intervention of thoughtful educators who recognize and challenge the deficit doctrines (Howard, 2000).

The danger of the Moynihan Report (1965) and other deficit-based literature is not just the role it plays in maintaining institutionalized inferiority for Black people and institutionalized privilege of White people and Western masculinity. It also skews the perceptions and realities of gender roles, while creating wedges between Black men/masculinities and Black women/feminists. Two debilitating and debatable conclusions, as highlighted by Angela Davis (1981), exemplify the legacy of Moynihan's document:

> (1) The root of oppression was … a "tangle of pathology" created by the absence of male authority among Black people! The controversial finale … was to introduce male authority (meaning male supremacy of course!) into the Black family and the community at large; (2) [Because] slavery had effectively destroyed the Black family …, Black people were allegedly left with "the mother-centered family with its emphasis on the primacy of the mother-child relation and only tenuous ties to a man." (p. 13)

Both conclusions articulate a breach between Black masculinities and Black families. Still, it is the first supposition that is most relevant to this discussion, since it actually demonstrates how the intentions and actions of Black men can be framed and maimed by others based on a White supremacist paradigm. The exasperated tone of Davis's (1981) conclusion that "male authority means male supremacy of course" reveals how the oppression of White male patriarchy (Western masculinity) creates distrust in all men—not just White men. In the next section, I describe and challenge Mutua's (2006) notion of "progressive Black masculinities" in order to reveal how dominant notions of Western masculinity influence and intersect with the personal experiences of the men I studied and their visions for the types of men they want to be.

Critiquing Progressive Black Masculinities

Mutua (2006) provides a vision for "progressive Black masculinities" that reveals the insidious nature of hegemonic masculinity, through its distrust and a deficit-based analysis of Black masculinity. Her discussions of "ideal masculinity as domination" position African American men exclusively within an American context (p. 16). Like most school lessons on Black history, her analysis goes back only to Africans in America—there's no acknowledgement of what ideal Black masculinity might have looked like before Black men were subjected to American slavery and capitalism, or what it currently looks like outside the United States. In fact, she states: "Domination over others is one of the central understandings and practices of masculinity. Stated differently, normative masculinity is predicated on the domination of others" (p. 17). By couching masculinity within the capitalistic trappings of the American economy and American history, she reintroduces Black masculinity through a deficit lens and demonstrates how Black masculinities have been historically produced and framed within a Western context, before asserting theories of "progressive Black masculinity" that call for Black men to embrace and pursue inclusive and socially just aims.

While Mutua (2006) strives to assert a stance that is affirming of Black men, her willingness to lump Black masculinity into "the American masculine ideal" from the start, without fully acknowledging the histories, distinctions, and "multidimension[alities]" of "Black identity" in various contexts, reflects the social and institutional power of dominant notions of Western masculinity to subsume *Others*. Lack of consideration for the unique historical and cultural distinctions of Black identity and Black masculinity is still common practice in how social institutions, including schools, function. In many ways, these realities not only typify characteristics of Western masculinity, they also serve to truncate the paradigms and discourses that could open up larger spaces for *difference* to be heard and appreciated. Toward a clearer understanding of how the participants in my study have been affected by these dynamics, I designed a study that was open to the unique ways that each man described his life history and defined success: Specifically, my decision to ask my participants to "tell me your journey from birth to boyhood to manhood" and my insistence on not prescribing a particular definition of success in this study are evidence of my intentional efforts to allow the diverse Black male voices and experiences to be heard. Ultimately, data from these males contributes to theory on Black masculinity by situating the personal identities constructed by the participants within and across larger discourses of power and systemic oppression.

Schoolhouse Pathways

Schools continue to be key institutions for the transmission of Western masculinity. For example, school discipline practices are a primary means of transmitting Western masculinity and controlling those who do not comply with these standards. Ferguson (2000), who studied the disturbing schooling experiences of African American adolescent males labeled "troubled," explains it this way:

> The punishing system is supported by nothing less than the moral order of society—the prevailing ideology—which simultaneously produces and imposes a consensus about a broad spectrum of societal values, manners, presentation of self including style of dress, ways of standing, sitting, tone of voice, mode of eye contact, range of facial expressions. It is also assumed that the rules, codes, social relations, and

behaviors adjudicated by a school's discipline system are about the transmission and enactment of a moral authority from adults, who are empowered to transmit and enact, to children, who are seen as lacking the essential values, social skills, and morality required of citizens. (p. 41)

In light of my study on the experiences of Black males, it is significant to note that Black males are disproportionately flagged and punished for violating school rules and, by extension, the standards of Western masculinity (Ferguson, 2000; Wilson, Douglas, & Nganga, 2013). It is significant to note that the schoolhouse is one of the first institutional settings where students get prolonged exposure to the characteristics of Western masculinity; for a long time, most Western students have been introduced to the institutional force of the media. Still, the prolonged exposure to the institution of schooling can be a traumatic experience for students whose cultural capital is incongruent with the dominant masculine culture. Certainly, not only do these variables and spaces influence how Bermudian males define success and distinguish the borders to be crossed, but they also likely frame how success and border crossing are perceived, experienced, and resisted in schools and in community-based pedagogical spaces.

· 3 ·

WE *AIN'T* NO FOOLS

Embracing the Breadth of Education

Across the Black Diaspora, the history of education reflects the legacy of struggle, sacrifice, and oppression that has also come to characterize significant elements of the Black experience (Anderson, 1988; Du Bois, 1898/1973; Morris, 2009; Ogbu, 2007; Woodson, 1911). In fact, schooling and education for Black people have historically been two separate experiences that intersect at times, but always continue to function independently of each other (Shujaa, 1994). Moreover, the history of education for Black people is one that has consistently occurred outside of traditional schooling. This reality is not lost on many individuals within Black communities. For example, the term *educated fool* is commonly used in Black communities to describe a Black person who has been schooled within mainstream structures but lacks the cultural relevancy or *street smarts* to be an effective agent for and within his or her community (Shujaa, 1994). This language is rooted in the understanding within Black communities that traditional schooling experiences alone are not sufficient for preparing Black people for life, resiliency, and service (Frazier, 1973; Hale, 2001; Shujaa, 1994; Woodson, 1911, 1933).

Throughout their history, members of the African Diaspora have produced a strong heritage of accessing education through community-based pedagogical spaces. Slaves, for instance, established educational networks within plantations and used clever subterfuge to learn to read. They did so often at significant personal and collective risk, as many Southern states established laws that made the education of slaves a heavily punishable offense (Cornelius, 1983; Webber, 1978; Williams, 2005). Black Bermudian slaves not only used creative means to become literate, but they even "turned the tables on their white masters by adopting the very method Englishmen had traditionally approved: the written petition" to formally request freedom (Bernhard, 1999, p. 276). In the post–Civil War segregated American South, educational opportunities for African Americans were severely limited (Anderson, 1988). Author Richard Wright, who grew up within those conditions, described in his autobiography how he gleaned much of his education outside of schools (Wright, 1945). Furthermore, to counter systematic prejudice, as early as the 19th-century, Black-owned businesses such as barbershops became central fixtures in the Black community as educative spaces that encouraged and enabled intellectual engagement, economic development, and cultural resistance (Harris-Lacewell & Mills, 2004; Mills, 2005, 2006).

As the struggle for Black freedom emerged to challenge overt racist oppression, protest groups engaged in social justice efforts that had essential instructional elements. As reservoirs for the recruitment of laypersons and locales to mobilize participants, community-based spaces (e.g., Black churches) were essential to these freedom efforts. For example, from 1961 to 1966 in the American South, the Student Nonviolent Coordinating Committee (SNCC) used participatory workshops to introduce community members to nonviolent tactics. The organization put these lessons into practice through sit-ins, and taught "freedom songs" that served as a binding emotional force (Carson, 1995). SNCC "freedom schools" provided free instruction to students poorly served in segregated schools (Perlstein, 1990), while media coverage of the SNCC freedom schools (such as Watters's 1964 *New York Times Sunday Magazine* profile) instructed the broader nation that powerful change was underway in the American South. In the later civil rights movement era, the Black Panther Party used an array of institutions and initiatives, including their newspaper, schools, and use of mass media coverage, to deliver political education to a vast and varied audience (Peck, 2001; Perlstein, 2002). Traditional schooling settings were not appropriate locales for mobilizing these efforts; instead, learning spaces outside of schools were employed.

Not only does this notion of *space* inform our understanding of various community-based *locales of learning*, but there are also global and geographical implications that have impacted and continue to influence the mobilization of those engaged in freedom efforts for peoples of African descent. Suggesting how the pursuit of education outside schools crossed borders, Frantz Fanon (1967) stressed the essential importance of political education, broadly construed, to Black freedom efforts in Algeria. The Black Power movement of the late 1960s and 1970s was also vibrant and impactful in Bermuda due to the influence of activists like the Black Beret Cadre and Pauulu Kamarakafego (Swan, 2009). According to Swan (2009), the meaningful relationships that were sustained between Bermudian activists and "revolutionary organizations across the African Diaspora such as the Black Panthers," are emblematic of the strong and steady "voice of Black [Bermudian] dissent" that could often be heard amongst the bellows of Black activists from "the wider Black world" (xi). For example, John Hilton Bassett Jr., "the long standing chief of staff" of the Black Beret Cadre, "raised money by writing and producing plays," and much like "activities organized by the Black Panthers, he used the funds to feed the needy in the Black community" (pp. 98–99). In these respects, Black Bermudians have not only tapped into the tradition of accessing community-based pedagogical spaces for peoples of African descent, but they have also crossed borders by remaining connected to the larger struggles for political, social, and economic uplift for peoples across the Black Diaspora. This historical context was significant as I considered how Black Bermudian masculinities are informed by other global masculinities and what the findings of this study on Bermudian Black males could mean for other Black men across the African Diaspora.

Over the last several centuries, music forms such as spirituals, work songs, and jazz fortified and instructed generations of Black peoples (Lovell, 1939; Manuel, Bilby, & Largey, 2006). Today, hip-hop music has emerged from the neighborhood-spaces of urban communities and crossed borders as a powerful influence on Black and other minority youth and cultures throughout the world (Gause, 2008; Lipsitz, 1994; Love, 2012; Morrell & Duncan-Andrade, 2002). Some scholars have advocated bringing hip-hop into the classroom as a means to more effectively engage students who have struggled in traditional academic structures (Emdin, 2016; Morrell & Duncan-Andrade, 2002). Hip-hop artists have also consciously accepted and presented their role as cultural instructors, speaking from the often marginalized—though highly impactful—*space* of lived experience. Boogie Down Productions (a.k.a. KRS-One), for instance, released an album whose title, *Edutainment*, accurately reflected the artist's twin goals of entertaining the Black community while also educating it about prevailing social issues (Boogie Down Productions, 1990). Similarly, the history and educative power of other musical genres, like Negro spirituals (Lovell, 1939) and the consciousness-raising lyrics of Afro-Caribbean reggae music (Manuel et al., 2006), affirm that education through music has been utilized across the Black Diaspora as a space and vehicle for speaking truth to/with power.

In the following two sections, I review literature on two of the four educative spaces that I explored in this study: The Black church and the Black barbershop. As stated previously, part of the purpose of this study was to explore the educational relevancy of spaces that have already been proven to be culturally and socially relevant. This brief overview of the Black church and the Black barbershop provides historical evidence of the educational relevancy of these two spaces, while providing a context for the research I conducted on the remaining two spaces—the sports club and the neighborhood—in this study.

Educative Spaces Outside Schools: Focus on the Black Church

Religion has been an ever-present and consistently influential force in Black communities (McAdoo, 2007). As the pre-eminent institution for the expression of spirituality among peoples of African descent, the Black church has been historically active as a socializing space and support system for African Americans (Drake & Cayton, 1945; Du Bois, 1898/1973; Frazier, 1973, 1974; Hale, 2001; Hill, 1971; Johnson, 1934; Lewis, 1957; Lincoln & Mamiya, 1990; Martin & McAdoo, 2007; Turner & Bagley, 2000). The centrality of spirituality and religion for peoples of African descent is a nexus for the diverse cultures reflected in African, Caribbean, South American, and African American people, whose ancestors "relied upon an African-based understanding of life, death, and creation to help them adjust to an unpredictable social environment" (McAdoo, 2007, p. 98). Drawing on African patterns of "multigenerational" interconnectivity and the "fictive kin (nonrelatives who are as close and involved in the family as blood relatives)" (McAdoo, 2007, p. 98), the Black church has served as a buffer and bridge for the sustenance and uplift of Black people. More than that, as Hale (2001) asserts, "[t]he African American church is the most important institution in the African American community and is supported and controlled entirely by African American people. African American churches were burned and bombed during and after the modern civil rights movement because they represented black power, independence, and self-determination" (p. 155). Serving as a space where spirituality and education converge, the Black church has been and continues to be a reservoir and resource for educational advancement for Black people. C. E. Lincoln noted,

> Beyond its purely religious function, as critical as that function has been, the black church in its historical role as lyceum, conservatory, forum, social service center, political academy and financial institution has been and is for black America the mother of our culture, the champion of our freedom, the hallmark of our civilization. (cited in Billingsley, 1992, pp. 354–355)

Several scholars (Billingsley & Caldwell, 1991; Lincoln & Mamiya, 1990) have acknowledged that a top priority for many Black churches has been educational outreach programs, including tutoring initiatives, preschool/daycare, General Equivalency Diploma (GED) programs, and private elementary schools. Notably, the educational focus of Black churches is not new. From its inception, the mission of the Black Sunday school was to promote literacy amongst slaves, newly freed African people, and (later) young people who had not been prepared for college admission (Hale, 2001). The interactive relationship between spirituality and education for African Americans is evident in the fact that when many historically Black colleges were founded, Sunday schools were also established, and faculty members were obligated to serve as Sunday school teachers as well (Hale, 2001; Stokes, 1972). Similarly, the Black church has been an educational, oratorical, and artistic training ground. Lincoln & Mamiya (1990) assert that "[t]he first public performance seen or given by many black children often occurred in church" (p. 312). Many contemporary artists and musicians attribute their early musical development to experiences in Black churches.

Educative Spaces Outside Schools: Focus on the Black Barbershop

The Black barbershop is a powerful institution in the Black community (Harris-Lacewell & Mills, 2004; Hart & Bowen, 2004; Mills, 2005, 2006). As a profession, business entity, and center of socialization, the Black barbershop has been a central fixture in the Black community from as early as the 19th century (Harris-Lacewell & Mills, 2004). More than seeing their profession as a fiscal stepping stone, Black barbers used their influence and opportunities for the betterment of their community. In fact, Harris-Lacewell and Mills (2004) assert:

> From slavery to freedom, barbers and hairstylists have constituted the overwhelming majority of entrepreneurs in the African American community. Both as slaves and as free men, black barbers used both monopoly and a white consumer base to their advantage.

Their profession provided them with power, prestige, and status in the black community. These men did not use this status and wealth solely for individual gain. African American barbers often used their earnings to actively engage in uplift activities. (p. 164)

Woodson (1932) explained, "[t]he cause of the Race can get a hearing in the Negro barber shop more easily than in a Negro school. In the barber shop the Negro has freedom; in the school the Negro must do what somebody else wants done" (p. 1). This ethos of service and community accountability continues today through the dialogue, networking, and mentoring that takes place in many Black barbershops. As a community-based pedagogical space, the Black barbershop has become a sanctuary where Black men can find community, camaraderie, and culturally relevant discourse—or "meaningful everyday black talk" (Harris-Lacewell & Mills, 2004, p. 167). Reminiscent of the codes and spaces that allowed slaves to communicate beyond the listening ear of slave masters, the contemporary barbershop is a sociopolitical space where dialogue can occur beyond the confines of the workplace and the home. For many Black men, communication with employers and family members is a complex experience. Similarly, for many Black men, the Black barbershop is the only space where they will be in the company of other Black men exclusively (Harris-Lacewell & Mills, 2004).

Based on a study of sex-role socialization in a Black urban barbershop, Franklin (1985) noted that "a wide variety of issues are discussed in the barbershop, ranging from international crises to neighborhood ruckuses" (p. 971). Franklin further contended that the barbershop is a powerful educational space that can both damage and empower, depending on the clientele on a particular day. Specifically, Franklin offered the following findings from his research in an urban barbershop: (a) "masculinity is negotiated actively by adult males and passively by male youth" (p. 976); (b) "barbershop[s] literally capture the 'minds' of Black youth for one to two hours approximately two times per month," during which time "vulnerable Black male youth are exposed to a predominantly male environment which reveals 'expectations' held for them by a cross-section of males with whom these Black male youth identify" (p. 976); and (c) messages of "physical aggression" and defeatism, such as stories about Black male failure due to external constraints (e.g., the White man, society), are presented without reference to the successes of Black men (pp. 977–978). These findings suggest that those who seek to utilize the pedagogical potential of the barbershop and other community-based spaces must also acknowledge and address some of the detrimental practices and unspoken rules that exist in these spaces. Others have identified the barbershop as a non-school–based educative venue, although published studies focusing on the barbershop as a site for educational intervention research targeting African American men are scarce (Hart & Bowen, 2004).

Educative Spaces Outside Schools: Focus on the Black Neighborhood and Sports Clubs

The neighborhood is an influential socializing space for good, bad, and everything in between in Black communities. In Ferguson's (2000) study of adolescent Black boys raised in neighborhoods they self-identified as "bad," the young participants were clear on the influence of the neighborhood: "They [the boys] assumed that where you lived shaped the knowledge base that generated different modes of being in the world" (p. 104). The young men in Ferguson's study are not alone in their perceptions. In fact, Karenga and Karenga (2007) highlight the intersections between the community and the family, which are entities that can never be disassociated from the neighborhood or the larger implications for the wider society. They assert:

> Quality relations are the hub on which family, community, and society turn. ... Indeed, in a real sense, the community is an enlargement of the family and the family a smaller form of the community, with each reflecting and reaffirming the strengths and weaknesses of the other in a dynamic interplay. (pp. 8–9)

Certainly, the discussion of the connections between community, family, and society become even more significant when we consider that the Black neighborhood is an indissoluble construct of/within the Black community and Black families (Billingsley, 1968; Nobles, 2007).

Much like relationships in many Black churches, interfamily relationships in Black neighborhoods have also drawn on the legacy of the fictive-kin, which are strong familial-like connections between nonblood relatives (McAdoo, 2007). Although these practices are not entirely dissimilar to traditions amongst other ethnic groups, it should be noted that there are distinct intersections between membership or participation in a particular Black *neighborhood* and an associated Black *community*; in fact, the constructs of *neighborhood* and *community* are often synonymous in Black cultural contexts, where the neighborhood serves as the resting ground of community spaces like Black churches, Black barbershops, and sports/community clubs. These traditions are also grounded in the persistence of African family traditions among many Black families, where intimate extended family relations are often manifested in relatives living in close proximity to each other (within and across multiple generations). Sudarkasa (2007) speaks to the origins of this tradition:

> African families were traditionally organized around consanguineal [i.e., biological kinship] cores formed by adult siblings. ... The groups, which formed around these cores, included their spouses and children, and ... [t]his coresident extended family occupied a group of adjoining or contiguous dwellings known as a compound. Upon marriage, Africans did not normally form new isolated households; instead they joined a compound in which the extended family of the groom, or the bride, already resided. (p. 33)

Though this tradition of living in close proximity appears to be less prevalent among Black families living in Western, postmodern contexts, the neighborhood has historically served as a bedrock of *the village* that, together, raised the neighborhood children (Sudarkasa, 2007). This "strong family tradition" has persisted through the institution of slavery, "legal segregation, discrimination, and enforced poverty," even as this tradition also undergirds the relevancy of the neighborhood as a significant space for Black people (Franklin, 2007, p. 5). In fact, poverty within Black communities has often been an impetus for community sharing and accountability amongst neighbors in Black communities.

While Black families are still overrepresented amongst the poor, the diminution of extended family traditions in some quarters—and perhaps, the weakening of Black communities in general—may be partially attributed to the shift toward more individualistic ideologies amongst some Black people, as byproducts of their participation in and progression up the social ladder in Western capitalistic contexts. Still, poverty also has implications for *space*— or the absence of it—and *spaces*, which serve as socializing contexts. Toward a better understanding and appreciation for the role of community-based pedagogical spaces in the lives of the Black males I studied, Stack (1974) declares: "Social space assumes great importance in a crowded living area" (p. 7). The significance of this assertion becomes clearer when considered against the backdrop of poverty in many Black communities and the urban contexts in which many Black people are socialized. Additionally, the notion of poverty can be extended metaphorically to discussions of culturally relevant practices in schools, where *a pedagogical poverty* presides over students whose cultural norms are incongruent with dominant social constructs. The pedagogical and cultural marginalization often experienced in school by Black students (and other members of nondominant groups) not only affects their identities and their conceptualizations of success, it also highlights the value of spaces that facilitate resistance to oppression.

In Bermuda, the sports/social club is another community-based space that is utilized by Black males, although there is a lack of literature on the role of sports clubs. Ironically, it was an American anthropologist, Frank E. Manning (1973), who conducted the most exhaustive work on the Bermudian sports/ social club; in fact, Justus (1978) credits Manning as having conducted "the first anthropological study of Bermuda" (p. 434). In his discussion of the roles of sports/social clubs in Bermudian life, Manning (1973) appears to reflect his positionality as a non-Bermudian, though his description is relevant to discourse on the role of space and literal border crossing for residents of Bermuda:

> In Bermuda, as a small place, the outlet is very limited. There's only a few things you can do. You could become active in these clubs, or turn around and just hang around the bars or something like that. It's not too much to do in Bermuda. It's very small. You don't have the outlet like other parts of the world, where if you didn't belong to a club you could go somewhere weekends, out of state or something, and find other interests … If I hadn't been in club life, I probably would have ventured to go abroad. (as cited in Crooker & Gritzner, 2002, p. 98)

Describing Manning's work in Bermuda as an "important contribution to the study of New World black cultures," Justus (1978) reiterates assertions offered in this book about the value of research in Bermudian settings in better understanding Black culture. Drawing from the work of Manning, she further describes the bars of the sports/social club as "places where conversations between younger and older men are frequent, where older men express great admiration for younger men" (p. 434). In this book, I contribute to this area of research on the role of the sports/social club in the lives of Black Bermudian males.

The roles of Black churches, Black barbershops, sports clubs, and neighborhoods in Bermuda as educative spaces for Black males have not been sufficiently evaluated. In fact, research that investigates these spaces and Black masculinity within a Bermudian context is minimal. Although Bermuda is influenced by other jurisdictions in the global community, it is significant to acknowledge some of the unique contours of Bermudian culture. Bermuda's educational system is one such area that requires attention, in light of the educational focus of this book.

Evaluating the Bermudian Educational Context

Bermuda's educational system provides an interesting and important context for this study and the subsequent pathways taken by Black males. There's a perception that the leadership of education in Bermuda has struggled to restore the rigor and reputation of its school system amidst growing disdain, distrust, and disillusionment with a reform process that produced major upheavals in both the structure and philosophy of education in Bermuda. The resultant shift in the demographic landscape of schooling in Bermuda is underscored by the assertion that the gap in quality between public and private education is growing, as perceived by the community and reinforced by the media. This perceived gap in quality cannot be disassociated from the conspicuous divide between public and private education in Bermuda and, by extension, the insidious divisions in race, class, and culture in Bermuda. Typically, private education is synonymous with Whiteness and public education is synonymous with Blackness, even though some Black students attend private institutions. These conceptualizations alone can influence how particular notions of success are perceived: For example, students may be labeled based on the schools they have attended. Although the racial demographics in Bermuda reveal that Black people account for 54% of the population, Black children make up over 90% of the population in what some would describe as a struggling public school system (Bermuda Department of Statistics, 2006).

Prior to 1996 in Bermuda, elementary school graduates were required to complete a high-stakes examination called the *transfer (or 11+) exam* in order to determine which high school they would attend. Public schools were academically stratified, and students were funneled to one of seven public high schools based on their transfer exam stanine score. Only two of the seven schools were considered *academic* schools: The Berkeley Institute, a historically Black school, and Warwick Academy, a historically White school[1] (Bell & Bell, 1946; Christopher, 2009). The other five high schools (St. George's Secondary, Whitney Institute, Northlands Secondary, Warwick Secondary, and Sandys Secondary) had varying reputations, though—at the time of the restructuring in 1996— none of the remaining five high schools were considered academically viable.[2] This configuration was rife with problematic dynamics, including the fact that an 11-year-old student's educational pathway and future life outcomes were greatly influenced by her/his performance on one test. This is significant context for the study that I conducted. In many ways, the transfer exam was the proverbial fork in the road that funneled students from their childhood neighborhoods to various high schools and life paths. We all had to border cross. The extent and implications of these border-crossing experiences on our perceptions and (so-called) attainment of success, our personal and collective identities, and our life pathways are the foci of this study.

Since 1996, there have been significant changes to the public education system, including the introduction of middle schools, the elimination of the transfer examination, and the restructuring of various schools (Bermuda Ministry of Education, 1993; Christopher, 2009). While the major structural reforms continue to be debated in public circles, there has been widespread dissatisfaction with overall academic outcomes. Of note, both academic schools have undergone significant restructuring as part of or in reaction to the government's controversial reforms: Warwick Academy has returned to its roots by becoming a private school, while the Berkeley Institute has been controversially transformed into one of two mega (public) high schools.[3] While consideration should be given to the social, economic, and family contributions to the origination of gangs in Bermuda, there is a sentiment that the recent proliferation of gang violence in Bermuda is directly related to the challenges of the educational system. There are few clear answers. What seems clear is that masculinity and identity are complex constructions that are influenced by pathways to and from the schoolhouse, and the borders crossed along the way. Ultimately, as I developed this project on how Black Bermudian males cross (literal and metaphorical) borders, form identities, and define success, I was interested to see how community-based pedagogical spaces, Western masculinity, and the schoolhouse are positioned in my participants' narratives.

In the next chapter, I detail my conceptual framework. I review key theorists and literature pertaining to the two theories I amalgamate to create my theoretical framework: border-crossing theory and postcolonial (PCBC) theory.

Notes

1. Coincidentally, my slightly above average stanine score of 6/7 was sufficient for me to have the option of choosing either Berkeley Institute or Warwick Academy. My parents chose Warwick Academy against my wishes because they wanted me to "understand how the [White] system worked."

2. This statement is not suggesting that these institutions have not produced their share of successful and productive individuals—intelligent students who learned under the watchful care of thoughtful and committed educators. Certainly, success is broadly defined and contingent upon a number of factors inside and outside of the schoolhouse.

3. Some would contend that Berkeley's status as an "elite" *academic* school has been compromised, leaving public school (mostly Black) students with diminished options (Christopher, 2009).

AMALGAMATING THEORIES, CONSTRUCTING A CONCEPTUAL LENS TO STUDY BLACK BERMUDIAN IDENTITY DEVELOPMENT

In general, identity construction is a complex and contested process (Gause, 2008; Giroux, 2005; Johnson, 2006; Schwalbe, 2005) that includes, but is not limited to, an amalgamation of difference across and within a continuum of races, genders, social classes, sexual orientations, religions, (dis)abilities, languages, political allegiances, and other culturally and historically contextualized markers (Bettie, 2003; Butler, 1999; Delpit, 1995, 1998; Fanon, 1967; Kimmel, 2006a, 2006b; Schwalbe, 2005). At times, identity markers can function somewhat separately from and in concert (or conflict) with other identity markers, as borders are encroached, pushed, redefined, and re-established individually, ideologically, and institutionally (Johnson, 2006). Herein lies one of the most significant benefits of using the intersections between postcolonial theory and border-crossing theory to study Black Bermudian masculine identities in this book. I will further explain and contextualize these theories and their intersections.

Before proceeding, the terms *geopolitics* and *subalternity* need to be defined and clarified, since they have ramifications for the construction of personal and collective identities, and they are significant for the theoretical amalgamation of postcolonial theory and border theory. According to the *Concise Oxford Dictionary* (1982), *geopolitics* is the utilization of political power over a territory or the influence that geography has on politics. Another definition is offered by Osterud (1988), who asserts,

> [G]eopolitics traditionally indicates the links and causal relationships between political power and geographic space; in concrete terms it is often seen as a body of thought assaying specific strategic prescriptions based on the relative importance of land power and sea power in world history. ... The geopolitical tradition had some consistent concerns, like the geopolitical correlates of power in world politics, the identification of international core areas, and the relationships between naval and terrestrial capabilities. (p. 192)

Historically, as well as in recent years, Bermuda has been a valuable geopolitical ally for the United States, Canada, and England. For example, in response to an 1861 blockade on southern ports by President Abraham Lincoln that interrupted trade between the Confederacy and Europe, Bermuda was used as a conduit for the continued transmission of goods, while also serving as a port for federal and Confederate warships (Zuill, 1999). From the Second World War until 1995, Bermuda housed military forces from Britain, the United States, and Canada, which included Canadian and American military bases (Zuill, 1999). The recent and controversial deportation of four Uighur refugees in Bermuda on behalf of the United States government exemplifies the link that exists between Bermuda and her neighbors. Contemporary definitions of *geopolitics* have become even more overt and expansive in terms of the way the definitions encompass the sociological power relations and multidisciplinary breadth of this term (Gray & Sloan, 1999; Hafeznia, 2006).

Another key term that needs to be explained is *subaltern*, which has been attributed to the scholarship of Antonio Gramsci (Kennedy, 2000) and defined as "nonelite or subordinated social groups" (Spivak, Landry, & Maclean, 1996, p. 203). Scholars such as Marx, Guha, and Spivak have utilized variations of *subalternity* to contextualize the nuances of social stratification and hierarchies in various communities and nations (Spivak et al., 1996). What is most significant about *geopolitics* and *subalternity* for this study is that both concepts intersect with various dynamics of the identity formation process of Black people. For instance, as citizens of a British dependent territory, Bermudians of African descent are challenged to form individual, collective, and national identities within the context of Eurocentric paradigms. The election of Black political leaders in Bermuda, much like the election of Barack Obama in the United States, has done little to change the economic power structures that undergird the systematic social and economic subordination of peoples of color in these jurisdictions. Similarly, Black Bermudians form identities in a culture where the election of Barack Obama, a *royal visit* by Queen Elizabeth to the island, and the music of Caribbean legends like Bob Marley and Byron Lee are all celebrated. Understanding what it means to be a Bermudian of African descent is a layered concept that exemplifies the confluence of geopolitics, subalternity, and identity. Still, it must be noted that an anti-essentialist paradigm demands that identity is never reduced to one identity *marker*: People embody and embrace social classes, religious traditions, and gendered orientations, and each marker fuels its own geopolitical war that can render a person part of the *subaltern* on multiple fronts. In this light, it is also necessary to acknowledge the social constructedness of identity markers, like race, class, and gender, which speak to the intentionality and malleability of geopolitics, subalternity, and the outcomes they produce.

Postcolonial Theory: Defined, Situated, and Explained

Nailing down a unified and universally accepted definition of postcolonial theory is both challenging and unnecessary (from a postmodern perspective). There is no universally accepted definition partly because postcolonialism is a burgeoning theory (Hickling-Hudson, 1998, p. 329) and partly because the term *postcolonial theory* is often subsumed under the larger label of *postcolonial studies*. Gresson (2008) offers a valuable definition that connects some of the labels associated with postcolonialism:

> *Postcolonialism* (also called postcolonial theory) is a term used to identify several lines of scholarship and research undertaken by those interested in the development of national and group identities and intergroup relations within geographical areas once dominated by colonial powers. Scholars writing in this tradition are concerned with the legacy of colonialism—what is life like for those who have been both brutalized and constructed or shaped by those whose primary goal was the exploitation of resources. (p. 130)

Postcolonial theorists include various analytical approaches that serve as bridges for understanding the history of imperialism, the various brands of colonialism as they have been historically informed by imperialism, and the connections linking the history of imperialism and postcolonialism today (Kennedy, 2000). Although the term *postcolonial* is often associated with scholarship that analyzes texts from various genres and cultural traditions, it can also be used more broadly to situate analytic approaches that inform and contextualize how we see "identity, ideology and cultural practice" (Hickling-Hudson, 1998, p. 327).

Postcolonial criticism and postcolonial theory are the two main strands that emerge from postcolonial studies, which all have links to "feminist theory, minority discourse, and cultural studies" (Kennedy, 2000, pp. 111–112). Villaverde (2008) provides a useful definition of postcolonial studies that buttresses Gresson's (2008) description by specifically naming key stakeholders of power while creating space for consideration of how and whom may be differentially affected. Villaverde's definition also grounds the intersections and extensions found in the descriptions offered by other scholars, since her definition is readily transferable for analyzing the interconnectivity, ideologies, institutions, and individuals whose lived experiences become the *territory* on which power and privilege differentials of the past and present play out. Villaverde (2008) defines postcolonial studies this way:

> Postcolonial studies examines the relationships between the British and French (as European superpowers) and the countries they colonized, as well as the subsequent development of Third World nations and indigenous knowledge. This is not to imply that colonialism is a practice of the past; on the contrary, postcolonialism allows us to understand the lasting impact of living under colonial rule. Postcolonialsim has contributed greatly to the ways we theorize about power and resistance, which has been extremely useful in shifting national conceptions of authority and privilege. (pp. 81–82)

While it is clear that postcolonial theory is derived from postcolonial studies, its application and emphasis on the intersections between theory and practice are contested amongst the three most prominent postcolonial theorists: Edward Said, Homi Bhabha, and Gayatri Spivak. What is significant for this discussion, though, is that all three theorists agree that theory and action are inseparable (Kennedy, 2000).

Key Postcolonial Theorists

Orientalism is undoubtedly Said's most important work as it relates to postcolonial theory (Kennedy, 2000). In an effort to make theory more accessible and practical for those outside of the academy, Said (1994) proposes "a strategy of *interference*" (p. 24, emphasis in the original) in order to, as Kennedy (2000) surmises, "[open] up … the culture to experiences of the Other which have remained 'outside' (and have been repressed or framed in a context of confrontational hostility) the norms manufactured by 'insiders'" (p. 116). By destabilizing what is considered normal, Said's work challenges the boundaries of whom and what should be heard and valued. This *opening up of culture* provides an important link to Bhabha's (1994) argument that culture is "a strategy for survival," when we consider that culture is so much more than ethnic dishes, unique dialects, and social practices. While cultures embody and embrace value systems, traditions, and beliefs, cultures are not static, monolithic, or all-encompassing. Difference, like change, exists inside and outside of cultures, as people and identities move, merge, and mutate (Gresson, 2008). In general, the process of "identity shifting" is not new, but assimilation and cultural shifting has been a particularly persistent motif for marginalized cultural groups (Goffman, 1959, 1963). As a "strategy for survival" (Bhabha, 1994) then, culture, like identity shifting, is relevant to *hybridity*—the capacity to navigate through/across a continuum or boundary—and the multifaceted implications for identity construction when considered within or in connection to postcolonialism.

Building on the work of Said (1994), Bhabha does not try to simplify the intersections between theory and practice, nor does he minimize the process of identity construction. In particular, Bhabha extends Said's groundbreaking theorizations to assert that "colonial power and colonial discourse are not monolithic or unified. Instead, he sees them as split because of a fundamental ambivalence in the colonizer's relations to the colonized and thus in the language or discourse in which this relationship is expressed" (Kennedy, 2000, p. 119). This is extremely important in terms of the production of the subaltern and geopolitics. Clearly, a significant appreciation of difference within and across discourses of power is registered in the ethos of postcolonial theory, and this theoretical characteristic is essential to postcolonial theory as an analytical tool for assessing individual and cultural identity construction. I see postcolonial theory serving as a lens to evaluate how colonial dominance continues to influence and extend across spectrums of identity—such as the identities of Black Bermudian males—much like refracted light passing through a prism elucidates the colors of the rainbow.

Postcolonial theorists offer linguistic and ideological constructs that can be used to interrogate vestiges of colonial influence. Bhabha's focus on "the colonial subject," which he describes as the "individual or collective psyche of the colonizer or the colonized," allows for analysis beyond the political and social realms (Kennedy, 2000, p. 119). Through Bhabha's "insistence on heterogeneity of the colonial and postcolonial experience, his concept of hybridity in the colonial and postcolonial experience, and his concept of mimicry" (Kennedy, 2000, pp. 118–119), I not only see links back to the foundations laid by Said's (1994) *Orientalism*, but I also see building blocks for analyses of the complex layers of difference. To appreciate the complexity of these *layers* requires that, like Bhabha, we not recoil from the ambiguity and "doubleness of colonial discourse [which] is not simply the violence of one powerful nation writing out the history of another," but is instead the geopolitical terrain where "an agonistic uncertainty contained in the incompatibility of empire and nation" is played out (Bhabha, 1994, pp. 95–96). I believe this "agonistic uncertainty" undoubtedly has ramifications for identity formation for citizens of colonized territories, since parts of their histories and identities have often been inscribed by the colonizer.

Spivak et al. (1996) shares many of Said's concerns for how the displacement of texts from their geopolitical realities can misappropriate colonized voices and representations (Kennedy, 2000). In particular, Spivak's recognition of the influence of "epistemic violence" on colonies is reflected in her discourse on the "worlding" of colonized countries (pp. 262, 270). This notion of "epistemic violence," which refers to the dismantling (or destruction) of non-Western ways of knowing and understanding, is particularly relevant to Black Bermudian males. As males of African descent in a British dependent territory that is heavily influenced by North American media and ideologies, Black Bermudian males are challenged to create identities amidst oppressive stereotypes and ideologies that marginalize their capacity to *know*, live out, or even see their Africanness. As I previously discussed in my critique of Mutua's (2006) notion of "progressive Black masculinities," Black males are not only Otherized by the dominance of Eurocentric paradigms that impose particular epistemological and ideological brands on them, they also have to "unlearn" the ideologies of self-hate that infringe on their capacity to even consider what it means to be both African and Bermudian, as participants like Kofi detail in chapter 5. This means, as Spivak et al. (1996) attest, "working critically back through one's history, prejudices, and learned, but now seemingly instinctual, responses" to find more authentic ways of being, knowing, and living (p. 4). Kofi's narrative provides an example of Black Bermudian male resistance; in his personal journey, Kofi is now beginning to evaluate "how to conduct myself, in every way, in an Afrocentric way" or "eat like an African" rather than embracing a European diet. This is the type of questioning that Spivak would suggest is necessary if colonized subjects are going to account for the "epistemic violence" wrought upon them.

Spivak is far more attentive to the roles and influence of gender than Said, even as they both try to offer "alternative historical narratives of the imperial process" (Kennedy, 2000, p. 125). I see Spivak's sensitivity to the role that gender plays as a vital acknowledgment within postcolonial discourse.

Although she rightly highlights the voices of women, her work is also a reminder that men have a gender. Spivak's work is a bridge for those of us who seek to eschew the privileged and essentialist positions which purport that colonialism affected everyone the same way. As a Black man who interviewed and listened to other Black men, I was challenged by Spivak to consider how my privilege had caused me to miss out on "Other knowledge: not simple information that we have not yet received, but the knowledge that we are not equipped to understand by reason of our social position" (Spivak et al., 1996, p. 4). I sought to unlearn my privilege as *my loss* so that when "speak[ing]" to Black males they would "take [me] seriously and, most important of all, be able to answer back" (p. 5). In this respect, I was able to embrace the hybridity of my "transnational" positionality as a Black male and scholar who sought to learn from the experiences of other Black males about identity development (Bhabha, 1994), while constantly interrogating the personal consequences of "epistemic violence" in my own experience (Spivak et al, 1996). In like manner, I also had to consider that culture, as Bhabha (1994) contends, is "translational"—this means that I had to account for the fact that the histories of various territories and peoples coupled with the "territorial ambitions of global media technologies" complicate definitions and understandings of *culture* (p. 172). Moreover, *culture* must be translated, defined, and understood contextually, much like a person who translates a foreign language into a familiar tongue must understand that some information can get confused and lost in the translation. Indeed, as I detail in chapter 6, Black Bermudian males have not been immune from the onslaught of global media influences given factors like the introduction of cable television, which broadcasts stations from the U.S. and other nations to the general populace.

Beyond the scholarship of Said, Bhabha, and Spivak, other scholars have also offered valuable insights on the meaning and functions of postcolonial theory. Some scholars frame postcolonialism simply as "the condition of societies 'after' and 'beyond' colonialism" (Hickling-Hudson, 1998, p. 328), while others emphasize the potential for postcolonial theory to elucidate the embeddedness of the cultural imprints left by the processes of colonialization and decolonialization (Hall, 1996). By extension, postcolonial literature suggests that "diasporic" phenomena can potentially be seen "through rather than around hybridity" as "the cultural consequences of the colonising process" (Hickling-Hudson, 1998, p. 328). Said differently, one's capacity to account for the consequences of colonialism may be enhanced by the postcolonial critic's capacity to consider what a particular identity/ideology/people group was prior to colonialism, while also using postcolonialism to envision what an identity/ideology/people group can be "after" or "beyond colonialism." The seeing "through hybridity" that Hickling-Hudson (1998) claims is necessary to understand diasporic phenomena refers to the postcolonial capacity to seamlessly and, when necessary, simultaneously evaluate cultural phenomena as having globally systematic and localized, separate contexts. This is what I sought to do in this study by seeking to understand particular dynamics within Black Bermudian culture while never losing sight of the Diasporic and Western imperatives that serve as unavoidable and undeniable context. Villaverde (2008) positions postcolonialism under the umbrella of transnational studies, while situating *globalism* and *internationalism*—terms that have very specific and important connections to postcolonial theory—as complementary concepts. Ultimately, Villarverde asserts (2008):

> Postcolonial theory acts as a pivotal tool of reflexivity to help us question the direction of power, who distributes it, who suffers at its hands, how it entangles everyone in complicity in the sustenance of existing hierarchies, and how to dispense with claims of truth. An entitlement to knowledge often extends a false and arrogant security about one's identity, which can prove disastrous in working through various communities of discourse or cultural national borders. (p. 83)

These dynamics not only inform the intersections between postcolonial theory and border-crossing theory, but they also situated and framed my analysis of how Black males form personal identities, define success, and engage in border crossing. Taken together, the theoretical points challenged me to critically interrogate the identities, definitions of success, and border crossing that the participants and I have formed, embraced, and engaged in as "colonial subjects." Plus, I was challenged to re-evaluate the processes of "learning" and "unlearning" truths as necessary steps in a Black Bermudian male's journey from birth to boyhood to manhood.

Border Theory: Defined, Situated, and Explained

As with *postcolonial theory*, finding a universally accepted definition of *border theory* is a daunting task. In fact, it can be argued that a single definition cannot fully capture the fluidity, breadth, and transience of border theory. Metaphorically and literally, border theory is a theory on the edge (Hicks, 1991)—on the borders or boundaries—that must remain flexible in order for theorists to recognize and rupture the "epistemological, political, cultural, and social margins that structure the language of history, power, and difference" (Giroux, 2005, p. 20). But this is not all.

While border theory has come to describe studies that are philosophical and cultural in nature, there are more specific branches of border theory that attempt to capture the multidimensionality of perspective, experience, and Otherness (Larson, as cited in Hicks, 1991). For example, Anzaldúa's *Border-lands: La Frontera* (1999/2007) and her concept of the "new mestiza consciousness" offer geopolitical critiques that situate the complexity of U.S.–Mexico border relations, analyze the implications of occupying a hybrid racial identity, and extend dualistic explanations to encompass the breadth of gendered, sexualized, and class-based difference. Otherization, which Villaverde (2008) describes as "the process of marginalizing difference, most times through negative stigmas and stereotypes" (p. 42), has been a method by which those who hold dominant positionalities have sought to silence *difference* and stultify subordinate groups (Bonilla-Silva, 2006; Gause, 2008; Johnson, 2006). Hicks (1991) contends that "border writing," "border text," "border subject," and "border culture" are manifestations of the transformational power of border positionalities and "polarities" to rupture dominant positionalities and deconstruct vestiges of the colonial/postcolonial, center/periphery binarisms (xvi). Similarly, Giroux (2005) utilizes the concept of border pedagogy to describe the power relations in educative settings that must be dismantled by students and teachers—border crossers—who are willing to challenge the "physical … [and] cultural borders historically constructed and socially organized within rules and regulations that limit and enable particular identities, individual capacities, and social forms" (p. 22). What all of the border theorists have in common is the belief that voices and identities live and are silenced within, across, and on geopolitical, gendered, and sociocultural boundaries and borders (Anzaldúa, 2007; Giroux, 2005; Hicks, 1991). This was significant for my study on the border-crossing experiences/life journeys of Black Bermudian males.

As the portraits of these men in subsequent chapters will show, the *expectations of manhood* that are formally and informally proposed to Black Bermudian males serve as borders that can be reinforced or challenged through their *experimentation/experiences in community-based pedagogical spaces*. Plus, through *exposure to life options* in school and community-based venues, Black Bermudian males are often encouraged to accept, reject, revise, and/or traverse the *expectations* that were proposed to them during their journeys to manhood. Participants' personal assessments of their individual success—or crossing over—is reflective of the expectations they have accepted, rejected, revised, and/or traversed. In essence, participants often judge their success based on their capacity to be *border crossers*.

Moreover, border theory encompasses the multifaceted approaches that use hybrid positionalities to problematize and reconfigure how power is distributed within and across difference. For instance, Hicks (1991) uses border writing and her interests in Latin American culture and literature to challenge "the distinction between original and alien culture" (p. xv); more than this, Hicks (1991) is dissatisfied with merely making a request for the admittance of marginalized literature into the "European/North American–dominated canon." Instead, through a strand of border theory, she partners with the "post-nationalist drive to smash the canon altogether" (p. xv). Hicks's machinations and response to destructive binaries like "original and alien culture" are a fitting exemplification of what Villaverde (2008) describes as liminal spaces: the "gaps created by the juxtaposition of binary terms" (p. 52). At stake here, then, are not just individual and ideological identities, but also the cultural and collective identities of peoples whose national and native histories have come under the onslaught of colonialism. When we consider the various layers and legacies of oppression in these regards, the exploration and utilization of the intersections between border theory and postcolonial theory becomes even more valuable.

Intersections Between Postcolonial Theory and Border Theory

Postcolonial theory and border theory share a common ethos. Postcolonialism is a theoretical approach used to highlight, analyze, and situate "how contemporary social, political, economic, and cultural practices continue to be located within the processes of cultural domination through the imposition of imperialist structures of power" (Rizvi, 2009). In essence, postcolonialism is a response to colonialism (Bhabha, 1994; Hickling-Hudson, 1998; Kennedy, 2000; Rizvi, 2009; Villaverde, 2008), which (at its core) has always been about power, domination, and conquest of Others as contextualized by race, class, gender, nationality, territory, and culture (Giroux, 2005). Said another way, colonialism is a historically oppressive construct that is also a synonym of and vehicle for Eurocentrism and the dominance of Eurocentric paradigms (Hall, 1996; Hickling-Hudson, 1998). Colonialism is a border-crossing ideology whose history reveals a legacy of consistent infringement upon the territory and identity construction of Others—including Black people—through marginalization, manipulation, and mutilation of cultures and peoples (Anzaldúa, 2007; Spring, 2005). Villaverde (2008) makes the theoretical intersections explicit by contending that "transnational studies and postcolonial theory widen the lens of the camera" so that accepted understandings of normal and "familiar" can be probed on an intentional and ongoing basis in order to promote "a larger network of coalitions transgressing many borders and boundaries ..." (p. 83). Villaverde's (2008) definition of *transnational studies* is significant since it brings together core concepts (i.e., colonialism, border crossing, the centralization of Western paradigms) that are discussed in this book:

> Transnational studies is a field exploring transnationalism (to connect and traverse national borders), its practices, intents, impacts, and range of perspectives about crossing political, cultural, economic, and religious borders. As a discipline it charts the effects of imperialism and colonialism and decentralizes the West as core axis. (p. 81)

Thus, by directly correlating Anzaldúa's (2007) call for greater understandings of *intercultural* and *intracultural* dynamics to Bhabha's (1994) call for greater consideration of the *transnational* and *translational* elements of culture, I see the most poignant intersection between border theory and postcolonial theory for Black identity development. Specifically, those who seek to better understand Black identities will not only chart the dizzying disequilibrium caused by the *trans*atlantic slave trade, but also explore the invasive, dehumanizing, and enforced border-crossing experience that ruptures African identities past and present, leaving in its wake the intercultural and *intracultural* wreckage on which Black people must now *find themselves*. "Decentraliz[ing] the West as core axis" is a vital border-crossing imperative of transnational and postcolonial studies because they provide conditions where we can "unlearn" the narrow ways of reading Black identities in the past, "learn" how to better understand Black identities in the present, and engage in more healthy, self-determined ideologies of knowing and envisioning the future.

Notably, the term *translational* refers to the process of interpretation across language, linguistic, ideological, and cultural barriers. Said another way, the term *translational* embodies the border-crossing ethos of language and, by extension, further establishes the links between postcolonial theory and border theory. Certainly, the prefix *trans-*, which means "across or beyond," more than hints at the global imperatives of postcolonial theory and border theory. Rizvi (2009) declaration is pivotal in this regard:

> Postcolonialism ... views culture as pivotal to understanding the nature of contemporary reality characterized by the expansion of global cultural interconnections,

which, even if they are powered by economic forces, need to be located in particular localities and interpreted through particular geometrics of power, in the dialectic between the local and the global. (p. 53)

Specifically, during the process of translation, there are often idiosyncracies and contextual dynamics that one must consider in order to extrapolate a more accurate interpretation/translation of a particular language, culture, or phenomenon. For example, Bermuda's geopolitical relationships with England, the United States, Canada, and the Caribbean all inform various aspects of Bermudian language patterns, culture, and educational systems. In the 1990s, public schools in Bermuda adopted the middle school structure made popular in the United States and Canada, in place of the British system previously employed. Similarly, Bermudian students are encouraged to sit American examinations (i.e., the SAT) and/or British examinations (i.e., General Certificate of Secondary Education—GCSE exams), depending on the school they attend. Furthermore, within the liminal spaces—again, the openings that emerge between divergent labels and ideologies (Villaverde, 2008)—there are disjunctures that exist between and within various languages and borders. Specifically, there are unique cultural and linguistic variables that are often endemic to the various communities that utilize the languages. Two communities that use the same language or share common borders are not immune from the need to consider how the translational process impacts language and interpretation—the usage and translations may be very different, even as they use similar word and cultural patterns. In Bermuda, much like how Ebonics and Standard English are used interchangeably within African American communities, there are particular slang words and patterns that are used by Bermudians. Some Bermudians sound more British than others, reflecting particular schooling, cultural and social class affiliations, or ambitions.

Although Anzaldúa (2007) uses the term *intracultural* to describe elements "within the Chicano culture and Mexican culture" and *intercultural* to mean the relations with "other cultures like Black culture, Native American cultures, the white culture and the international cultures in general" (p. 233), these terms can be reframed and reused to center the experiences of any other ethnic group. The potency of Anzaldúa's (2007) border-crossing theorizations for other Otherized cultures grow exponentially when partnered with Bhabha's (1994) notion that:

Culture as a strategy of survival ... is transnational because contemporary postcolonial discourses are rooted in specific histories of cultural displacement, whether they are the "middle passage" of slavery and indenture, the "voyage out" of the civilizing

mission, [or] the fraught accommodation of Third World migration to the West. ...
Culture is transnational because such special histories of displacement—now accompanied by the territorial ambitions of "global" media technologies—make the question of how culture signifies, or what is signified by *culture*, a rather complex issue.
(p. 172, emphasis in the original)

Due to advances in communication and technology, border crossing and "border people" are far more common than in previous generations (Anzaldúa, 2007). So when I utilize the terms *intracultural* and *intercultural* within the context of the transnational and translational survival mechanisms of culture, not only do I expand my vocabulary for describing the geopolitical influences of our highly technological society on identity construction, but I also glean a clearer understanding of how subaltern positionalities for many people—including Black males and other marginalized groups—can be established and reified across a socioethnic diaspora. For instance, within a Black Bermudian context, intracultural dynamics, such as the recent proliferation of Black-on-Black gang violence, cannot be separated from the intercultural influences of dominant, Euro-Bermudian/Euro-American economic and educational structures that have provided many ingredients for the vicious cocktail of gun crime and Black male educational failure in Bermuda. But the upswing in gun-related deaths of Bermudian Black males cannot be disassociated from the transnational influences of how Black identity construction is experienced in relation to other cultures in Bermuda and, based on the media's transnational influence, other jurisdictions. Specifically, the overrepresentation of Bermudian Black males in the penal system is disturbingly similar to the disproportionate statistics on males of color in other jurisdictions, including the United States, Canada, Britain, and the Caribbean (Mincy et al., 2009). But the analysis cannot stop here. The unique history of cultural displacement for Black Bermudians when juxtaposed with the media's global influence and portrayal of Black identities reveals the complexity of Bermudian culture as a translational construct (Bhabha, 1994). Certainly, there are socioeconomic and geopolitical dynamics at work that can be more carefully explored using the intersections between postcolonial theory and border theory. Through the amalgamation of these theoretical considerations, I can begin to "problematize the familiar (i.e., colonial infringements on the construction of identity) with the unfamiliar" in my research study (i.e., the utilization of language and frameworks that recenter the voices of the subaltern) (Villaverde, 2008, p. 83).

Ultimately, postcolonial theory coupled with border-crossing theory offers opportunities for the recentering of marginalized groups while resisting the

tendency to essentialize difference—particularly as it pertains to Black identity development (Hall, 1993, 2003, 2005). Certainly, the Black experience
is not monolithic—and neither are the perceptions of the various people
affected by colonial/postcolonial relationships. Moreover, the intersections
between postcolonial and border-crossing theorizations allow the "voices" of
Black males to push back against the forces that (have) encroach(ed) the borders of their island (in the case of Bermuda) and their identities.

Putting Theory into Practice: Black Identity and Bermudian Males

Although race is a social construct that cannot be supported biologically, it
has real implications for how history and identities have been experienced
and framed in the Western Hemisphere (Bonilla-Silva, 2006; Johnson,
2006; Wright, 2004). Race and Western racism were systematically created,
and they are systemically maintained (Bonilla-Silva, 2006; Johnson, 2006;
Wright, 2004). Not only have these realities created a hierarchy that obfus-
cates Blackness, but also, as a subordinate identity within the dominant Eurocentric context, "Black identity has been produced in contradiction" (Wright,
2004, p. 1). Through history lessons, textbooks, and dominant discourses that
continue to ignore and separate the African experience from the African
American/African Bermudian identity, *Blackness* is framed as a dangling or
misplaced modifier for peoples who have been told they have no home, no
culture, and no humanity. Colonialism, as a vehicle for the mass dissemination of Anglocentric dominance, has left an indelible mark on Black identity
construction and *race* relations. Stripped of its connections to Africa, Blackness becomes an identity of no fixed abode. Colonialism has been a conduit
of intercultural and transnational racism that has systematically compromised
Black identity construction.

The literature on postcolonial and border theory reminds me that Bermuda is still a colony of England. Having been born and raised in Bermuda, I
knew this information; it is part of my lived experience, but somehow I forgot.
In many ways, my *forgetting* reflects the insidious merging of oppression and
normalization through the colonial "master narrative" that has become the
uncritique discourse (Bhabha, 1994) of what it means to be Bermudian—or
a *British dependant territory citizen*, since the popular label *Bermudian* can be
contested based on Bermuda's dependent status. Certainly, the valuable intersections of postcolonial theory and border theory for critically interrogating

essentialist politics about race, gender, and class while situating the production of the subaltern and geopolitics are revealed in an analysis of Bermuda's unique history and colonial ties.

In Bermuda, "God Save the Queen" is played at "national" events, and an appointed British governor still resides on the island, although he is more of a figurehead than a major political actor. Many Bermudians, particularly Black Bermudians, feel that England does little for Bermuda; and yet, despite ongoing discussions about independence, there seems to be a discomfort and fear (in many sections) about severing ties with England. These dynamics certainly influence personal identity formation in Bermuda, since our "national" identity is somewhat obscure—we participate in sporting events like the Olympics and World Cups as if we are an independent nation, but our flag and currency are constant reminders that we are still subjects of England. In many respects, these phenomena are mutations of the "hybrid hyphenations" such as "Puertorican-mullato, … Chicano-mestizo" (Bhabha, 1994) and even *African American* that "emphasize the incommensurable elements—the stubborn chunks—as the basis of cultural identifications" (p. 219). Bermuda's political, social, economic, and cultural ties to the United States, Canada, and (to a lesser extent politically) the Caribbean further complicate Bermudian identity and the dynamics of race, gender, and class within the context of the production of the subaltern and geopolitics. In fact, the case can be made that Bermuda's colonial status is a subaltern positionality that further complicates Black identity construction in that context, and, according to Bhabha (1994), challenges

> the performative nature of differential identifications: the regulation and negotiation of those spaces that are continually, *contingently*, "opening out," remaking the boundaries, exposing the limits of any claim to a singular or autonomous sign of difference—be it class, gender, or race. Such assignments of social difference—where difference is neither One nor the Other but *something else besides, in between*—find their agency in a form of the "future" where the past is not originary, where the present is not simply transitory. It is … an interstitial future, that emerges *in-between* the claims of the past and the needs of the present. (Bhabha, 1994, p. 219, emphasis in the original)

For a "nation"/dependent territory like Bermuda that is still under colonial rule, postcolonialism is a hybrid theorization that can link our colonial past and present with a vision for a liberated future, since postcolonialism "refers to the condition of societies 'after' and 'beyond' colonialism" (Hickling-Hudson, 1998, p. 328). Perhaps this is also why postcolonial theory and border theory can be useful lenses for critically analyzing Black Bermudian masculinity and the intercultural, intracultural, transnational, and translational mechanisms they employ. Notably, Bermudian businesses import nearly all of the goods and products made available to the people. In many ways, Bermudian identities and masculinities are also imported, through human interaction during travel and via the media. As citizens of a British territory that is an amalgamation of North American, European, and Caribbean cultures, Black Bermudian males, in many ways, are socialized to be border crossers. This reality is evident in the strong Bermudian support of other nations in the soccer World Cup finals (because Bermuda's national team is not in the tournament), or in the crossing of literal borders by plane in order to earn a university degree, since Bermuda College has limited undergraduate and graduate degree program offerings. Metaphorically, because *success* is often defined based on a Euro-American construct, some would argue that Black males who supposedly *succeed* do so by adhering to or *crossing over* to a Euro-American paradigm. Similarly, educational *success* in Bermuda is often validated by non-Bermudian agencies and standards, whether it be the SAT, GCSEs, or a Ph.D. In light of the translational nature of culture, it must also be noted that my examples are not intended to oversimplify how border crossing plays out in Bermuda; nor is it my intention to place value judgments on various practices, which are often precipitated by Bermuda's small geographical and population size. Instead, as a responsible researcher, I sought to account for Bermuda's unique context in order to better understand the identities that Black Bermudian males form. Re-examining how Black Bermudian males define success is critical to better understand their identities, especially within the unique context of Bermuda's geopolitical positionality. How particular groups or individuals within a group define success is a reflection of outside ideologies influencing the group or individual's ideologies; similarly, how one pursues or resists these definitions of success is an expression of the internalization and/or rejection of particular definitions of/approaches to success. Numerous borders can be crossed during these processes, and in a Bermudian context specifically, these "crossings" represent ideological terrain or liminal spaces between the colonized—in this case, the identities and ideologies of Bermudians—and the colonizing forces of non-Bermudian entities, identities, and ideologies. Moreover, I see the intersections between border theory and postcolonial theory as "hybrid hyphenations" (Bhabha, 1994) that can be used to create more spaces where Black males (in Bermuda and beyond) can think, live, and learn "beyond" colonialism.

In this chapter I have sought to focus on and unpack the specific theories that help form my conceptual framework. The breadth and depth of the theories being used demanded specific attention in this chapter. I have highlighted the most significant themes and theorists as they relate to my investigation of Black Bermudian masculinity. Prior studies on Black identity have focused on other people groups across the African Diaspora. As I sought to learn about the complex dynamics of Black Bermudian identity, I recognized that the theoretical amalgamation of postcolonial theory and border theory in my study would have significant implications for future investigations of Black identity, particularly for those researchers who, like me, seek to avoid essentialism while navigating the nuances of Black identity construction in their research across the Diaspora.

In the next chapter, I offer narrative portraits of five of the twelve participants in the study to frame some of the most prominent findings in relation to Question 1: How do Black Bermudian males form personal identities as they journey from boyhood to manhood? There are four overarching themes drawn across the narratives and the entire data set: the men's *expectations of manhood*, *experimentation/experiences in community-based pedagogical spaces*, *exposure to life options*, and *expression of identities*.

· 5 ·

EXPECT THE (UN)EXPECTED

In this chapter, I evaluate the formation of life *expectations* of Black Bermudian males that emerges as an impactful process that informs the identities they embrace as they journey from boyhood to manhood. The expectations participants had of themselves and others vary significantly depending on the context of their lived experiences. Often, the expectations were a reflection of the expectations they embraced as a result of the counsel, examples, and/or shortcomings of others. Through the narrative portraits of five participants, I explore and extrapolate the diverse ways that this first theme—*expectations*—has been experienced and lived out in the men's journeys to manhood. I introduce each participant through the lenses of their familial and schooling backgrounds. I then briefly discuss their varied involvement in community-based spaces.

While elements of the four themes (expectations, exposure, experimentation/experiences, and expression) were evident in the narratives of all twelve men, I have chosen to position the participants and their narratives within the themes that were most relevant to their lives and their stories in order to present a representative or thematic collage drawn from their individual stories. Specifically, in this chapter we meet Jeremiah, whose "high expectations" for himself and others paint an intriguing parallel when followed up by the rollercoaster ride of Dexter's enthralling narrative of "low and shifting expectations." We then meet Kevin, who clearly articulates how "unfulfilled expectations" in the journey to manhood can be precipitating factors in "dead periods" and disconnects that often lead to unfulfilled life expectations. Finally, we meet Giovanni and Malcolm, who both demonstrated the power of their "daddy's" expectations as important sources of counsel and as examples of the dangers of trying to live up to the *competing expectations* of *others*. Taken together, each story and each theme is meant to highlight a particular characteristic or common experience for Black Bermudian males, as informed by the data. What follows is my best effort to present the panoply of perspectives offered by the participants about their journeys.

Jeremiah's Journey: High Expectations of Self, Doing Things "the Right Way"

Jeremiah is a Black Bermudian male in his late 30s who would describe himself as a Bermudian born and raised. He is married with two children, and until being made redundant recently, Jeremiah had been enjoying what many would describe as a successful career as a high-ranking professional in the financial services industry. At time of the interview, Jeremiah was unemployed after being inexplicably "let go" by the company for which he had faithfully worked for over a decade. Jeremiah believes that race was certainly a factor in his company's decision, noting that they kept on staff many foreign employees of his "ilk," "standing," and "seniority," and even hired a less qualified, White professional who moved into Jeremiah's former office the week after he was relieved of his job. Based on the expectations Jeremiah developed for himself and others during his life journey, this professional disappointment confirmed what he thought but did not want to believe about White people, in general, and corporate Bermuda, in particular. The "professional embarrassment" and realities of redundancy placed Jeremiah at a crossroads in his journey as a Black Bermudian male who unexpectedly found himself with lots of time to reflect on his past, re-evaluate his present, and revise his expectations for his future.

Jeremiah believes he paid the ultimate professional price because he has never been willing "to do more than meet people halfway" or to "sell out" in order to succeed in a White corporate environment that makes these demands of Black males—this is a border he is unwilling to cross. He explains: "To some extent … the [Black] guys who have made it [in my industry] to one extent or another have had to sell out. You know? And you have to live with yourself." For Jeremiah, professional success now means "not having to be in that position [i.e., not being able to leave a company on his own terms] again." In light of his journey from boyhood to manhood, as I detail below, one can begin to understand why he described himself as "surprised" when his professional expectations were not met: Jeremiah has always set high expectations for himself based on the influences of his upbringing, and he typically reaped positive results by "doing things the right way," sacrificing short-term interests for "delayed gratification," and being true to who he says he is: "[a] Christian, Black Bermudian, social conservative, politically radical male."

Jeremiah's journey from boyhood to manhood was characterized by clear expectations laid out by role models in his family, including his father, who Jeremiah sees as his chief example, closely followed by the examples of his older siblings. He explained:

> I'm the youngest of four children, 2 older brothers and an older sister …, and I attended [Cooper Academy—a prestigious academic high school]. And of course, my whole life has to be viewed through the lens of [being] the youngest of four siblings who were significantly spaced out. I've always had examples of Black masculinity and Black manhood …, and I always had plenty of role models as to what it meant to be a Black male.

Jeremiah's family life of consistency and order grounded his life expectations for himself and served as the backbone of the personal identity that he forged, including his academic pursuits which he used to frame much of his journey. He continued:

> Through elementary school and going through [Cooper], every step of the way that I took, someone else had already done it. So I had an older brother that went to [Cooper] and so I took the [Cooper] route. I wore his old [Cooper] tie, and by the time I started at [Cooper], he was starting university. … So in terms of having a direction and a path—[I am the] son of a working-class father …, [who is a] husband of one wife, father of only four children—quite a straight guy, salt-of-the-earth type of guy— no outside children, nothing like that. Very loyal, dedicated to his family.

Jeremiah expected no less for himself, because he saw many examples of people close to him who he believed had "done it the right way." Though Jeremiah's family was characterized by order, his family faced their share of challenges. In fact, the orderly family structure was necessary for his family to meet the needs of his disabled sibling. These dynamics impacted the man that Jeremiah sought to become:

> My older sister is severely handicapped. My family was always solidly bonded together because there was a need in our family to always have that stability and that teamwork

to be able to care 24/7 for someone who is severely, severely handicapped. So as a Black young man, all I knew was a good family life, a tight family life. Routine and order. If I could sum it up, I would say with my dad being there, my mom being a housewife, my older brothers setting the example for me and generally steering away from any major antisocial behaviors—for me there was always a path, a well-worn path to walk in.

Though the path to manhood was pretty clear for Jeremiah inside of the home, developing a sense of self outside of the home was more complicated because of his small physical stature, which led to "social awkwardness" as a teenager. In spite of his social awkwardness, Jeremiah was clear about his academic plans and his strong sense of Black identity due to the high expectations articulated at home and at his predominantly Black elementary and high schools. He internalized these high expectations and they became his own. As such, Jeremiah was keenly aware of who he was, what he believed, and where he wanted to go. As a teenager, he could articulate his views on social issues and his self-expectations for the type of life he would one day enjoy. In fact, not only was his identity forged amidst the high expectations that he set for himself based on the influence of influential people and spaces, but many of his perspectives on race, politics, and spirituality could be characterized as *black and white*. He explains:

> I always knew I was going to go to college, from the time I started [high school]. My oldest brother embarked on a financial services sort of path, and I always had a very keen sense of what's right and what's wrong. Always knew that financial services was going to be a career path that I wanted to pursue. I read books by Martin Luther King, read Nelson Mandela's autobiography when it came out years later, but I had read Malcolm X's autobiography by the time I was 15–16, always been interested in Black/White issues. Being the youngest around the dinner table of older people, my emotional and my intellectual IQ obviously was brought up along quickly because I was always in brother-adult, semi-adult conversations and company in a very politicized family, who weren't necessarily involved in the PLP [the Progressive Labour Party] but were strictly progressive, staunchly progressive Labour Party supporters, and very, very much in tune with Bermuda's history and where it placed us as a family, and where it placed Black people, and the disadvantages over the years and what had to be done to overcome it through education and also through being, you know—I wouldn't say proud, but being firm in who you are and your sense of identity as a Black man.

Jeremiah embraced the high expectations set for him by his family and his schools, and he would meet these expectations that he had internalized as fundamental to the man he wanted to become. He graduated from top institutions, passed his certification examinations the first time around, and would describe himself as a being part of the Black intelligentsia. He has considered getting involved in Bermudian politics through elected office or as an advisory committee member for the PLP, which is an historically Black political party that held the parliamentary majority from 1998–2012, after winning the general election for the first time. While his future involvement in politics is unclear, Jeremiah is clear about his commitment to his church, which served as an impactful space on his journey to manhood, much like the family and school. He is a regular church attendee who attributes his achievements to his faith in God and the high expectations that were set for him.

Jeremiah's personal identity development was heavily influenced by his family's conversion and commitment to a conservative Christian denomination. As a boy who transitioned to a faith system that promoted high expectations, Jeremiah developed an identity that was consistent with in his faith system. In fact, the church served to strengthen his *black and white* outlook on many issues, especially as he would have to face various life *experiences* that challenged him to live out his faith during times of duress. He states:

> The other part of it I hadn't mentioned yet was Christianity and how it affected my family. All I knew growing up was going to church. … To a large extent, going through [a public high school] in parallel with growing up in a particularly conservative Christian way of life kind of shaped who I was.

For Jeremiah, attending a public high school rather than a parochial school actually did "something for [his] faith." He was buoyed by the example of his older siblings, his father, and family to see the lifestyle promoted in church as the way to go. He continues:

> If you are convinced that this way of life actually makes sense from a young age—yeah, this is actually where your peace and harmony [comes from]—the routine, the structure … the sense of hope, the optimism, all those things that come from being part of the church and having Jesus in your life. … When you see all of that making sense, and then you are going to school, where not everyone believes the same way … you can kind of, like, weigh out for yourself, it doesn't make sense to be going in the trees at lunch time smoking weed, guys showing you marijuana seeds, like, does this make sense? People talking about parties and sex they are getting into at age 13, 14, and 15, and doing a pack of stupidness, like, does this really make sense? And for me, the resounding answer always came back, this doesn't make sense. When I compare what my peers are doing and what's normal for my peers in terms of … stories that you hear when you went back to school Monday morning, after me spending it at church, you kind of get to see for yourself, "Okay, am I going to ruin my identity as a Black

male in Bermuda, Black Bermudian male, who wants to go to college, who wants to become something in life—is this the path I'm going to follow? The worldly path, with the pleasures that it affords, or am I quite comfortable and happy and fulfilled in becoming a man in the church, and that sort of tradition?" So for me, it made the most sense for me to kind of continue in the Christian sort of way of life and to grow up as a Black Bermudian Christian male. So throughout my high school years, because I was brought up peculiar in my beliefs and how I lived my life—different, in that sense of peculiar, not strange or weird, just different—it gave me a very firm sort of backbone spiritually and resolve that this is what I want to do, this is what I want to be—this is the man I want to be in life.

Jeremiah's consistent exposure to high expectations in various settings, like church, provided the conditions for his strong sense of personal identity: The repetition of positive messages seemed to have deepened the impression on the canvas of his character, to the extent that he had a firm sense of self, even when placed in environments that were divergent from his belief systems. Taken together, Jeremiah's family, schooling, and church environments shaped him to be a man with strong faith, a strong sense of Black identity, and a strong desire to pursue his life's goals.

While Jeremiah seems to have reached the high expectations that were set for him in various contexts, he admitted that he sometimes wrestles with the high expectations of some of his Black male contemporaries at church who do not believe he is sufficiently involved in the work of the church. Jeremiah struggles with what many see as "grassroots" work, such as approaches to addressing gang violence amongst urban Black males in the community. He states: "I am not doing anything to address gun violence, other than maybe advocating for a three-strikes-you're-out policy right now because I am actually invested in this country." His "vestedness" in Bermuda is undergirded by his personal interests as a citizen and husband who is not an advocate of "victimology" as a means of blaming everything on White people and excusing the power of personal choice. He continues: "If somebody breaks in here [my house] … I am not going to really enjoy that—I am not going to excuse it, either … [and] I am not interested in hearing the guy's [intruder's] background."

Jeremiah does not believe he can relate to the "grassroots" experience based on his upbringing and social class background, and he would prefer to not try to perpetrate an identity that is not—as he sees it—legitimately his. He does not feel he can authentically relate to the urban Black Bermudian experience, and he feels it would be disingenuous to think otherwise. He continues: "I have to be authentic to the Black man that I am, even in these circumstances. As sad as these guy's realities are, my reality is this … I can address who I am and be who I am." As a result, Jeremiah has remained on the fringes of these efforts, choosing instead to offer constructive criticism to those who think they can relate to "grassroots" communities, if and when his opinion is solicited. This has created tensions and disconnects between him and other Black males at church due to their ideological differences in how to approach "grassroots" work, and their perceived motivations for doing or not doing this work. For example, Jeremiah asserts that he is viewed with some degree of skepticism by some "brothers" at church, while Jeremiah is suspicious that self-promotion in the name of community work is the impetus behind some programs and individual actions. These perceptions contribute to his disconnect in crossing over to this type of work, though he is hopeful that common ground can be forged in the future.

Connections to border crossing—in this case, his inability to border cross—abound in Jeremiah's struggle to relate to "grassroots" Black Bermudian communities and in the ideological differences that appear to exist between him and some of his contemporaries at church. But the discussion of border crossing transcends his church experience. In addition to wrestling with how his personal identity positions him for certain agendas at church, he is also selective and reflective about how he positions himself and the language he uses during visits to the barbershop. For example, he explained that he usually does not reveal his professional credentials unless someone specifically inquires, though he has happily shared information with the barbershop proprietor when he sought counsel on how to more efficiently manage his business. For instance, he stated:

> The barber wanted to talk to me about how [he] can make [his] barbershop more profitable. ... I know how to do that stuff and I know how to give advice. And what do I sit there and do? Give the guy 15 minutes free advice ... give me a call if you ever want to do it. ... So, actually, I used the elitist class—whatever you want to call it—that knowledge that I had gained over the years ... [to] impart a little bit of knowledge to ya' boy [the barber] that he wouldn't have got from a White boy because a White boy wouldn't have been in his chair.

Additionally, Jeremiah chooses not to intentionally use Bermudian slang or incorrect grammar in the barbershop, believing instead that he would be doing a disservice to his community by not providing a counternarrative to colloquial Bermudian language usage in urban settings. He explains:

> The guy [barber] is a sharp business man. Every time I talk to him, he talks about a business idea he has got ... [and] goes through the math of it while he is cutting my hair. ... So, I am not saying that they are dumb. [But] in order to access and tap into

opportunities in this country, you have to be able to frame and express yourself in certain ways. And I am not really helping him ... if I try to sell a lie ... that you can talk like this and still access everything that Bermuda has to offer economically. Because it is just not gonna happen. ... So, I can code-switch raw Bermudian [speech] when I need to and mid-Atlantic business speech. With them [at the barbershop], I have taken the decision ... [that] the message still has to ... get across that this is all good for the barbershop talk, but in order to get ahead economically or whatever, you have to be able to switch it up.

These dynamics reveal that even for a man who believes that he has a clear sense of his identity as a Black Bermudian male, border crossing can be a difficult process. Jeremiah wrestles with the intracultural tensions and translational dynamics of culture (Anzaldúa, 2007; Bhabha, 1994) that affirm, as I mentioned in chapter 2, the complexities of identity, masculinity, and expectations derived from one's social class, educational background, and exposure to life options (Dodson, 2007; Gause, 2008; Johnson, 2006; Kimmel, 2006a). As I later describe in chapter 8 in my discussion of how Black Bermudian males define success, Jeremiah believes that his strong faith has helped him navigate the highs and lows of climbing the corporate ladder, while his strong sense of Black identity has served as both a buffer and a barrier to the subtle and not so subtle tentacles of racism in corporate Bermuda.

Notably, other participants in this study referenced high expectations that were derived from influences in various settings, including the family, church, and particular schools (i.e., academic schools like Cooper Academy). In the case of Dexter, whom we meet next, high expectations were common in his journey. In fact, he was often forced to adjust to shifting and/or low expectations because of the instability of his experiences in boyhood and adolescence.

Dexter's Journey: Shifting Expectations, Low Expectations

While Jeremiah's journey to manhood was characterized by consistency and high expectations, Dexter's background can be described as the antithesis of Jeremiah's stable family and school environments. Having been raised in various foster homes in his early childhood, Dexter quickly learned how to adapt to shifting environments as a means of self-preservation. Dexter, who is now a school teacher in his early 30s and headed towards his second divorce, began his narrative this way:

I was born in Bermuda, [and] growing up until the age of 7 or 8 years old it was a ... what is the word ... some things were foggy in my understanding of who am I, and how I got here. [When] I went to New York to live for 2 years I found out that I was adopted, because my cousins were like, "Why are your parents so light-skinned and you are so dark?" I was like, "I do not know." Then, I started thinking about it and I asked my mom, "Why am I so dark and you and daddy are so light?" She was like, "You were adopted." I was like, "What does that mean?" She said, "You did not really come from us." I was like, "What does that mean? What are you talking about?" Then, they broke it down for me, and ... I had a sense of embarrassment/a sense of foolishness since I didn't see it.

Dexter's shifting family dynamics impacted his sense of self in early childhood and elementary school. His early memories are fragmented by the various shifts he encountered as a young boy. His transition to his adopted family was less than smooth. He remembers having to move to various foster families and not being able to travel overseas for vacations. He now understands that many of these circumstances emerged while his adoption was being processed, but as a boy he did not understand what was happening. If his foster family traveled outside of Bermuda, Dexter would be moved to another home temporarily. He recalls:

I have been with this family since I was 1 years old, but my memories start from when I was 3. I have pictures from when I was 3 or 4, ... and I had a different last name at the time and didn't even know it, like I had no connection that it meant something different, like cognitive[ly]. ... I went to Legacy Springs Primary for P1 [grade school, year 1], and then my parents had to go away, and I didn't realize the legality of it, but I wasn't their legal child so they couldn't take me. So then I had to go to another foster family, and then I went to [Carter] Primary [School] for P2. I lived with two different foster families in the course of that year, so basically it was a lot of turmoil [and] I felt unsettled at [Legacy Springs] Primary. ... [I]t was very difficult. ... I didn't understand, but there was something in me, despite the uncertainty, that always made me tough, if that makes any sense.

Being tough took many forms for Dexter as he sought to forge an identity amidst the shifting contexts of his family structure and lived experience. Often, smiling and being a *joker* were his strategies of choice as he sought to make sense of different expectations in different contexts.

Like, I remember going to these different foster homes and walking into the door, and the first thing I did was I had a big smile like what a man would do, like what you would teach a man to do, like, to smile in people's faces and then just [be] kind [to] a certain degree, to just feel that way [my pain] afterwards. It was like someone trained me for that, I don't know, I hadn't been trained by anyone. "How are you doing? We are your new family," [I would] give them a hug, a happy big smile, and then I would go to my room and put down my book bag and just cry for about 2 minutes, and then never cry again. I would just get up and wipe my eyes, and just go out and live my life with my new family.

But living with his new families and understanding the shifting expectations was not an easy task. Often, his failure to adjust had painful consequences. He continues:

[I would] get licks [spankings] because there was a different set of rules, get beaten for doing things that was probably okay in another family; like, leaving your toys out in one family might be okay, and another family that was a no-no, licks. [They were] not understanding [that] my academic aptitude wasn't as high as it should have been for my level at the time, probably because of the confusion, so, like, I would get tricked. … I always thought "yes" meant "yes" unconditionally and "no" meant "no" under any circumstance. … So if you say, "You don't want me to take off my belt, do you?" The answer should be, "no," but "yes" sometimes. … "Do you want to stay out of trouble?" "Yes." "Do you want me to take off my belt?" "Yes." "Oh, you *do* want me to take off my belt?" Depending on how it is asked it could be trouble, and I did not have the fortitude to know the difference when I was 4, 5, 6. Early on, I was always confused when I was asked these double-negative type things, and I was always getting licks for stuff that I was just answering wrong to, not how I felt. Days of the week: "What comes after Saturday?" I didn't know. "You don't know your days of the week?" I better say "yes." "Yes, then you are lying to me because what comes after? You said you did [know your days of the week]." Like these types of things [resulted in] licks, so I had to adjust.

Dexter was eventually adopted by a Bermudian family with whom he had previously lived as part of the foster care program. Once Dexter was adopted, he and his adopted family lived in New York for a few years before returning to Bermuda, where he finished elementary school. The instability of his family life impacted his academic performance as a student, even as it also impacts his present perspective as a teacher. He explains, "I c[an] hear my primary school teachers saying, "You play too much. You are intelligent, but you play too much. … You are not serious, you are not focused." Even now as a teacher … I am saying the same things, to the same [type of] boys, that are [the] same age that I was [when I was] being told [I play too much]."

Dexter's teachers could see that he was a student who had the potential to be a "'high flyer," but he was more committed to protecting himself through the façade of the class clown than to his school work. Dexter's desire to be socially accepted impacted his academic performance, his academic goals, and his expectations. Although he believes he could have qualified for acceptance into one of the academic high schools, he was not interested in pursuing that path. He states:

> I really didn't care. Like, it meant nothing to me. As a matter of fact, my early dream in life at that time was to go to Hope Academy [a nonacademic school that had a reputation as a bad school, unlike Cooper Academy, which Jeremiah attended]. It was all I ever wanted. That was my first choice. I could've got a [stanine of] 9.9 [the highest possible score on the transfer exam for high school placement] and I would've gone to Hope Academy. I loved the idea of Hope Academy. I was just fixated on it. I just think, once again trying to fit in, I wanted to be cool.

There is a striking irony when Dexter's expectations and goals are compared to Jeremiah's. The recurring motif of the school uniform—in particular, the school necktie—as an emblem of honor and a symbol of a school's reputation is profound. Dexter further explains:

> Hope Academy kind of had a tough reputation. I wanted to put on that tie and [I knew] nobody would mess with me. [And that's] pretty much what actually happened. If you put on a *Hope* tie and look the part ... the stigma was that they will stab you, like, they don't care, like, ... they will fight you, they don't have anything to live for, [and] they are renegades. ... I wasn't really like that, but I had on the tie ... [s]o it worked for me.

The stigma and stereotypes of Hope Academy and other schools with similar reputations impacted the identity that Dexter formed as he transitioned from boyhood to manhood. Dexter used Hope's tough reputation as a means of protection from those outside of Hope. In essence, the tough-guy persona became an acquired identity that held social capital amongst his peers. Even as an adult, there are individuals who have admitted to Dexter that they thought he was "crazy" and "smoked weed" when he attended Hope. As a student, he embraced "the stigma."

Dexter was proud to attend Hope Academy. He believed that Hope was "a good school." It wasn't until later in life that he learned more about Hope's curriculum, and although he had no desire to attend an academic school, it is interesting that he chooses to compare his performance with the performance of students at an academic school. As I will discuss later through the narrative of Malcolm, competition seems to be an important aspect of the Black male's journey to manhood—particularly in a small space like Bermuda. Dexter states:

> Years later I [learned that] Hope was a trade school. ... It wasn't meant for academia. It was meant to prepare people for work, for trade skills ... and hands-on type of

work. I started thinking about all the different classes and I'm like, "Whoa, I never saw that, it was a trade school." I never knew that, never, ever. I don't know if I knew that [information] that it would've made any difference to me anyway. I wanted to be an architect, and they had architecture in Hope Academy. ... Matter of fact, I beat out the kids in Ivy Secondary [an academic school]. I wanted to go to Hope [and] my stanine [5.4] was right on point.

Because of his athletic ability, Dexter claims that he was offered places at the academic schools despite the fact that his test stanine was slightly below the admission requirement. Besides their different entrance requirements, the high schools had varying reputations, and student identities were influenced and perceived differently depending on the school they attended. For example, as Dexter notes, Ivy was also an athletic rival of Hope Academy because of the close proximity of the schools and the tensions created by the schools' reputations: Black students who attended Ivy were often seen as "sell-outs" or "nerds" who were not as tough or athletic as students at Hope. Ivy Secondary was a historically White public academic school (when Dexter was of school age) that has been the academic rival of Cooper Academy (Jeremiah's school) and other private academic schools. Though many students of color attended Ivy Secondary, they were never seen quite the same way as the Black students at Hope Academy, who had the reputation of being tough and athletic, or those who attended Cooper Academy, who had the reputation of being both academic and athletic. Dexter purports:

They [the academic schools] wanted me for sports. [T]here was no way in hell I was going to go to Ivy Secondary. Ivy was the enemy. Ivy was the school that rolled up their noses at Hope Academy. Why would I betray all that I worked for? All my honors at Hope were equivalent to a C at Ivy Secondary, based on [the] low standards because it's a trade school, but I never knew that. They told us to aim low. I'm not going to lie to you. I was told at school, we were told as 5th years [the equivalent to U.S. high school seniors] [to aim low], because they were desperate to have us just graduate and it is kind of good that they had us aim so low because it might have overwhelmed some of us. Do you see my mindset? It was absurd. They [would] say to us, "Look, you guys, you need 39%" ... to pass, to get a D ... in math, to pass high school! I will never forget it. I mean, it was just a tactic to get us to feel safer, that we can do this. Either way, for me it was a bar. And I aimed for that bar, so much so that I stopped my test [when] I thought I had at least 50% right. ... That's how my mind was wired at *Hope*. ... I'm like, "big deal," that is what D meant to me. It's still a pass. It wasn't frowned upon as a grade you wanted to avoid. ... As a matter of fact, it was scorned upon you when you got an A. Peers would say, "You geek. Don't hang around with us anymore, because you get all of your work right."

Dexter's narrative speaks to the way students were tracked into various schools and exposed to varying academic and social expectations that significantly impacted the identities and life outcomes of students. As we learn from Brandon (in chapter 7), who initially attended Ivy Secondary for high school, social and physical survival trumped academic development, and many young Black men who liked to work with their hands at a trade school like Ivy were more likely to be encouraged to pursue a career in construction than inspired to use their hands as a doctor or an engineer. Embedded in the educational system and psyches of the people were explicit and implicit forms of racism and classism. For example, most students in Bermuda's public education system are Black, while many White students, whether academically gifted or not, have been able to attend academic private institutions. Many Black Bermudians have embraced the stereotypes and reputations of the schools and students to the extent that the type of *intracultural* oppression that scholars like Anzaldúa (2007) discuss has emerged and been insidiously sustained, even as the complexions of the ministers of parliament and system administrators have browned.

The identities formed and the experiences Dexter had in boyhood and adolescence have certainly influenced his identity and experiences as a man. His academic performance during his initial stint at Bermuda College was poor because his expectations were not met; he was frustrated that his family did not have the money to send him overseas to college, and even more disgusted that students who were academically and athletically weaker than him at Hope were able to go overseas to school because their parents could afford it. This experience caused him to "see the world differently." He explains:

> I had to go to Bermuda College, and I think I resented that … so I acted out accordingly, with my grades and my attention to class. You think I didn't care in high school? I didn't care in college. I got kicked out my first year. … I had like a 1.11 after my first semester. You'd think I would pick it up, right? I jumped to a 0.9 something the second [semester].

The data above suggest that Dexter's identity was shaped by low and shifting expectations, but also that his life decisions often were manifestations of low and shifting expectations: He shifted from succumbing to the low academic standards of his high school to embracing expectations of noble overseas college dreams, only to shift back to low personal expectations when those he trusted failed to meet his expectations. This theme of unmet expectations was a recurring and persistent motif in many of Dexter's relationships and in the lives of other participants like Kevin, who I discuss later in this chapter. The manner in which Dexter was introduced to members of his biological family is another example of how instability affected the expectations of his past, and, as he sees it, some of the failures of his present. Today, he continues to question whether the disconnect with his biological family is related to the challenges he has faced in his two failed marriages. He describes meeting his biological family:

> I met my biological sister on Facebook. She asked me … "Were you adopted as a child?" And I was like, "Who wants to know?" And she was like, "Someone who may be your little sister." And when she said that I knew it had to be her. I actually went to high school with my brother, my biological brother. He was one year ahead of me. We never had a relationship. We knew we were brothers in high school, from the first day I knew he was my brother. I remembered his name. His last name was my former last name. … I said, "Oooh, that's my brother." I never said anything until I told my best friend. … Then someone asked him and he's like, "Yeah, that's my brother," he knew my name … he knew who I was. And we never had a relationship, ever.

Dexter's introductions to his biological family members were consistent with the low expectations of his youth. Underscoring the significance of space in Bermuda, Dexter's biological brother would later be his barber at the neighborhood barbershop, and his odd introduction to his biological sister over cyberspace was "topped" by his distasteful introduction to his biological mother at the neighborhood grocery store—crushing any interest he may have had in developing a relationship with her. Dexter explained that when he was a teenager, both he and his biological mother worked at a neighborhood grocery store: Dexter as a grocery packer and his biological mother as a cashier. Up to that point, though, they had never been formally introduced, and Dexter— having been warned by his stepmother that his biological mother was working at the grocery story—wasn't quite sure which of his colleagues was actually his biological mother. To Dexter's chagrin, his biological mother "introduced herself [by] sen[ding] a [fellow] cashier to [Dexter] to be a mediator." Dexter was incensed and embarrassed by his biological mother's poor judgment.

Clearly, Dexter and Jeremiah have had divergent upbringings that have impacted their personal expectations and the expectations they have of others. For example, learning to adapt to shifting expectations helped Dexter to develop "foresight." He claims he is highly sensitive to his environment and the need to ensure that it is always secure. He attributes this sensitivity to his childhood experiences and believes that being attentive to his environment helped him to prepare for changes in the economic climate. His successful transition to a teaching career in pursuit of professional success is one example he cites. Kevin, the next participant introduced, has struggled to fulfill many of his personal and professional expectations because of a variety of life circumstances.

Kevin's Journey: Unfulfilled Expectations

Kevin is a Black Bermudian man in his early 40s who has formed an identity amidst expectations that have remained somewhat unfilled. Kevin's journey from boyhood to manhood was impacted by his parents' divorce, his father's alcoholism, and a turbulent schooling experience that saw him spend time at numerous elementary schools in Bermuda and even a boarding school in the United States. Kevin is happily married to his second wife; his first marriage ended in divorce. Although Kevin does not have any children with his present wife, he did parent his ex-wife's children, and sought to maintain contact with them after the marriage was dissolved. Kevin offers a narrative that casts light on the distinct connections and disconnects that emerged in response to his father's struggles and triumphs. Kevin grounded his narrative in the various neighborhoods and communities where his family lived, which is significant for my examination of the role of neighborhoods later, in chapter 5. Kevin began his narrative this way:

> I am Bermudian born and raised. I started out my life up in [Brenau] Parish ... on [Haven] Road. I was a bit too young to remember that. What I do remember is when I lived on Jewelry Road. I came up with what started off with what we would term "complete family": mother, father, supportive grandparents, aunts, and uncles, and as time went on, for various reasons, the family broke. My father was removed from the home. But in doing that, my mom was ensuring that we maintained a form of [a] relationship as [best] we could. ... He used to drink a lot. She would allow us to maintain contact with him in whatever way we could. We moved around a lot. On [this] 21 square mile I think I have lived in every parish at least once; some of them, four or five times.

Kevin attended Cooper Academy, but his experience there was a bit different from Jeremiah's experience at Cooper, in that Jeremiah was a bit more docile in dealing with the social disjunctures of being slender and "peculiar" during adolescence, while Kevin was far more aggressive in navigating his identity as a big guy donning thick glasses. Kevin opines:

> I just stopped going [to] high school for a minute. I think it's like 200 and something days of the year you are suppose to be in school; one year I missed 150. Just not

going to school. ... I would go and—once they started realizing that I wasn't coming school—I'd go, get signed in to school, leave, come back at lunch time, get signed out after lunch, leave. So they wouldn't know I was gone until people would say, I haven't seen [Kevin] in my class for weeks—"Oh, but he is here on my attendance records." So when they started to catch up, then I just kept using what I had, as far as natural intellect, to keep trying to circumvent the system. ... So I ended up kind of being put back once I got in my fourth year of high school.

Much like Dexter used humor to fit in at Hope Academy, Kevin embraced the persona of the "daredevil" in order to carve out an identity in school that would be appealing to young ladies. This approach, which is reflective of some of the typical notions of Western masculinity I highlighted in chapter 2, had ramifications for his schooling experience and his later decisions as a man who would participate in a criminal act that led to incarceration. He explains:

[There] was one time that my perspective had gotten so skewed that I would basically try almost anything, no matter how crazy it sounded—not drugs or alcohol or any-thing—but just, like, dares. Doing things no matter how crazy it seemed at the time to establish this person I wanted to be seen as, you know, somebody who was kind of edgy. Part of it was kind of girls. Girls always wanted that guy who is kind of edgy. And the quote-unquote nerd that I was coming up as—the guy with glasses, the guy with intelligence, guy who didn't have all the best stuff [i.e., clothes]. You got labeled in a certain vein and wanted to break out of that box, and you can go completely to the other direction. Nowadays they would call it a kind of gang mentality; it was kind of a show of force. I used to carry weapons to school ... and one day, out of a joke, I actually pulled one of the weapons on a guy; it was a knife and ... I had six or seven of them on me at any given time. And so, at one point I pulled one out and the guy backed off, and he came at me again and I had another one. ... I had paid someone 50 cents to choke him for half a minute. And like, that was the level of whatever [I] could [do to] just to kind of get a feeling, to feel something, because it was kind of like a dead period [in my life], my father was out and all the rest, and so I just wanted to feel connected to something. And if these guys thought that that was cool, then hey, here's the 50 cents.

Kevin's acknowledgment that he was feeling "dead" due to the confluence of his father's absence and other turbulence in life is very significant to under-standing the process of identity formation for many Black males who, like Kevin, grasp onto anything or anyone who makes them "feel connected" during these "dead period[s]." Kevin's transparency in this regard is particu-larly important because elements of his story—namely, his disconnect with his biological father and his decisions during his "dead period"—are represen-tative of the experiences of other participants in this study who we meet in chapters 5 and 6. What makes Kevin's narrative so significant is that he seems to have processed how the absence of his father impacted his early identity formation in a way that some of the other participants did not identify, or at least struggled to articulate.

Kevin was nearly expelled from Cooper Academy for his knife-wielding show of bravado, which typifies how *physical aggression and force* can become a default means of gaining respect for Black males who embrace the destructive stereotypes of Western masculinity. Kevin avoided expulsion for this incident because of the intervention of a Black male administrator who believed that he had "a lot of potential." Ironically, Kevin not only made significant enough improvements to graduate with honors but also was given leadership positions in his final year of high school. With expectations of a successful business career, Kevin left Cooper having embraced the school culture which suggested that he was to become a part of the Black intelligentsia. Sadly, a combination of circumstances—including a lack of funds for college and a stint in prison—impeded his journey.

For Kevin, forming an identity as he transitioned from boyhood to manhood also meant dealing with the unfulfilled expectations of a father who often failed to follow through on his promises because of his struggles with alcohol, and a mother who did her best to keep the family together. He explains:

> My mother was great. You know, when it comes to trying to be a mother and a father and an example, she constantly tried to do what was right. And in trying to do that, nobody succeeds 100% of the time. But she succeeded a lot. In my adult life, learning more about different things through counseling and whatnot, especially when it was coming to getting married and trying to be better than the person that I was before, you learn that your family of origin has a lot to do with how things happen and how your life starts to turn out. If you don't know that, you will make mistakes. I realized later on in life that while I loved my dad, I didn't like him as a person. We didn't have that, you know, son-and-father-hugging, come-to-see-my-sports-games [relationship]. It was constant disappointments. Constant not showing ups. ... Coming through as a young man, you seek your father's approval, so it was always, you know, "I love my dad, I want to be around him." But as I [grew up], it was so much of not wanting to be like him that I tried to do everything the opposite of how he did; and strangely enough [I] ended up repeating a lot of his mistakes. My dad was a hard worker. He always had a job. Sometimes two. He always tried to financially provide for his family. He just had some other issues that he had to deal with, and those issues clouded my judgment about the type of person that he really was.

Kevin's judgment and personal vision of who he really was as he journeyed to manhood was also clouded during periods of his life. As he transitioned to adulthood, the distance between the career in law that he dreamed of as a young man watching *Matlock* and his lived experience began to expand. Further underscoring the theme of *unfulfilled expectations* in his life, Kevin's inability to progress academically, professionally, and financially were precipitating factors in his decision to engage in a drug deal that went bad. Ironically, his decisions were leading him to become the man he never wanted to be—his father. He explains:

> In trying to get away from everything that he [my father] did wrong I found out that I went and duplicated a lot of his stuff. My dad was a bouncer; I didn't know that until years later, like recently. I became a bouncer when I got older. He had been incarcerated for a period of time, but I didn't know. People seem to kind of believe that if you have an idea of your history you won't repeat it, but it is almost as if without knowing his history I was predestined to repeat it anyway, so it was weird. And now in my adult life, talking to him, and we worked together for a while, we got a lot of time to really shoot the breeze and find out what and why and where besides alcoholism. … You come to find out that we had more in common. While I was running away from the man that he was, I basically ran smack dab into a similar lifestyle.

The lives of Kevin and his father have converged once again—this time at church, where they are both active members in the same congregation. The church was certainly an influential space in Kevin's journey to manhood, as was the barbershop and the prison. I briefly return to his narrative in chapter 6, drawing on his vast experiences, including how his journey was impacted by the church—a space where, as a boy, he learned that contradictions are just as common as conversions to Christianity, and where, as a man, he was able to reconnect with both his earthly and heavenly Father.

Giovanni's Journey: "Working" With Other People's Expectations

Giovanni is in his early 30s and has never been married. He is presently in a committed relationship where he serves as a father figure to his fiancée's two children. He is a self-proclaimed "mama's boy" who, as a result of the close relationship with his mother, has had challenges in some of his previous relationships with women. Giovanni characterized his journey from boyhood to manhood as "very structured." In fact, contrary to Kevin and Dexter's narratives, Giovanni has lived in his upper-middle-class neighborhood for most of his life, and many of the Giovanni's life expectations were prescribed by his parents. He states:

> Parental-wise, I think everything, up until college, was planned out. It was always set that I was going to college. I was going to get good grades. I was going to be here [at

home], [under strict] discipline. In my younger years, I don't really remember having much fun. I just remember a lot of discipline, a lot of reading, a lot of homework. And as I got older, I kind of rebelled away from it for that very reason, because I was just sick and tired of it. But I still—I think I—the reason I wanted to go away to college so bad was just to get away from all that discipline. So, yeah, I just remember a lot of structure, you know, set schedules, set times. Be here, be there. Extracurricular. That type of thing.

Perhaps Giovanni's parents could be excused for being overprotective and, in his eyes, overbearing. Giovanni was the lone survivor of a set of twins; his twin brother died soon after birth from complications during the pregnancy. Additionally, Giovanni was diagnosed with scoliosis (a spinal disorder) as a young boy and had to wear a full body cast after having surgery to help him to stand up straight. Giovanni remembers having to sit on the side while other children enjoyed bike riding and swimming during the summer. He eventually learned to ride and swim with other neighborhood children, but he experienced a disconnect with his cousins and neighborhood friends once his family moved to a new house that his father built in a more affluent neighborhood. As a young man, Giovanni spent many weekends in the yard helping his dad maintain the property. Even today, he still feels obligated to meet his dad's expectations of helping in the yard—though he now embraces the responsibility as the future heir to the estate. Giovanni's transition to manhood was a process that took place as he assisted and learned trades by working with his dad at home. Though he feels it negatively affected his play time as a child, it also impacted his sense of manhood in a positive way. He shares:

I think a lot of what has made me what I am is I had a lot of responsibility as a young child. I was here [at home] on the weekends. That was my day at the house, so like things that I think are average and a child didn't know, I kind of knew. Like I was up on a roof, painting a roof at eleven [years old] ... scrubbing the roof, cleaning out the gutters. ... I learned a lot, you know, and so I didn't get to much play. I was always working, cutting trees, cutting hedges. In a way it kind of helped me, and in a way it kind of—I think it kind of hindered me. ... I have chores to do, you know, responsibility. And like, you get to my age, and now I am completely tired of it. Like, I really don't want to do that. ... I don't have to do it. But I feel like I have to do it. It's my yard ... and, like, my parents have always been there for me. ... I did help all day Saturday with my dad in the yard working. After all this time, and what my parents did for me ... I will do what I can do to tell them that I appreciate what they did. You know, that's what my character is.

Giovanni attended Ivy Academy (a historically White academic high school) where he struggled to fit in socially; this negatively affected his self-confidence. He states:

> Primary school was cool. … [High] school was rough, you know, because at the time … I had this confidence issue at school. … I was scared to go to school. Not from school, but from a social aspect. I think I could learn a lot. … As far as looking at myself, how it has affected me as a man, I think about stuff like that, it's just—I mean, it took me a long time. I don't know. I remember being picked on … and maybe, like, that's why now I am, like, kind of like, nurturing. I can tell when somebody is not feeling [good], or comfortable. So I think that's one of the biggest things that [I got] from school.

Data suggest that Giovanni was able to turn his negative high school experiences into positives, and in this, his narrative challenges typical notions of Black men as uncaring, insensitive brutes. Through his caring spirit and his sensitivity to the hurts and needs of others, his narrative serves as an important counternarrative to the dominant discourses about Black males that were discussed in chapter 2. Rather than using his oppressive experiences as an excuse to hurt others, Giovanni seeks to put the needs of others before his own as an expression of his agency and love for humanity.

Giovanni's narrative is also consistent with the literature in chapter 2 on the value of the extended family in Black communities. While Giovanni sought to reach the academic expectations of his parents—and in particular, his "daddy," Giovanni's mother and extended family were also sources of support and balance. For example, Giovanni's parents asked him to wear his cap and gown off the airplane upon his return to Bermuda from university so that his grandfather, who could not travel to the graduation due to illness, could see him deplane in his graduation regalia. Giovanni has worked in the business field since his return from college, choosing not to return to college for a master's degree—much to his parent's chagrin. In this particular instance, he chose not to chase the expectations of others to pursue another college degree, but in most areas of his life he has fallen in line with the social norms and expectations of his family.

One expectation or family tradition that many of the men enjoy in Giovanni's family is social drinking, particularly on holidays and Sundays when his extended family convenes for various social events. Giovanni has embraced this tradition fully. He characterizes himself as a family guy who is comfortable and happy with a simple life. Upon his return to Bermuda from university in the U.S., Giovanni was able to develop greater self-confidence as a man by participating in the local soccer league and by reconnecting with some of his acquaintances from his childhood neighborhood through the sports club. He has reached many personal athletic goals as a member of his soccer team, and he is now embracing leadership responsibilities on and off the field, including serving as a board member for a scholarship program that his sports club runs.

Though Giovanni had some similar experiences to Jeremiah as far as expectations and family support, Giovanni does not appear to have the same strong sense of Black identity that Jeremiah forged at Cooper Academy. Moving from a predominantly Black, working-class neighborhood to a more affluent, White neighborhood and attending a historically White high school appear to be factors in his sense of identity. This is consistent with the discussion in chapter 2 on "cultural capital" and the influence of "prolonged exposure to the institution of schooling" (Ferguson, 2000; Shujaa, 1994). Additionally, the cultural norm of alcohol consumption amongst Bermudians, and Black men in particular, is a theme that emerges from the narratives of other participants like Kofi, who is introduced in chapter 6. This theme is evident in the narrative of the next participant, Malcolm, whose story—like Giovanni's—reveals how his father's expectations impacted his journey to manhood.

Malcolm's Expectations: Hard Work, Hard Liquor, and Hard Losses

Malcolm grew up in a Christian family in a house his parents owned in a tight-knit Black community. Now in his early 30s and the father of a young child, Malcolm claims that he has "backslid" from the Christian principles that he was raised to follow as a young boy in the church. Though his present girlfriend is not the mother of his child, he is intentional about spending quality time with his daughter and maintaining a healthy relationship with the mother of his child. Notably, like many of the other men in the study, he takes his role as a father seriously, which challenges some of the typical notions of Black men as disappearing, disinterested deadbeat fathers (Dodson, 2007; Livingston & McAdoo, 2007; Perkins, 2000).

Like Giovanni, Malcolm learned about the *expectation of hard work* from his father. He also struggled to appreciate his father's constant insistence upon completing chores around the house and ensuring that he was attentive to detail in his work. His father owned a business, and Malcolm was taught early the value of prioritizing and taking responsibility. This work ethic is now evident in Malcolm's commitment to hard work and his declaration that "I have no problems trying to make a dollar." In fact, both rounds of our interviews were interrupted by calls from his employer to inquire whether he was able to work overtime that evening. In both instances, he happily obliged. He describes his childhood experiences this way:

> [My dad] just wanted to bring me up as a man from being a boy, he wanted to show me what's more important in life as far as bills and chores, and stuff like that. So coming up as a boy was kind of hard, but … I look back and see what my old man was talking about. … I take care of business first and chill later, so I see all that now. It is easier for me now to appreciate all that.

Unlike Jeremiah and Giovanni, who both migrated to middle-/upper-class neighborhoods and academic high schools, Malcolm has embraced employment as a blue-collar worker, which may be partly due to the opportunities that were available through his dad's business and the de-emphasis on academic achievement in his schooling experiences. Unlike Jeremiah and Giovanni, Malcolm attended a high school that had a nonacademic reputation, before transitioning to a mega-school as part of the restructuring of public education. Much like Giovanni, Malcolm was challenged to meet expectations of doing hard work around the house. Malcolm, however, was not presented with the same emphasis on academic achievement—he encountered less social pressure for academic achievement during his high school experience than Giovanni experienced at Ivy Academy and Jeremiah and Kevin experienced at Cooper. Malcolm states:

> I would say [my schooling experience was] average, but to be honest, I blame the system, because I was doing better when I was at [my local high school], and then they wanted to bring in this mega-school and bring everybody all in one area. I kind of lost my focus. I lost my focus on school, like I [got] caught up with other bredrens [friends] and family, so I wasn't really focused on my work like I was supposed to. They had three lunches [lunch periods]. As a young guy, three lunches [meant] I would take all three. It was easy to cheat the system, like not go to class and all that. It just made [cheating the system] much easier than it was at [my previous high school], because you had ten people in a class, you knew if somebody was missing, but at the mega school [with] all the kids, you never knew who was missing. It just seemed like they didn't really care, and I didn't [care] because I went up there the first year [the mega school opened], so it wasn't really organized properly, and they are probably more organized now.

Malcolm failed to graduate from the mega-school and he has not yet earned his GED. In many ways, Malcolm's schooling experience mirrors some of the disconnects Ferguson (2000) highlights in her study of Black boys in public schools in the United States. For example, Malcolm's decision to skip class with friends in order to enjoy "three lunches" reflects the reality that social relationships in school often trump the completion of school work, and "transgressive behavior"—for example, breaking school rules—"is that which constitutes masculinity" in schools (Ferguson, 2000, p. 170). At the very least, Malcolm's failure to successfully complete high school—like over 50% of the Black Bermudian male school population (Mincy et al., 2009)—adds credence to Carruthers's (1994) assertion that "[t]he crisis in Black education is, indeed, worldwide" (p. 41). Still, as a result of many hands-on experiences and his personal buy-in to the expectation that men should work hard, Malcolm is proud to have developed into a competent construction worker who is proficient in many trades. He plans to commence studies at a GED community school in the near future.

Rising to meet expectations is a recurring motif in Malcolm's life and in the lives of other Black Bermudian men. When asked to describe what it means to be a Bermudian, one of Malcolm's most resounding descriptions was "Bermudians like to drink." Reinforcing the power of expectations, the consumption of alcohol is a pervasive cultural norm in Bermuda that, as I detail in a later chapter, is imbedded in local traditions and further celebrated through pedagogical tools like a popular local song called "Bermudians Love to Drink." This song, which was created by Bermudian comedian Bootsie, not only reflects the pervasive culture of alcohol consumption in Bermuda, but also exemplifies the power of informal pedagogical tools which reinforce ideologies that are absorbed by the populace as acceptable appendages of identities. As other participants in this study attest, Black Bermudian masculinity has been significantly impacted by the normative ideology of alcoholism.

Malcolm claims that he experimented with liquor at the sports club, and like others in the study I discuss later, had to learn some hard lessons as a result of his use of alcohol. Underscoring the potential positive aspects of the sports club, Malcolm also noted that his journey from boyhood to manhood was enhanced by the "experience [of playing] football and cricket as a youngster against different teams, because [he] got to know different people from different parts of the island." From these encounters, Malcolm claims that he learned to appreciate "competition," which, as discussed in chapter 2, is a typical ideal of Western masculinity (Hatty, 2000; Whitehead, 2002). The connections that he makes between competition and identity in Bermuda are relevant to understanding how *space* impacts how Bermudians, in general, and Black males, in particular, form and negotiate identities. He states:

> Being a Black man is like always challenging the next brotha, especially when it comes to sports it is about challenging with the next brotha. Especially, when it comes to girls [attracting women]. … If I am passing the ball, I want to be better than you when it comes to football [soccer]. Even just playing a Game Boy, I want to be better than you. When it comes to writing, I want to be better than you, anything like that, and it could go on and on and on. … For Bermudians I think it is more [than] just men being competitive, I think it probably happens more often day to day, because it [Bermuda] is so small. … If you see someone popping their bike [doing a pop-a-wheelie], you want to jump on your bike and beat them [pop longer than them].

Malcolm's narrative elucidates another significant experience for Bermudian teenagers: The tradition of owning a motorbike at the age of 16 serves as an informal rite of passage for Bermudian teenagers, representing the transition to greater responsibility and autonomy. For Black Bermudian males, many of whom are often encouraged to "work with their hands," finding ways to make their bikes faster is a popular pastime. While these traditions are fun, they can also have deadly consequences, much like other traditions around the world that can be associated with the expectations of Western masculinity. Notably, for generations in Bermuda, many Black families have lost their sons as a result of motorbike accidents on Bermuda's unforgiving roads. In fact, Black Bermudian males are the most likely demographic to be killed in a motorbike accident in Bermuda (Raynor, 2009). In this particular respect, trying to live up to the expectations of what it supposedly means to be truly masculine in Bermuda—taking risks, loving speed, and claiming to have no fear of death—has led to the undoing of many Black Bermudian males. Malcolm explains:

> Another experience I can say was when I first turned 16 I got a bike, and your first thing to do is, go, go, go, speeding all over the place. That was a great experience. I was always going at fast speeds, fast speeds! I just wanted to get out of here and just go. Like I said earlier, I appreciate my dad coming down on [correcting] me [about speeding], because that's why I am where I am at today. So, a bad experience was experiencing one of my mate's passing, because he was always speeding on his bike, so I saw why my dad was coming down on me … he didn't want [me] to go do that.

Malcolm learned both positive and negative lessons based on the expectations of the individuals in his family and social circles, and in the communities that he was socialized in. Like other participants in this chapter, he struggled to always understand or appreciate the expectations placed on him as he journeyed from boyhood to manhood. In many ways, Malcolm experienced a delayed appreciation for the expectations and values instilled in him as a boy. As a man, Malcolm's gratitude for the counsel provided by his father underscores a sentiment alluded to by many participants: They did not always know what was best for them as they journeyed to manhood; thus, they were vulnerable to the expectations and guidance of others to help them forge personal identities. While participants like Dexter figured out later in life that some of the expectations of particular foster families and schools were problematic, Malcolm—like Giovanni—now sees that his dad was trying to make him into a responsible man and protect him from some of the dangers that claim the lives and compromise the life outcomes of Black Bermudian males. Notably, Malcolm's understandings of the expectations of manhood—for example, "competition"—are consistent with many of the typical notions of masculinity I discuss in chapter 2, and the perspectives of many other participants in this study who demonstrate how Western masculinities are contextualized in Bermuda.

Additional Theoretical Connections

Together, the Black Bermudian males in this chapter form a diverse group, yet they have many compelling similarities that speak volumes about how *expectations of manhood* impact the personal identities Black Bermudian males form as they journey from boyhood to manhood. Ultimately, each man—through the expectations of manhood that were implicitly or explicitly set before him during boyhood, adolescence, and early adulthood—formed personal expectations that then became a target for his own self-evaluation of success in his own journey to manhood. Notably, the target itself—manhood, or what it means to be a man—was also largely constructed by the expectations each participant was exposed to. In this sense, both the means to the goal of manhood and the definition of the goal itself—what it means to be a man—emerged as highly nuanced, overlapping processes that were complicated or clarified based on the consistency and coalescence of their individual personalities, their family histories, the institutional pathways they took, the local environment of Bermuda, and the standard of masculinity which they were expected to reach and challenged to pursue.

While the overarching theme of *expectations of manhood* matters, the diversity of the specific expectations, as highlighted through the themes and narratives of each participant, is equally vital: *High expectations, low or shifting expectations, others' expectations, unfulfilled expectations,* and *working or competing expectations* are significant themes not only because they capture the variance and diversity of the journey to manhood for many Black Bermudian males; taken together, they also represent the intricacies embedded in choosing life pathways and forming identities.

In chapter 2, I acknowledged scholarship that suggests some of the typical notions of Western masculinity and highlighted how these realities may impact the identities and ideologies of Black males. Descriptors such as "competitive," "dominant," and "violent" are written on printed pages and challenged in the works of Whitehead (2002) and Hatty (2000), but they are also engraved on the psyches and lived experiences of Black males' lives as identities that they may choose to embrace or eschew at different stages and in different situations along their journeys. For example, harkening back to Kimmel's (2006a) point about the social pressure that many males face in trying to live up to the typical masculine ideal of developing "large and intimidating male bodies," Jeremiah struggled socially at Cooper because he was neither large nor intimidating; these were *high*—though problematic—expectations that he could not reach. In fact, his small stature was the subject of many jokes during adolescence, much like the teasing Giovanni experienced at Ivy as he struggled to live up to *other people's social and scholastic expectations*; for both Jeremiah and Giovanni, the high expectations of others in adolescence had both positive and negative effects that significantly impacted each man's personal identity and sense of self as a man.

Though his small stature excluded him from some of the social and athletic circles that were a part of the culture and identity of Cooper Academy, Jeremiah was able to tap into other forms of collateral that were valued at Cooper and promoted in the spaces of his home and his church: namely, his academic development. Consistent with McAdoo's scholarship (2007) on the relevancy of the church as a vital socializing space and support system for people of African descent, Jeremiah was able to forge a positive identity as a Black Bermudian man who was encouraged to see his masculinity and his identity through a lens that transcended the expectations of his peers and the typical notions of masculinity that scholars like Kimmel (2006a, 2006b) and Connell (2005) describe.

Kevin, on the other hand, did not have the same level of non-school–based support to provide counterdiscourses to the dominant ideologies of masculinity that were being transmitted in the social institution of the school. Not only did he struggle to meet the expectations of typical Western masculinity, but because of his feelings toward his father and the "dichotomy of two religions" that he experienced, he did not have the same level of security in or encouragement from people in nonschool venues. Kevin resorted to a violent show of force and dominance over another male student as a means of survival and expression of his masculinity. Whitehead (2002) describes some of the typical characteristics of masculinity as ownership, money, and the possession of various accoutrements; Kevin had none of these, and the impact of this reality on his identity in adolescence and his decision making in early adulthood are evident: He nearly got kicked out of school because of a violent act, and he later served time in prison for a bustled drug deal that he believed would relieve the financial pressure that he and his family faced. Still, it is vital to heed Whitehead's (2002) counsel that "complex gendered power relations [should not be] reduced to an 'oppressor-victim' dualism, in which multiple subjectivity and self-identity processes are made invisible by the power of political categories of gender ... and their ideological and material forces" (p. 99). Said differently, Kevin's identity and journey to manhood cannot be summed up by particular events, decisions, or outcomes. To do this would be to take for granted the myriad "ideological and material forces" that impact identity construction and cheapen the complex processes and borders he navigated as he journeyed from boyhood to manhood.

Moreover, questions still remain if we are to comprehensively consider how Black males form personal identities as they journey from boyhood to manhood. For example, being careful to avoid the essentialist tendency to truncate complex constructs, discourses, and identities into narrow, hegemonic monoliths (Anzaldúa, 2007), we must begin to ask questions like, Who are Black Bermudian males in competition with? Are Black Bermudian males violent, and if so, who are they violent toward? Do Black Bermudian males seek to dominate others, and if so, who? Data suggest that many Black males are often in competition with each other, and only certain Black males—for example, those who see themselves as part of the Black elite—are overly concerned with competing with White males. For example, Cooper Academy students often referenced how they were encouraged to compete against Ivy Secondary students in the number of GCSE examination passes. Ironically, as a student at Hope Academy, Dexter's hatred of "snubby" Ivy students seemed to be reserved for the Black students who he thought were *acting White* because they attended a historically White school. Malcolm's narrative answers some of the questions I raise in this paragraph, as do other participants in later chapters in their discussions about violence and the influence of the media as a source that sets and then propagates low expectations for Black males.

Consistent with Whitehead (2002) and Hatty's (2000) discussion about "competition" as a common characteristic of Western masculinity, Malcolm suggests that Black Bermudian males are often in competition with each other, and that this reality is intensified because of the size of the island. It is interesting to note the subjects or *objects* that Malcolm claims Black males compete for. Recall that Malcolm stated: "Being a Black man is like always challenging the next brotha, especially when it comes to like sports it is about challenging with the next brotha. Especially, when it comes to girls [attracting women]. ..." Notably, Malcolm does not reference being in competition with "the next brotha" over the acquisition of his GED or his academic pursuits—though this may be the experience of some males. Instead, bragging rights are based on conquest in "sports" and "girls." Malcolm's acceptance of the notion that he should "work with his hands" or engage in "blue-collar work" is also reflective of typical masculine notions. Many Black Bermudian males embrace this ideology, based on the data in this study. In this respect, Black Bermudian males—based on Malcolm's experiences—have been impacted by typical gendered expectations, Western societal norms, and institutional influences (Bahr, 1976). What appears to be a major factor in the expectations Black Bermudian males encounter are the pathways that are promoted in schools and other social institutions they attend. Notably, while impressing girls was an important part of the identity-forming processes of the males in this chapter, the extent to which participants embraced hegemonic masculinity—as defined as "the dominant position of men" or "the subordination of women" (Connell, 1995)—was not evident.

Consistent with the research on schools as social institutions where typical notions of masculinity are transmitted, Dexter was accepted by his peers at Hope Academy based on his identity as the jester and his perpetuation of typical, yet damaging, forms of Western masculinity. His humorous jibes gave him access to social collateral that he used for protection and survival. Other times, in order to maintain his reputation, he utilized his lyrical arsenal to hurl pejorative—and sometimes homophobic—remarks like "shut up you faggots" at other students who he describes as "twice my size, twice as crazy, [with] nothing to lose in life," but who would not hurt him because he was "funny." The language Dexter used to describe other males in school also speaks volumes about the expectations and influence of Western masculinity on Bermudian masculinity and sexuality: Toughness, as reflected at schools like Ivy, not only meant that you were expected to not value academics, but it also helped create the context where those who did value academics could be chastised as being effeminate. Notably, through his use of the pejorative label "faggot" and his brief mentioning during the interview of a male in his neighborhood who he described as being effeminate during adolescence, Dexter is the only participant who mentions homosexuality in his narrative. These notations are worth highlighting, though not enough data was provided to further interpret the topic of sexuality and Bermudian male identity. Perhaps the absence of references to nonheterosexual identities speaks to the dominant ideologies in the four spaces highlighted in this study and the conservative nature and Caribbean influences on Bermudian masculinity and culture. Many Black Bermudian males between the ages of 30 and 40 would have grown up listening to reggae music, which during the 80s and 90s often included songs with strong antihomosexual lyrics and sentiments.

While the notion that the school is a masculine institution is relevant to data in this chapter, it is also significant to note that the church is another institution that is structurally masculine: Like schools, churches are hierarchical and often led by men in the highest positions, even though there are more female parishioners than male parishioners, much like there are more female teachers than male teachers. Notably, all five participants in this chapter attended a church or Sabbath/Sunday school during boyhood and early adolescence, though only two of the five participants would be considered active church members at the time of their participation in this study. The reasons for their continued participation in a church or disengagement from a church are beyond the scope of this study, but data suggest that each participant—to varying degrees—considered the time spent in church to be valuable to their personal identity development and some of the expectations they now embrace about living a meaningful life, even if they chose to not actively participate in a church in adulthood. Ironically, all three of the participants who do not presently attend church expressed some level of desire to eventually re-engage with a church community as a space where they can grow and be educated on matters of spiritually. The impediment most consistently noted by the three nonchurch attendees was "life," suggesting that the church was not central to their daily experiences, their conceptualizations of success, and their personal identities as Black Bermudian males.

Conclusion

The data in this chapter suggest that the expectations that Black Bermudian males encounter as they journey from boyhood to manhood are significant to the identities they pursue and eventually embody, irrespective of whether these expectations are high, low, shifting, consistent, competing, or others'. In fact, the expectations and identities Black Bermudian males and people in general embrace come from others, at least initially. Said differently, we are all impacted by the expectations of individuals in our environments, or in the words of the poet John Donne (1624), "No man is an island"—not even in Bermuda.

Still, Black Bermudian males do not encounter the expectations of individuals in isolation. *Experiences/experimentation* are also highly impactful in the identities they form. In fact, *expectations* and *experiences/experimentation* are not mutually exclusive dynamics in the identity formation process. Often, the experiences that Black males have and the things they choose to experiment with are directly related to their personal expectations and those of the individuals who have the most significant influence on them. Similarly, in many ways, many of the choices that Black Bermudian males make play a role in choosing identities for them. How *experimentation* and *experiences* impact the identities that Black Bermudian males form during their journey to manhood is explored in the next chapter, with more specific attention given to the role of community-based pedagogical spaces in their processes.

· 6 ·

BLACK BERMUDIAN MALES
AND COMMUNITY-BASED
PEDAGOGICAL SPACES

To gain a greater understanding of how Black Bermudian males have personally experienced education in learning spaces outside schools, I draw on descriptions of their experiences and experimentation as active participants in various community-based pedagogical spaces. As a Black Bermudian male who has also been influenced by community-based pedagogical spaces, I was impacted by the life journeys of the participants and inspired by their wisdom and insights. The results of the study reveal that nonschool educative venues are impactful centers of learning, socialization, and support, as indicated by the first five participants profiled in chapter 4. Findings from the data also suggest that some of these community-based spaces may in fact have had a more substantial impact on the subjects' lives than schools have. To further illustrate how my participants discussed these spaces, I provide brief portrayals of the participants' educational *experiences and experimentations*—in school and out.

While chapter 5 highlighted the influence of *expectations* on the identities that Black Bermudian males form, the data in this chapter suggest that Black Bermudian males also form identities through experiences in community spaces and positive and/or negative experimentation within those spaces. Below, we meet Kofi, who offers a colorful array of experiences as a result of his *unsupervised experimentation* in the neighborhood and sports club. In addition,

I introduce three other participants, Shaka, Allan, and Devon, who were all also greatly influenced by the neighborhood, while also reintroducing the voices of some participants from chapter 5 to highlight their experiences in the Black barbershop and the church. Indeed, asked the open-ended question, "Can you tell me your journey from birth to boyhood to manhood?," all of the participants talked without prompting about the significance of a neighborhood, a church, a sports club, and/or a barbershop in their personal development. Yet, as I later describe, other spaces such as those found in the confines of prison complexes or in the freedom of dance groups proved important to two of the men's journeys as well.

Kofi's "Unsupervised" Experimentation: Boys Being Boys

Kofi is a proud Bermudian male with a strong sense of African and Bermudian identity. He eschews the label "Black" and describes himself as an "African" who is proud to have been born and raised in Bermuda. Now in his 30s, Kofi is newly married, a thoughtful father figure to his stepchildren, and a successful business professional and educator in corporate and community settings. But the seemingly mature, conscientious gentleman who sat across from me during our interviews is a far cry from the teenage menace he described himself as having been: a young man who neighborhood mothers encouraged their sons to avoid at all cost. Kofi's journey from boyhood to manhood was grounded in unsupervised experimentation in his neighborhood and an array of experiences in other community spaces like the sports club. He explains:

> In my teenage years, I, [like] the average Bermudian male, [couldn't] wait until [I was] 16 to get a bike [motorcycle]. ... I learned from someone how to hotwire a bike. So me and my "band of merry men" ... would go [to] "town" [the main city area] and steal bikes and ... we would ride [stolen] bikes around in the neighborhood. The neighborhood people all knew, besides for my momma. You know, mommas have that blindness to their child. They [neighbors] would call the police. ... On Halloween we used to [throw] eggs [at] their houses and we used to [steal] oranges [from their yards]. ... I was the negative influence in the neighborhood.

Kofi noted that most of his friends had "nuclear homes" of a "mother and father" or "in the absence of a father, [his friends] had older brothers that were able to be that male figure for them." Conversely, Kofi was raised in a single-parent home where he learned by his "own experimentation and whatever

[his] imagination would allow [him] to do." His mother worked two and some-times three jobs, which meant he was left in the care of his older sister. He states: "I had a lot of free time and no one to purposefully guide me in any direction. So it was learning by mistakes and God's grace." Kofi's father, whose marriage to his mother ended while Kofi was very young, lived in another part of the island and became actively involved in Kofi's life only during times of crisis. Kofi's living arrangement greatly affected his decision making inside and outside of school. As a student at Handel Elementary and Cooper Acad-emy, Kofi loved many sports, but he believes he underachieved academically because he was not pushed enough. In describing his schooling experience, he reveals not only some of the typical differences between the interests and decision making of boys and girls, but also how border crossing as an ideolog-ical and pedagogical imperative informs his approach today as a sports coach:

> It was weird. My sister and I had different upbringings. She would come home [and go] straight [to] doing her homework. I would come home ... and go outside [to play] football [or] cricket in the church yard. ... I was a good student. I never worked hard. Things came easy to me, educationally, so I just did enough to get by. ... In my coaching, I [encourage] practice that is just outside of [the athletes'] reach so that I am constantly [helping them to] striv[e] to do better. I don't think that as a boy I got that influence.

Notably, the sports club and the neighborhood were more significant spaces in Kofi's journey than the schoolhouse. In his words, the sports club meant "everything" in his journey to manhood, while the neighborhood was a very significant second. In fact, every one of his most important learning spaces—his schools, sports club, and church—were "walking distance from [his] house," and the people he encountered in these neighborhood spaces impacted him in various ways.

When speaking of church, Kofi claims that he was "drafted into church," in part because of the proximity of the church to his house and because of the informal community educators who "forced" him and his friends to participate in church activities. He explains:

> I fell in love with sports in the church playground. ... It was just a little patch of dirt ... but it felt like a World Cup stadium. ... The people may "make off" [complain] to you every once in a while but ... they just let you be a kid. I [accidentally] broke several windows at the church [but I] never got a bill for any of it. I don't know [how but] that type of thing just got fixed ... [even though] it wasn't my church.

While Kofi values how the church playground served as a vital community space that influenced his physical and athletic development, he can also now see how his spiritual development was initiated through the influence of conscientious church members. He continues:

> So it's a Sunday morning now, … the church yard is our home base. … We are riding
> our bikes … making noise and having fun, and I will never forget this woman, Sister
> Place—may she rest in peace—came and took us [into church]. She didn't call our
> parents. … She just said, "Park your bike right here," and … from then on we went
> to Sunday school and vacation Bible school [VBS]. I don't think I was ever actively
> registered … [b]ut I was always there. I knew all the songs: "I'm glad I came to VBS"
> [singing].

Kofi believes that Sister Place's activism as an informal, spiritual mother represents "the type of collectiveness, nationhood and sense of community that … has escaped us [Bermuda] now." Kofi claims Sister Place's actions "grounded me in Christianity" and filled a gap that his biological mother did not fill at the time. He asserts: "My momma thinks it is a failure of hers [that] she never made me go to Sunday school. And I told her, 'No way!' … I got all of that. I got that [spiritual] foundation." The guidance provided by Sister Place demonstrates the positive influences that can be organically encountered in community spaces. Kofi was fortunate in this particular instance, since there are no guarantees as to the quality of the influences when the experiences of youthful fun and unsupervised experimentation are the primary pedagogues.

Much like the surrogate spiritual/community mother (Sister Place) who led Kofi to attend Sunday school, there were also a handful of men who served as mentors and father figures in various spaces. In the absence of his father, Kofi's uncle was the most impactful male mentor in his early development. For example, after wetting his pants on his way to his first day of school, his uncle taught him the vital lesson to "use the trees" when he needed to use the potty. Kofi's uncle was also a father figure and disciplinarian for other neighborhood boys in need of guidance. In fact, during another neighborhood experience, the "hand of Kofi's uncle" took center stage. Kofi recalls this story with enthusiasm:

> After school one day "the boys" were playing in the trees behind my yard and one of
> them said "Let's light a fire." So we lit a fire … [and] almost burned down all the trees
> in the backyard. So my uncle comes out and he puts out the fire and took us all down
> into hallway of my house. These are old houses so the hallway may be 3 feet wide.
> But I remember clearly, all four of us boys were able to fit side by side in that hallway.
> And my uncle was able to slap all four of us in our faces with one swing: "da da da da
> da da!" And I don't know if it was the first guy that got hit the hardest, but he was the
> only one crying. The rest of us were trying not to laugh.

Kofi's uncle died when Kofi was 10 years old, meaning that Kofi lost his most significant male role model when he needed him most.

The absence of a positive and consistent male role model after Kofi's uncle's death impacted his decision making. Without supervision and sound counsel, he found models in the form of negative experiences and experimentation in his neighborhood and sports club. For example, Kofi was arrested because he and a friend were "stripping" parts off a bike his friend had stolen. It was during this experience that Kofi—drawing on his familiarity with the contours of his neighborhood—ran from the police, jumped off a cliff into the ocean, and "curled up" in a cave until nightfall. Though he remembers sincerely praying, "God, if you get me out of this, I will never steal again," his ambitious "getaway" was unsuccessful. His mother sent him to live with his father after this embarrassing incident, which was an awkward border-crossing experience given that his father was "involved passively" in his life up until that point. In the absence of his father's influence, Kofi had drawn many of his lessons from peers in nonschool venues and schoolhouse influences, but now he was forced to move from his neighborhood to live with a father he scarcely knew. Kofi's recollections about this period of his life reveal some of the inner tensions and questions that Black males rarely share but that impact their identities and sense of self. For example, he thought it "strange" that his birthday and his father's anniversary to his second wife are on same day. He states: "I don't know if it was the actual day I was born … [that] he was marrying someone else or a year later on my birthday was his marriage date. [I] never asked the question."

Kofi believes that other key questions—in school and out of school—went unasked as he sought to forge an identity. In spite of the fact that he was always in top classes at Cooper Academy, he had to obtain his high school diploma directly from the Department of Education because he did not meet the graduation requirement for Cooper. He declares: "How does a person doing five GCSEs not graduate? … I was falling through the cracks and there wasn't anyone there to catch my fall. … I was absorbed socially. I was absorbed in sport."

Kofi also cites a non-Bermudian "high school place test" that "was supposed to tell you what career field that you were geared toward" as significantly detrimental to his self-esteem and beliefs about his career options. His test result declared that he should pursue a career in "farming," which left him "distraught" because farming was not a "viable" career option in Bermuda. Echoing similar sentiments to those expressed in chapter 2 on the use and impact of non-Bermudian assessments, he states: "That wasn't a Bermudian test. … So why are we giving it to our Bermudian children?" In the absence of any follow-up from a school counselor or other adults, Kofi asserts that he did not have much guidance when he chose to attend a community college in the United States. Though he would earn "two associate's degrees," he wishes that he had been guided toward a career as a P. E. teacher, which is in line with his passion for sports. Also disappointing was the reality that his father did not financially support him when he attended community college, which created family "tension" because his mother had to fund his college fees by herself. In fact, his mother did not invite his father to attend Kofi's graduation from community college in the U.S., which Kofi did not understand at the time. Though delayed, Kofi now has a good relationship with his father. He states: "To his credit, he wasn't there in childhood, but in adulthood he has done well by me."

Much like Davis's (1981) discussion of how the Moynihan report promoted the notion that "Black people were allegedly left with 'the mother-centered family with … only tenuous ties to a man'" (p. 13), Kofi's narrative exemplifies the odd reality that sons often see their mothers in a more positive light than their fathers. Far too many fathers are disassociated—by circumstance or choice—from the daily lived experiences of their sons, only to be summoned when trouble comes or when accolades and special occasions arrive. By comparison, neighborhood influences—whether positive or negative—are consistently present; the 'hood is always there to dole out lessons, and whether active or in absentia, fathers and father figures exert an influence that sons feel and experience. For example, Kofi attributes his womanizing in youth and early adulthood to the legacies of his father and grandfather, and his experimentation with alcohol to his uncle, who was a bartender and "party guy." At 15 years old, Kofi and his friends would regularly get drunk from drinking Guinness, in part because they bought into the popular slogan that "Guinness is good for you," and the idea that "Guinness will make you perform well with women." More than this, it appears that Kofi bought into the typical identities that signify what it supposedly means to be a Western man, including the *highly sexualized posture* described by Kimmel (2006b) Plus, more specifically, Kofi seems to have embraced what it supposedly means to be a Black Bermudian male, as an extension of Western masculinities and promoted in spaces like the sports club: a socializer, a drinker, a ladies' man, and a sportsman.

Kofi acknowledges that there are clear intersections between his experimentation with alcohol and the sports club. He admits that "a lot of my experiences were trial and error," and he specifically remembers "drinking in public" at the sports club with his friends and returning home drunk. In many ways, the acting out of Kofi and his friends are clear examples of how "particular masculinities"—in this case, Black Bermudian masculinity in a sports club context—"are combinations of actions and signs ... performed in reaction and relation to complex material relations and emotional demands; these signify that this is man" (Hearn & Collinson, 1994, p. 104). Kofi's unsupervised experimentation as a teenager in the neighborhood and sports club led to alcohol and marijuana abuse during his early adult life. He declares:

> So from [age] 15 until I was 31, I was an alcoholic. ... [At] 19 we were introduced to marijuana. I remember my cousin ... coming around with marijuana. [Prior to] then, I remember telling him clearly, "I will never do drugs. No." Because then, the slogan "Say no to drugs" was reinforced in school. So I think the school did a good job at that point.

But at 19 years old, he had graduated from the influence of school antidrug slogans. Through the influences of peers in the neighborhood and the culture of his local sports club, he embraced a lifestyle practiced by far too many local sportsmen: partying, womanizing, and alcohol/drug abuse. In fact, Kofi claims that his drug abuse got worse as a result of his overseas travels with Bermuda national teams, which are affiliated with the sports club teams. He claims that the threat of being drug tested by the local sports governing bodies prior to the overseas tour initially curbed his marijuana use, but then he was never tested and he fully embraced the culture of smoking marijuana and drinking. He candidly states:

> "Bermudians like to drink."[1] That's the slogan, and culturally that's almost accepted by Bermudians. ... [A]t the time I bought into it [the mentality] totally. [W]e went on the tour and smoked every day, all day. I remember ... [a] team [official] ... had to come [to a player's] hotel room, and a puff of smoke went out the door. [The team official] surely didn't report it, but he wasn't too pleased. [Another team official] at that time was an alcoholic. All the other teams had an 11:00 or 10:00 curfew. The Bermudians didn't have a curfew, so we were going out to get herb [marijuana] and prostitutes. ... I remember one time I was getting back, 4:00 in the morning now, and the alcoholic [team official was] at the bar. He calls me over [by] my nickname, and he's buying pitchers of Heineken. ... Needless to say, we didn't do very well on that tour.

Kofi claims that he experienced the negative and positive peer pressure of the sports club space. He admits that marijuana and alcohol were prevalent at his sports club, and that during what many would call his "glory years," when he "ascended high and quickly in sports," he was a "functioning alcoholic" who also experienced some of the other trappings of playing sports in Bermuda: "notoriety, women, and power." He also believes that he underachieved in school academically because of the imbalance of negative nonschool influences and a lack of guidance and drive while he was a student. He has become a border crosser as he has developed as a man. For example, he no longer spends as much time with his childhood friends, though he still considers them his "bona fides." He explains:

> I don't see them as often. And in doing that, I've been able to grow, and spare time I would have had with those friends is … dedicated to my personal growth. In school, I wasn't an avid reader, but now, I read anything I can get my hands on.

Not only is Kofi a voracious reader, he is a student of life who is trying to make up for lost time to maximize his potential and help young people make better choices. More than anything, the process of maturation appears to be an important border-crossing experience that must be noted. Kofi has crossed over from an immature and irresponsible school boy who "could" learn in school to a conscientious and capable man who now loves to learn. Perhaps greater surveillance and support from schoolhouse and nonschool actors could have led him to a more positive pathway sooner.

To his credit, Kofi draws on his experiences to mentor young people today through his coaching, community work, and connections to schools. Still, he admitted that he has not escaped the unsupervised experimentation and experiences of his past unscathed. He has lost many friends to road traffic accidents as a result of alcohol abuse. He also acknowledges that there are "complications" in his young marriage because he "battered th[e] bridge of trust when I would … get drunk and not come home [to] my girlfriend [now wife]." He accepts her distrust as fair, perhaps—in part—because the lack of literal *space* in Bermuda (21 squares miles) means Bermudians struggle to escape their past while living on the island. With only three major roads and one major city, you can always encounter reminders—in Kofi's case, women— of the past. These are all borders to be navigated that can complicate the lives and identities of Black Bermudian males. Kofi's profile reminds us that Black Bermudian males who are allowed to engage in unsupervised experimentation in community-based spaces are exposed to influences and experiences of varying qualities that have a lasting impact on the identities they form.

Shaka's Journey: Surveillance and Experimentation

Shaka is a Black Bermudian male in his early 30s who, like Kofi, has a strong sense of African identity but is far less patriotic about his Bermudian identity.

Shaka is a school teacher who is divorced from his wife, with whom he has three children. He also has one older child from a previous relationship with a woman he still believes is "the one." Shaka's journey from boyhood to manhood was characterized by the surveillance of a conscientious mother and father who refused to allow their son to underachieve or fall victim to the ills of his neighborhood. Shaka had numerous childhood experiences that impacted his identity and made him feel unsafe or unsettled, including his parents' troubled marriage that ended in divorce.

Shaka has vivid memories of his childhood. His most notable early memories include moving from the Webster's Cliff neighborhood in Bermuda to the East Coast of the United States while his mother was in university. He disliked this border-crossing experience because he thought the U.S. was violent and he was afraid of being abducted by someone called "the killer." He also remembers his father visiting for his mother's graduation and reacting violently to the presence of "some guy." It was at this point that Shaka first got the feeling that "things were not good in my life." After his mother's graduation, his family returned to the Webster's Cliff neighborhood in Bermuda and he attended grade 1 at Webster's Cliff elementary school.

Shaka claims that he had a very positive school experience from elementary to college because his family encouraged his academic pursuits and he excelled. But while he was performing well in school, his family was not doing so well. In response to the tensions at home, sports became an important outlet. In particular, playing football (soccer) provided a peaceful, fun space of positive experimentation. He explains:

> I remember my family falling apart. ... There was a lot of arguing. By the time I got to primary 5 [about age 10], I was a football addict; [it] was like my new heaven: football every day, all day. ... As long as I did [my] work, I played football.

In spite of his parents' divorce, Shaka describes his overall home and school experiences as "really structured." Like many boys, he loved physical education. In fact, he claims "the best thing in my life outside of my parents when I was a child was my gym teacher: "[I] still can hear him saying, 'Follow through after [making] the pass.'" He can also still hear the constant chiding of his parents, who ensured that he had his priorities in order. He states:

> I had my mother who I was petrified of, [and] my father who I was petrified of. I knew in school I couldn't do a pack [of foolishness]. Playing football, sometimes you get around some of the tougher, rowdier guys. In class, those guys thought I was a freak [a nerd]. [They] couldn't even believe how I got on the [soccer] field. Why? [Because]

my parents had me petrified of not being respectful, petrified of not trying my best with my education, petrified of whatever, doing what I shouldn't be doing.

Much like the experience noted in Jeremiah's narrative in chapter 5, Shaka followed in the footsteps of an older brother to attend Cooper Academy. He describes his Cooper experience and the pathway leading to it this way:

> I remember doing my stanine test and I got a 5/7, [which was] good enough to get into Cooper. ... I remember my first day going into school [at Cooper Academy] I cried ... just from the overwhelming feeling I got [from the] new environment. ... When I got to my class[room] I saw some people I knew from my neighborhood. ... I got caught up for like the first two years in the social life. By the fourth year, I remembered [why] I was in school and started doing my work again: academics—no problem, sports—no problem, enjoyed playing football. [I] didn't play much cricket in high school because [cricket] gear was too expensive and the school didn't provide it for you anymore [like it was provided in elementary school].

Shaka's mention of the cost of cricket equipment limiting his access to the sport provides vital context to understandings of how economics, sport, and border crossing converge. Many Black Bermudians males—particularly those who are economically disadvantaged—have limited access to a diverse set of extracurricular activities. This reality underscores the value of football as an important sport for Bermudian youth and the powerful influence of sports clubs that serve as social conduits and vital educative spaces for Black Bermudian males. Notably, most Black Bermudian males participate in a youth football program during their journey to manhood.

In addition to being a football enthusiast, Shaka—like Jeremiah, Kevin, and Kofi—is a proud alumnus of Cooper. In fact, being a "Cooperite" means more to him than being a Bermudian. He describes his disconnect with his Bermudian identity:

> What does it mean to be Bermudian? [Are we discussing this] in the sense [that] Juan de Bermudez [the Spanish explorer credited with discovering Bermuda] had just dropped off slaves in the new world when he spotted Bermuda? Because what that would mean [is] that we are named after a slave trader. Not even what that *would* mean, what that *does* mean is that we're named after a slave trader! So ... to be a Bermudian, it means to have a "blood-seed" passport that allows you travel around the place, that's it, nothing else. Because I don't want to be a Bermudian, I can't be called a Bermudian. I can't be called a Bermudian and be happy.

Shaka's consciousness and critique of Bermuda's colonial history was undergirded by his overseas travels for his own cultural development and his educational experience while attending an HBCU in the U.S. He is acutely aware of the divergent perceptions and "intracultural" tensions (Anzaldúa, 2007) between peoples of African descent. For example, he recalls how he and his Bermudian intramural soccer teammates in university were seen as arrogant and affluent by Black males from other countries. He also noted being chastised by a Ghanaian professor in the middle of a final exam because he arrived late for the test and "colonized all the chairs" with his wet jacket and book bag. He explains:

> I show up to the test [with] about an hour and a half left. Now the test is going to take about 20 minutes ... and I come in all soaking [wet]. ... [E]verybody's seated doing their test quietly, so I walk into the classroom ... take off my bag, put it on the back of this chair. Now I'm like the last student in there so there's about 15 more seats. ... Take off the jacket, put that on another chair [along with] some other stuff ... [so] by the time I sat down to where my test was, I had like about five desks. This is a final—so this guy [the professor] in the middle of the final says, "Hey, hey!" I'm like, "Okay, he's talking to me." He says, "Where you from?" I said, "Bermuda." He goes, "You must have been from somewhere like that. I see your colonial mentality." I said, "F*ck." I'm thinking, I'm busting free [and] breaking chains. But it's embedded. ... [A]fterwards, I talked to him, and he says I "colonized all the chairs," and in general, he could tell I was British.

Educational experiences like this have caused Shaka to critically interrogate his identity and his conceptualization of history. His schoolhouse education at predominantly Black elementary and high schools has been buttressed by his conversations with activists like Pauulu Kamarakafego, who I mention in chapter 2 as being an impactful Bermudian leader during the Black Power movement (Swan, 2009). Having returned to Bermuda after college in the U.S., Shaka's in-school and nonschool educational experiences have led him to have stronger allegiances to his neighborhood than to the label "Bermudian." Plus, his neighborhood not only significantly impacted his sense of personal identity, it also gave him a socially conscious lens that informed his observations and understandings of life in Bermuda. Using a metaphor from his experiences seeing "crack addicts" in his neighborhood, he describes Bermudians this way:

> We're just going around, going on as [if] all things are well. And really, we're not. We're being taken advantage of. We're being disrespected. We're standing for less. We're eating food that's not healthy. We're living in toxic environments ... but we're smiling. We're smiling in part because we have enough money to keep smiling. ... We're like cocaine addicts. ... I've seen two types of crack heads: The one crack head ... who don't

know where his next 50 dollars is coming from to get that crack. He's looking bad, he's never smiling unless he's hitting, right at that time. The cocaine guys who come in a TelCo [electric company] truck ... [are] functional crack heads, they're suffering and smiling. ... Nobody knows I'm on crack as long as I get my hit before I start scratching. That's what it's like in Bermuda. ... Everybody's trying to keep [up an] appearance. ... I could stop everybody here and say, why are we suffering? And everybody would give a different reason, and they're walking away smiling. You know why? Because they know what they're having for dinner, and they know where they're staying tonight; they know what channel they're watching when they go home.

Clearly, Shaka's personal lens and keen critique has been informed by the realities he has observed in his neighborhood and the dysfunction he feels Bermudians are unwilling to own and address in their own neighborhoods and families.

While many would describe Shaka's Webster's Cliff neighborhood as "bad," Shaka is far more complimentary. In fact, he describes Webster's Cliff as the "best neighborhood on the island," citing as evidence neighborhood block parties, "pop-a-wheelie races" and "fairly tight living quarters," which meant there were always people outside playing cricket, swimming, and fixing bikes. Shaka claims he was often away from home "for hours" experimenting in the neighborhood, and that every neighborhood influence was not positive. He credits his parent's surveillance for keeping him from totally losing his way when he was a rebellious 14 year old who would leave home, without permission, on Friday night and not return until Sunday night. He claims he was "just roaming the neighborhood" because there were so many people outside to play with from the houses and apartments. He notes that, unlike today, there were a lot more "grannies" and "uncles" around, which facilitated generational connections, community fun, and neighborhood accountability that kept children "settled." Shaka's recollections are akin to the African family traditions of intimate extended family connections (McAdoo, 2007; Sudarkasa, 2007). More precisely, Shaka's experiences and feelings of attachment in his neighborhood are relevant to the claims of scholars like Stack (1974), who asserts that "[s]ocial space assumes great importance in a crowded living area" (p. 7), and Sudarkasa (2007), who highlights the importance of *the village* or neighborhood for Black families.

During the summer vacation, though, Shaka notes that kids were often unsupervised while playing and swimming in the neighborhood. It was common for four or five children to swim for miles along the length of the shoreline while holding onto "black car inner tubes." Shaka's mother never condoned this unsupervised experimentation, but he did it anyway while she was at work. As Shaka got older, he began to test his boundaries, much like Kofi did at about the same age. But there was one significant difference between Shaka and Kofi's relationships with their parents: Shaka was "petrified" of his parents—particularly, his mother! Shaka's mother saw no need to send him to his daddy's house, like Kofi's mother did. Instead, Shaka says his parents would "chase me down" from any location at any time of day or night. Shaka explains:

> My mother used to look for me. [If] I wasn't at home, I would show up at a place, [and] they would say, "Yeah, your momma's here." "What do you mean?!" … [I] took off [running]. … [Another] time I was up there hanging out on the wall [with] the hardest guys … and what did I hear? My momma's bike [motorcycle]. I said, that sounds like it [her bike]. So I went over to the side, looked around, looked in the alley, but I saw the bike and didn't see her, and that was the worst thing, to not see her … I [was] knocking on 16 [years old], bigger than my momma [but] … petrified that this woman I can't see [is after me]. So I … jumped down the cut [the alley], ran through the park, hopped over the [elementary school] wall, ran along the school field to the gate at the bottom of the hill at Webster's Cliff. … So I'm walking up the hill, I heard my momma's bike coming, right? So I'm thinking … I've got her. Yeah, right … she put down her little helmet, got off the bike, [and] just started attacking, "whew, whew, whew, get yourself here, rah, rah, rah." [She] searched my pockets looking for marijuana. One time, she smelt marijuana on us, or she saw our eyes were red or something—she called the policeman; the police search[ed] my bedroom … on my momma's call. She made me and my brother walk from Webster's Cliff to the hospital one late, late night … to get drug tested. So all that type of stuff was how she fought—like she weren't having it.

Clearly, Shaka was not left alone to navigate through the negative influences and experimentation of his neighborhood. His parents exerted a powerful and positive influence on the identity he was forming, particularly as it related to his social and academic development. Shaka's parents, however, were less active in his spiritual development. He says surrogate parents in the neighborhood who provided positive experiences to support the spiritual journeys of the children, and the accumulation of positive influences and surveillance when he was in community-based settings, helped Shaka cross many educational borders: He successfully completed high school, Bermuda College, and university abroad at an HBCU.

In fact, Shaka's border crossing from Cooper to a U.S. college offers important context when compared to Kofi's transition. Both men matriculated to Bermuda College; yet, on the back of an anonymous scholarship from someone at Cooper who believed in him, Shaka crossed over to Bermuda

College with his confidence in his academic ability intact. Kofi, on the other hand, crossed over to Bermuda College as a young man whose confidence in his academic ability had been shattered by a test that declared he should be a "farmer," and as someone under the heavy influence of the sports club culture. While Shaka declared that "at Bermuda College I really got a love for learning," Kofi said he wasted a lot of time in the college student center and failed to make adequate academic progress. Notably, both men now admit to not having a clear sense of their options or the best pathways to take once the routine of mandatory schooling was complete. Later, football and academics converged for Shaka again. His participation on the Bermuda College football team allowed him to travel on an overseas tour that exposed him to a U.S. college campus for the first time. Seeing a college campus in the U.S. was an important experience for him. He explains:

> [I] got to get a good feel for it [the college environment], saw it, and seeing something, you can more easily visualize yourself walking the halls or sitting in the yard, going to classes. You will see, okay, that's where I'll be going, that looks doable all of a sudden. So it gave me a reality check on how possible university was.

In fact, Shaka's uncle, who also attended this same HBCU, was the person who helped him to choose between the two HBCUs he was considering. This is the kind of specific advice that Kofi now identifies as missing in his educational journey.

Notably, Shaka does not claim allegiance to any particular religious tradition, though he, like Kofi, claims he got "a good foundation [about] right and wrong, stories in the Bible, [and] little songs from vacation Bible school." Like Kofi had Sister Place, Shaka had Mr. King—a church member who corralled neighborhood children in his car for Sunday school. He explains:

> Webster's Cliff was a neighborhood that had a lot of children who lived in tough situations, but the environment was very loving. ... I remember feeling like the adults there [cared] ... I trusted them, I loved them. Spiritually, something was going, too. This is when Mr. King used to go around and make two trips in his blue station wagon and take everybody to [the church] where he was the pastor ... that's like the foundation for me, and [it] was seriously important ... that I developed a conscience based on so many stories in the Bible, what's right and what's wrong, and what's acceptable. I'm not a Christian, but I'm thankful for Mr. King taking us to Sunday school [and the] spiritual influence.

Data indicate that Shaka's schooling experience alone was not enough to ensure his safe passage to manhood. Though he was academically proficient in school, his life outcome could have easily been very different had he been left to the experimentation and negative influences in his neighborhood. The surveillance of his parents and the positive influences of nonschool settings preserved Shaka when he was choosing a self-destructive path. Today, Shaka believes his spiritual consciousness helped him avoid the lifestyle and violence that has claimed the lives of many of his former neighborhood peers. Additionally, his personal faith protected him from social anarchy when he did engage in neighborhood experimentation and hang with "some bad dudes." On many occasions, he would "cut a trail" (leave) when he sensed that "something was about to go down." On other occasions, his parents' surveillance interrupted his experimentation, and their proactive utilization of mentors from community spaces, like the barber, served to counterbalance the negative neighborhood elements. He states:

> I also remember … some of those tougher times where I was doing stuff my parents didn't want me to do, my mother actually brought the barber—brought Ricky over to my house. [He] sat down at the kitchen table, and [she] had him talk to me and my brothers … you know, just getting some influence and things. [S]he brought police up there to talk to us when we weren't even in trouble. She brought a reverend up there.

Shaka's discussion of the influence of his barber is particularly relevant to this study. His mother recognized that the schoolhouse and her personal surveillance were insufficient if her son was to forge a healthy identity. She needed other safe educative spaces for her son. Shaka's experiences at his barbershop are representative of the value of an *education by committee* approach, where mentors in various spaces make key contributions to the identities of Black males. He states:

> I remember going to Ricky's barbershop … [and] he [the barber/shop owner] became an influential person in my life. He used to look out for us. Momma used to just drop us down there. I remember he used to try to keep a clean environment, you know, clean in terms of language and all of that type of stuff. … [Y]ou've got conversations about sports, … about life, … about politics, and you will hear things. I always felt safe there. … Yeah, [the barbershop] was just another place where I got see Black men in conversation and whatnot. I'm going to always remember the conversations.

Shaka's visits to the barbershop became more and more infrequent as he got older. Still, the influence of the barbershop as a safe space where he "never [felt] anxious" cannot be understated, particularly when considered within the context of the fears he described as a boy living in the U.S. and his feelings of "danger" as his family fell apart. One can never minimize the value of meaningful encounters in positive spaces: Ricky's barbershop was a location where his mother not only knew Shaka was safe, but also knew her messages were being reinforced. Moreover, Shaka was able to forge a strong personal identity and enjoy a positive educational experience overall because he was not left to navigate the negative influences of community-based spaces alone. In fact, through parental surveillance and the support of other parents/guardians, Shaka was able to find *safe spaces*, such as Ricky's barbershop, Sunday school, and the neighborhood, when supervised by responsible adults, which provided a sense of security during seasons of instability caused by familial challenges and his own decisions as a young boy trying to form an identity.

Allan as Outlier: Education by Any Means Necessary

Allan is what many would describe as a "conscious" Black Bermudian male. In his mid-30s, Allan sports dreadlocks, has a very peaceful demeanor, and embodies a strong sense of African and Bermudian identity. He is a lover of nature, with a gentle and humble spirit. Through the use of rich personal examples and his strong Bermudian accent, his cadence and word choice suggest that he is a man of deep reflection. Allan is very proud of Bermuda and its culture, but he does not make major distinctions between being a Black man in Bermuda and being a Black man in another country. When asked specifically about his identity, he offered a definitive response: "One word: African. That's my identity. ... Yes, we are Bermudians as a whole. This is where we're born, [but] I'm an African born in Bermuda the same way that a Portuguese man born in Bermuda, you still call him a Portuguese." Allan reflects a border-crossing ideology in that he sees his African identity as one that transcends his present location to remain connected to Black men across the Diaspora. Like Giroux (2005), who challenges "essentialist constructions of difference," Allan problematizes labels like *Black* and *Bermudian* as too simplistic to account for the complexity of his African identity and too limited in their capacity to allow him to identify with men of African descent in various jurisdictions (p. 99). Allan is happily married and the father of one child. He is a mason and proud home owner who, through ambition, sacrifice, and his masonry skills, was able to purchase and renovate the home he now lives in. But this was not always his story.

While Allan mentions a pedagogical space I highlight in this study—the neighborhood as a space of experimentation—he identifies two additional community-based educative institutions that serve as both potent pedagogical forces in his life and outliers in this study: prison and the gombeys.[2] Disturbingly, prison is a space Black males in Bermuda and across the Diaspora consistently and disproportionately experience. As I detail below, much of what he has acquired was accomplished after he was released from prison after serving time for attempted murder and he determined to "accomplish more in a one year than [others] accomplish in a lifetime." Like Kevin in chapter 5, Allan's transformation occurred in the solitude of the prison space where he was able to reflect on his manhood and recalibrate his personal vision. Allan also acquired his GED in prison, where he served nearly 4 years of a 10-year prison sentence for "defending his [biological] brother" who was attacked at a public venue. As I detail later, the restraint of the prison space—which offers an interesting contrast to the free expression of gombey dancing—eliminated the distractions that had conspired against the completion of his high school diploma in public schooling. Allan admits that a combination of a lack of personal focus and poor schools impeded his educational border crossing during adolescence.

Allan was raised in a close-knit family that he described as "poor," though, as other participants have noted in their narratives, he did not realize it until later in life. He has fond memories of family gatherings where his nuclear family and his extended kin gathered often to share food, play marbles, and enjoy the ocean. Like Shaka, the close living quarters in his urban neighborhood created a strong sense of community (Stack, 1974), and in Allan's case, many of those who lived closest to him were extended family members who shared the multi-unit house his parents rented; the "strong family tradition" that has persisted in Allan's family is consistent with the persistence of neighborhood and African extended-kin traditions in many Black families where the ideology of *the village* serves as a vital space for the rearing of children and the preservation of culture and identities (Sudarkasa, 2007). If, as Bhabha (1994) suggests, culture is a "strategy of survival" that facilitates the hybridity that the subaltern need to traverse various borders, then a healthy neighborhood can serve as a powerful nexus for Black families, Black identities, Black agency, and Black history.

Allan is a lover of history, particularly Black history, which he feels has been "desecrated" by Europeans who stole many of "our symbols." Ironically, Allan hated history in school, like many other Black males who are exposed to history lessons only from a Eurocentric perspective. He explains: "[History is] my favorite subject [now]. Not in school—in school they never really talked about anything that interested me ... but as I got into my older years, I really started to learn more about my history." Allan admits that he "was [not] interested in school," but preferred to use his hands and do anything that was "artistic." This ideology is reflected in the fact that his discussion of his schooling experience was minimal in comparison to his discussion of other educative spaces. He merely named his elementary school and the high schools he attended, specifically taking time to note the "straight up zoo" that was Hope Academy, and, after prompting, the fact that he earned a 3/3 on the transfer/high school entrance exam. In fact, Allan claims that he saw the "destruction of education" when the first high school he attended was closed down and he was forced to attend Hope. He asserts that he was forced to move from a technical school, where he was learning both academic and practical skills, and where teachers would "snatch hold of [discipline] you," to Hope Academy, a school that he claims "was being run by students," and where some "teachers were shooting hard drugs." He says the lack of control at his high school meant he had a lot of time to experiment with "racing bikes" while "skip[ping] school." In light of the high school experience he describes, Allan was fortunate to have positive experiences in other spaces to buttress his development.

The fact that spaces like the neighborhood and individuals outside of the schoolhouse were very impactful in his life is not uncommon in this research study. For example, like Jeremiah and Giovanni in chapter 6, Allan remarks that his father was very significant in instructing him to become an independent, God-fearing man. Allan notes that his father was intentional about preparing him for manhood, even calling him "a man" from as early as 10 and 11 years old. In fact, he notes that his dad never called him or his brothers "boys." Unlike some of the other participants, Allan experienced a positive, steady influence from his father, which he believes is why he and his brothers are very independent today. Yet, despite the positive influence of his father, Allan admits that he wandered down the wrong path at times, in part because he often chose to hang with "rough people" in the neighborhood.

Allan is adamant that he was "never a follower," but he is not naïve about the influence of neighborhood experiences on his identity during his journey to manhood. Like other participants, Allan was exposed to some of the negative influences and experiences of "street life" in his neighborhood as a teenager, including getting into a "couple of fights" to defend others, and experimenting with marijuana—though he does not see marijuana as a drug, and is quick to distinguish it from cocaine, heroin, and other drugs that are criminalized by "them" (those in power). Allan says he has not smoked marijuana in nearly a decade, and he claims he has always been a peaceful person who simply hung out with "rough guys." Consistent with one of the themes that emerged in this study—learning through experiences and experimentation—Allan embraces life's mistakes as "the only way to learn." In fact, his father was intentional about instilling this experiences-based mantra in Allan's thinking by sharing statements like, "I make mistakes, you know? You can't do everything the way I do it. … You might find a better way." Allan believes he learned to improvise and adjust to various circumstances because of his father's approach. In fact, Allan believes his capacity to use the setback of prison time as a setup for his comeback as a new man is directly related to the messages that his father instilled in him to acknowledge mistakes and build on them.

Allan takes full responsibility for the events that resulted in his arrest and imprisonment, though he believes the charge of attempted murder was "bogus" and that the high-profile, public nature of the incident is what prompted authorities to try to "make an example" of him. The fight, which occurred in front of politicians, other dignitaries, and hundreds of fans, has been framed as a watershed moment in the gang violence that has escalated recently in Bermuda and resulted in the proliferation of gun crimes and shooting deaths of numerous Black males.[3] Images of Allan brandishing a weapon during the fight flooded the front pages of the newspapers and television reports. Allan asserts that many of the details of his case were exaggerated, and he believes the media has been highly influential in drumming up and helping to create gangs in Bermuda. Harking back to the work of Kimmel (2006a, 2006b) who identifies the narrow and destructive conceptualizations of Western masculinity that cross cultural and national borders through the media, Allan is under no illusions as to the transience and invasive tendencies of foreign masculine identities on Black Bermudian males. He describes his thoughts on being labeled a gang member:

> [T]hey [the media] started putting it out [that] "the Crips are in Bermuda." No way, [Bermudians] would have never thought of that. You would have never thought of yourself as a gang. Maybe we guys came [grew] up together, we're going out together, that's it. A gang? No way. That's what people look for, labels. If it's not got a label to it, they don't understand it. People want labels. I never looked at it as a gang.

He also has a different account and interpretation of the events that led to his arrest and conviction. While many believed the fight was between rival gangs, Allan is clear that the plot was far less sensational. He was simply defending his younger brother:

> At first people thought it was a "town" [central parish] and "country" [Western parish] thing. … I remember clearly. I was talking to somebody about the game [and someone]

said something to my brother. ... Before you know it, they were fighting [and] fell onto the field. When they fell onto the field, that's when I hear "crack," and I look down, it was my brother down on the ground. So everything went haywire. From there everything just went—chaos. I exploded on that day, yeah. Not to the fullest potential, but I did explode.

Allan believes that there are individuals in power who are intentional about maintaining the oppression of others—particularly Black males. Within a Bermudian context, Allan's identification of the oppressive tentacles of a colonial mindset and existence is an important rereading of "identity, ideology and cultural practice" (Hickling-Hudson, 1998, p. 327); his rereading of the present is grounded is his critical reflection of the past and his acute awareness and identification of how power is disproportionately held and how Others are differentially affected (Gresson, 2008). His critique has connections to the notion of border crossing, in that he believes there are individuals whose corporate interests are enhanced by the inability of Black Bermudian males to travel freely and access work across the island because of supposed gang affiliations. He states:

> The media directs what they want you to think. This is another part of manipulation—
> if the media could make guys in different neighborhoods ... look affiliated with some
> sort of gang activity or whatever, they'll shut you down from work. You go look for a job
> and say you're from this neighborhood ... they [interviewers] automatically—when you
> leave—you're scratched off that interview: "No we don't [have a job for you]—we ain't
> crossing [getting into] that. He lives too close to [a particular neighborhood]."

Allan is highly critical of the approaches being used in response to violence that he says are designed to "hurt," "destroy," and "punish" rather than educate. Still, he admits his time in prison was a turning point in his life that led him to a deeper understanding of his identity. He explains: "I think I experienced a real sense of spiritual awakening when I was locked up [and] had the time by myself; that's when I actually experienced a real sense of, 'yeah, this is what you are.'"

Allan further underscores how the prison served as a learning space, in part because there were few distractions, and because—heeding his father's counsel—he has always been willing to admit and learn from his mistakes. For Allan, that is what a man does. He states:

> [I] had a lot of time—a lot of thinking time—a lot of studying. I don't blame nobody.
> It's all my doing, all my creation, all my choices. I'm a person that won't blame the
> devil, because that don't make me a responsible person. I've made all the choices in my
> life, got the consequences, dealt with them. For the good choices, [I] got the rewards.

Clearly, a house is not the only thing that Allan has renovated since his time in prison. Allan has truly renovated his life and embraced education by any means necessary—mistakes, experimentation, and negative experiences included. He would not change any of it. To change some is to change all, and Allan is far too optimistic about his present and future to cry over the mistakes of his past. Allan has demonstrated his capacity to learn however and wherever he must, and he is intentional about acknowledging the significance of his wife's support in his journey; now, as a mentor and instructor of young gombey dancers and a role model to his younger brothers, he is demonstrating his capacity to teach. Gentle and genuine, he is truly his brother's keeper. He declares:

> I've learned a lot of lessons with my time [in prison], you know, time to think. My situation even startled my brothers. But I always told them when I was up there [in jail], "Always remember, don't dishonor me. Don't make my time [in jail] a waste of time." Don't you ever [retaliate] ... and then you're coming up here [to prison] for some dumb stuff. You might as well have come [to prison], I would have stayed out. So I came out [of prison], I bought this house, [and] my brother bought a house.

While Allan is now taking full advantage of the freedom he temporarily lost while incarcerated, he feels most free when he is "dancing gombeys," which is the other significant space and outlier that emerged in this study. Grounded in African cultural traditions, the gombeys are popular—typically, all male—Bermudian dancers/dance troupes who, dressed in distinctive, colorful costumes and masks with tall hats and peacock feathers, dance and parade through the streets to syncopated and captivating drum beats. During parades and festive seasons, hundreds of smiling and dancing Bermudians can be found *followin' de' gombeys* through Black neighborhoods, with exuberant shouts of "ay-oh!" ringing from the crowds as they and the gombeys twist and turn through alleyways. Sounds of men blowing into conch shells and empty beer bottles produce flute-like accompaniment to the drum ensembles that create the core beats that entice *locals* to leave their immediate neighborhoods to join the procession—in trance-like fashion—for miles.

Consistent with his strong African and Bermudian identities, Allan has been an avid gombey dancer from the age of 2. He now teaches other Black males how to *dance gombeys* and choreographs creative routines. The gombeys are central to Allan's personal identity as a practice or space of positive experimentation and expression. He explains:

> The masquerade is a slow [gombey] dance that I do. ... I know how to do every single dance [but] when I go [into the] masquerade it's like another whole other world I am

[in]—people are like, "Oh, wow." [I] flow like water, like I ain't got no bones in my body, just flow.

Few spaces allow Black males to "just flow." In fact, most mainstream or traditional educative spaces—like schools—are intentional about stifling free-flowing creativity, expression, and play. The organic expression that Allan describes when he does the masquerade dance is also consistent with the improvisational attributes of Black people who have historically had to make something out of little.

Allan describes gombey dancing as his "passion." During our interview, he enthusiastically showed me his handcrafted, one-of-a kind gombey suits, and he is proud to be viewed by many in the community as one of the best gombey dancers in Bermuda, having been introduced to this African-orientated practice by his grandmother, who made his gombey suits. Allan's experiences as a gombey highlight the reality that, for generations of Bermudian males, the gombeys have been a source of positive Black male mentorship and African-Bermudian identity formation. Acknowledging the gombeys as an educative community institution/space is significant to this study and representative of the fact that some Black males are educated in community spaces besides the four emphasized in this study.

Allan's narrative reveals the complexity and beauty of border crossing for a Black male whose story of transformation and redemption challenges many of the stereotypes about Black males—especially those whom society is all too willing to lock up in prison and throw away *the key*—but also highlights the humanity and humility of a Black man who actually offers *a key* to more fruitful pedagogical practices that respect the cultural identities and masculinities of Black Bermudian males. Allan's experiences reveal the importance of both freedom and restraint: Through the positive experiences of the gombeys, he found a space to "just flow"; through the enforced environment of the prison, he benefited from the time to *just stop*. These polar opposites are pregnant with pedagogical possibilities. Educational stakeholders must critically assess and address the questions that Allan's learning experiences posit: How and where are Black Bermudian males and Black males in general given the time and space to *just flow*, and when and where—besides the prison—are Black males able to *just stop* in order to (re)assess and (re)position themselves toward healthy identities and wholesome outcomes? By border crossing from the dark to light side, Allan's transformation provides a hopeful counternarrative to dominant discourses that rarely consider the potential of Black male renewal and redemption.

Devon's Journey: Neighborhood in Isolation, Experience(s) as Teacher

While most participants noted the significant influence of multiple community spaces, Devon's narrative highlights the influence of one space: the neighborhood. Devon is a Black Bermudian male in his early 30s who consistently referenced the strong influence of the neighborhood on his upbringing. In fact, he declares, "My neighborhood made me, you know, shaped me into what I need to be to become a man. As far as everything big in life. Trials and tribulations through life. You learn it, you see it." When asked the broad question of what spaces were most influential in his life, Devon asserts that "the street ... had the most influence on me," underscoring the primacy and isolated impact of the neighborhood. Unlike other participants in this chapter who referenced multiple community spaces as being significantly impactful, Devon's journey is representative of Black males who have limited access to a wide variety of positive educational experiences and spaces. The neighborhood was Devon's primary teacher, filling the vacuum created by the absence of strong guidance from his family or significant influence from school. He states, "Well, I didn't know the right directions, nobody showed me the right directions. ... I had no figure around to be like, you know, okay Devon, let's go this way, let's go that [way], or, Devon, what do you want to be?" There was no significant sports club influence in Devon's neighborhood like those that helped some of the other participants feel a sense of connection growing up; no experiences to note of a surrogate mother or father leading him to VBS or Sunday school; no gombeys; and no Ricky's barbershop to reinforce positive lessons. Instead, Devon found sanctuary in the neighborhood where he would simply "do whatever, just hang out with the boys, you know, do whatever."

Devon describes himself as "calm and humble," and asserts that family—his "daughter and wife"—are most important to him. He is proud of his Bermudian identity, particularly the friendliness of the people, and he believes that "a Black man in Bermuda is the same as a Black man in America or Germany or somewhere." In fact, the notion of neighborhood encroaches upon the language and lens he now uses to frame the interactions and identities of Black Bermudians. He states: "Bermuda is like a neighborhood. ... Bermuda is like a village in Africa. It seems like we're just a bunch of village people just running around on an island."

Of the twelve participants, Devon most frequently mentioned the absence of strong family support during his developmental years. As a result, his community, his neighborhood peers, and *trial and error* became the most dominant teachers. Devon began his narrative by sharing the following:

> I was raised on Thompson Street, Gilchrest Parish. I used to play football. I was a good footballer. ... I went to Blake Secondary. I wanted to be a lot of things, like [a] lawyer and stuff like that. But then stuff happens. You go around the wrong people and stuff like that. You go the wrong way. Some people go different ways. You learn from your experiences.

Barely in his 30s, Devon often speaks in retrospect, as if he believes he has missed his best opportunities and now must make the best of what is left. Devon is married to an educator, and is the father of one child, from a previous relationship. He has primarily worked as a lower-level employee in various service industries, though he wishes he had heeded his grandfather's counsel to learn a trade. In comparison to the other participants in this study, he spends the least amount of time discussing his family background. His ability to sum up nearly 30 years of life in one paragraph elicited nervous laughter (from both of us) during our interviews as I sat quietly waiting for him to share his journey. He continued:

> So now you see what you should have done back in the day, but sometimes it is too late, so you try to better it from now. I am a plain and simple type of guy. I live my life plain and simple. Have fun now and then, but I try to do what's right as a person. No one is perfect. I don't know what else you want me to say?

After a moderate pause, he then continued by revealing some of the pain of his experiences, before discussing his most influential teacher—life:

> I don't stress out about too much. I don't grumble about too much. There are a lot of things out of your hands, so you must cope and get over the hurdles. If I was to die tomorrow, I would say I have lived a good life. I have been through a lot of stuff, like my mama had a kidney transplant, and stuff like that. I went away with her. ... I have seen my grandpa die in front of me, so I have seen a lot and been through a lot.

Lost amidst the experiences and challenges of life, school was not memorable for Devon. He attended Legacy Springs Elementary, and like Kofi, who often engaged in unsupervised after-school activities in the neighborhood, Devon also had lots of free time to experience the neighborhood without adult guidance. He explains: "My momma never really told me go do my homework or really, like, study ... she was a single mother, she had to go do other stuff. ... She had me when she was ... about 16 [or] 15."

Underscoring his detachment from his schooling experience, Devon barely remembers the *transfer exam* that funneled him to Blake Secondary, a school that did not have a strong academic reputation. Referring to my inquiry about the transfer exam, he claims, "I don't remember that type of stuff," before describing his overall schooling experience this way: "It was school. It was experience. ... I can't say it was glorious. It was just your experiences in life you have to go through." Like Dexter in chapter 5, Devon also attended Legacy Springs Elementary and employed the persona of "the joker." He had no ambitions to attend one of the schools known for academic excellence. Devon explains:

> Whatever school basically where my friends was going, that's the school I wanted to go. ... It never was because of the education. ... Obviously you're there to be taught something, but for me I was the joker. Not that I didn't really know the work or whatever, but I couldn't understand why they [other students] were doing it.

Devon's father moved abroad to the United States when Devon was a boy, leaving him in Bermuda with few male role models besides his grandfather and the guys in the neighborhood. Devon states that he was "raised around mostly women," and no one taught him simple lessons like "how to save money." He had to become a man and fend for himself early in life, and fending for himself meant findings ways to support himself financially after dropping out of high school. This is a common reality for many Black males, including Troy, who we meet in chapter 6. Devon declares: "I became a man young—maybe 12 or 13 [years old]. You know, you have to go out and do something, you know, if you have to go cut grass or something to make any money or something, that's what you call becoming a man." Devon's "or something" was the sale of narcotics in his neighborhood, and he believes he was "lucky a couple of times" to avoid being caught with drugs by the police. He explains:

> I have sold drugs a couple of times. You know, I sold drugs and sh*t before. ... I have had times when the police have searched me and I have had stuff right there on me and just by being lucky they didn't find it or look in the right place; so you learn from those types of experiences: I am not going to carry it no more, stuff like that, or you realize that's not me, or you realize what would have happened if you would have gotten caught—I wouldn't be in this interview right now.

Experience(s) has/have continued to be his teacher. While the most enjoyable neighborhood experiences for Devon included "everybody partying together" and "playing football together," there were many hard lessons to be learned in the neighborhood as he forged an identity by learning from his experiences. For example, he asserts:

> I think I grew up kind of too fast. ... I didn't really live out my youth; hanging around older people and stuff like that. But sometimes it is a good thing. They teach you *the game* about basically different stuff. Older people would say "When you get older you will find who your friends are and ... [p]eople change." And when it starts happening, you say "People use to say that."

Troy—another participant from Devon's neighborhood—also uses this exact term of "the game" in chapter 6 to describe this common neighborhood lesson.

Devon once had to get 50 stitches under his eye after being hit in the face with a bottle at a club. He does not believe he was the intended target, but because of his neighborhood associations, he was "in the wrong place at the wrong time." Devon knows who threw the bottle, but he chose not to retaliate because he is "a people person" who thought it best to "let God deal with it, [and] kill him with kindness," which he says are lessons he does remember from church. Part of his learning curve has been coming to the conclusion that he could not continue to make the same decisions and expect different results. He has had to modify who he spends time with, which has meant distancing himself from his childhood friends from the neighborhood. In this respect, Devon had to choose to cross parish borders by moving to another part of the island, in part because he realized that street life only leads to two places: prison or the grave. He states:

> Now I am trying to do what I need to do ... save my money, take care of my child and live life like that. You can't do the same thing all the time. I don't even hang around all my friends. Well, I'm not as close [to them] as I use to be. ... I am moving on. ... [I'm] married and ... becoming a man. You get tired of the same stuff: being a player, being a gansta. It is true—you either die or get locked up. ... You distance yourself once you start seeing different things, going through different things. Some people learn earlier than others. Sometimes you have to go through things or see something that makes you want to change.

Devon's maturation to manhood is apparent, particularly when compared to the narratives of other participants who also desire to transition from street life but finds this border crossing out of street life a daunting task. Devon continues:

> Everybody wants to be the guy—"*Scarface*"[4]—everybody wants the best of things, have everything: cars, houses, money, everything, but you have to do it right. That

goes to show, you either die or go to jail trying to be Scarface. But if you do things right—save when you are young, work when you are young—then you will have those things when you get older.

His references to *Scarface* reveal the border-crossing influence of the media (Bahr, 1976) on Black Bermudian identities. Consistent with the claims of Kimmel (2006a), Devon's references to *Scarface* also demonstrate the manner in which males of color have been influenced by these Mafia-style, gangster identities that have been portrayed and embodied by White males, such as the main characters in the original *Scarface* film, but have now been associated and identified with Black males and other males of color.

Devon is a border crosser who has sought to make many changes in his life. His identity is the most mobile of the participants, perhaps because of the limited role of community spaces during his journey and because he has learned from experience that his most significant community space—the neighborhood—and the associated lifestyle promoted there cannot lead him any closer to where he wants to be. Clearly, he wants more, from himself and others. He states: "Now I am trying to get around the right people: positive people, so positive things can happen." Though he still "has a draw" (smokes marijuana) occasionally in the privacy of his home, Devon's narrative reflects the border-crossing possibilities of a Black Bermudian male who is fighting to detach himself from the negative influences and ideologies of a community-based pedagogical space he has outgrown. His description of the neighborhood is telling. He states:

> The neighborhood means nothing, really, it's just where you come from. It's not like it means everything to me. You know, because it makes my character, it's made my character and stuff like that, and there are different things, you know, but it's just the neighborhood, a place where you live. You can't really help where you live.

On the surface, the sense of detachment that is evident in his reference to the neighborhood may appear to be contradictory to his previous descriptions that highlighted the centrality of the neighborhood to his identity development. But there is more to it. Devon is still on the border; he is transitioning from the boyhood ideologies and space that short-circuited his dreams of being a "lawyer" or "learning three trades"; he has learned from the literal and emotional scars of his experiences; in essence, he has become a man ... a man who claims "I missed out on a lot" by "not making the right choices"; a man who still harbors dreams of being a lawyer, though he does not have a GED yet. He continues:

> It's not just a neighborhood, it's a period in your life. ... Do you learn from your mistakes or do you keep making the same mistakes? So it's all about being a man and learning to be a man. ... I learned late. I've learned the values of life ... so now that I've learned them, I'm on the road. That's all I could say.

Like every man, Devon is a work in progress. He is doing his best with the resources he has and the experiences he has learned from. From his narrative we are reminded that while participation in the church, the sports club, and the barbershop are optional, the family, the neighborhood, and the school—as experienced within the various unique arrangements that can exist—are default institutions or mandatory spaces for Black Bermudian males. We are also reminded that the influences of these optional and default space spaces vary. Besides the neighborhood, Devon had few significant institutional and community-space ties growing up. He briefly attended Sunday school and was involved in sports teams as a boy, but neither his participation nor the influence of these spaces were particularly enduring. He does credit the church for helping him understand the difference between "right and wrong" and the importance of "forgiveness," but for the most part, Devon has learned most of his lessons in the isolation of neighborhood experience(s) and experimentation rather than through his childhood visits to the church. His connection to the barbershop is equally tenuous. He describes the barbershop this way: "It's a place to go get my hair cut. I just want to get in and get out. [For] some people, [the barbershop is] their comfort zone where they talk about their stuff or whatever, that's not me." Whereas some participants like Jeremiah and Kevin value the barbershop as one of many engaging learning spaces they have encountered, other participants—like Devon—have found their education in the isolation of neighborhood experience(s).

Revisiting Space(s) as Place(s) of Learning

In this chapter, I have sought to explain how the identities that Black Bermudian males form during their journey to manhood are influenced by community-based pedagogical spaces (i.e., those outside of the schoolhouse). Through the narratives of Kofi, Shaka, Allan, and Devon, we have learned much about the identities they have formed and the spaces that mattered most in these processes. The salience of the neighborhood, church, and sports club spaces to the participants was evident and consistent with many of my expectations upon undertaking this study, though understandings gained from the data are not comprehensive. Still, there was consensus across the participants as to the relevance of these three spaces, and there were commonalities in the experiences and experimentation that were associated with these spaces. As I detail below, data on the barbershop was less consistent.

Cutting to the Chase: The Organic Nature of Barbershop Experiences

While six participants in the study noted the value of their barbershop experience in their life journeys, Kevin's narrative includes the most affirmative discussion of the value of the barbershop as a space/place of learning. Conversely, Devon, like four other participants, did not find the barbershop to be a significant space in his journey to manhood. Troy shares Devon's sentiment that the barbershop is simply a place to "just get a haircut." Whereas for some of the participants the barbershop is valued as an engaging learning space, other participants find their education elsewhere. Moreover, while each participant noted that he had spent time in a barbershop, data suggest the educative significance of the barbershop is not consistently meaningful across the participants. The organic nature of the barbershop means that—much like the haircut—the barbershop experience is individualized based on the personality and preferences of the patron.

The participants' recollections of the barbershop provide compelling insight into the uniqueness of their experiences. Kevin's enthusiastic overtures about the barbershop reveal the educative impact of the barbershop in his life:

> The Black barbershop ... ha, ha, ha! That is the Black hub. ... You would go, and you would sit down, and ... every topic is meat for discussion in a barbershop. There is no taboo, there is nothing off limits. ... It was just a perpetual place to just hang out, chill, and sometimes you would be in there sitting for hours and you didn't mind.

Much like Shaka's experience at Ricky's barbershop, Kevin notes specific lessons he remembers learning in his barbershop. He continues:

> [The barber] Mr. Clark, he always taught us guys when we were younger that when you go out, you represent more than yourself ... you're representing your family, you are representing your bloodline. ... And then the other thing it taught me [is] the art

of agreeing to disagree. ... [I]t's all right to have a difference of opinion with a person, and it didn't have to break down into a fight, a curse fest, because he didn't allow cursing in his barbershop. It taught you how to be a gentleman, as opposed to sitting off on the street, you know, saying "F" this and "F" you, drinking or whatever you did, all this other stuff. And it taught you to be a really good debater. You couldn't come into a barbershop and talk about your team without some facts and figures. You had to know what was what.

Notably, the typical Black barbershop is often viewed as a grassroots, urban space. Data suggest that for some Black men who have border crossed out of grassroots, Black neighborhood spaces, the barbershop may serve as a locale where they can feel connected to classes of people with whom they do not associate in their normal travels. For Black males like Devon and Troy, there is no need to attempt to remain connected to the grassroots, Black neighborhood space—they *are* connected to this space. Caleb, who we will meet in chapter 7, has observed that some Black men—he mentions politicians as an example—transition out of what would be considered the neighborhood barbershop once they ascend the social, political, or economic ladder. There appear to be social class dynamics at work here that are worthy for future evaluation. Furthermore, Kevin also reported, "I get my hair cut by my wife now, and have been for some years, but I miss the interaction of the Black barbershop." Such a statement suggests how border-crossing ideologies impact one's participation in various spaces: Said differently, the venues where individuals access lessons may change over a lifetime.

Heralding Outliers, Hearing *Others*

Notably, the organic emergence of the prison and gombeys in participants' narratives as relevant educative spaces/experiences was unexpected but not shocking. Certainly, Allan's description of two spaces that transcend the four specific spaces I set out to investigate in this study is an important border-crossing imperative that further underscores the value of qualitative research methods to allow participants to define themselves for themselves. By not allowing the relevancy of the gombeys and his prison experience to go unheard, Allan "ruptures a politics of historical silence and theoretical erasure that serves to repress and marginalize the voices of the Other" (Giroux, 2005, p. 97). Narrative research methods created the vital dialogic space where the pedagogical power of two understudied spaces—Bermuda's prisons and the gombeys—could be considered. In so doing, I was able to avoid the "erasure" or exclusion of two significant community-based pedagogical spaces that impact the identities Black Bermudian males form. This was vital, since the data affirm that spaces play different roles for different people, and some participants had more memorable experiences in one space with little association to another space. More than this, by allowing Black Bermudian males to name and frame their realities, this study border crosses from *me*search to *we*search.

Additional Theoretical Connections

Each participant in this chapter embraced a strong African identity that undergirded how he saw himself as a Black male living in Bermuda. From Kofi, who is very passionate about being a Bermudian, to Shaka, who "cannot be called Bermudian and be happy," the profiles in this chapter exemplify the breadth and complexity of the "fluid and multiple" masculinities and identities that, according to Gause (2008), rest on and respond to "historical, political, racial, and sociocultural contexts" (p. xiv). In his own voice and in his own way, each participant in this chapter represented aspects of the postcolonial commitment to resisting the vestiges of colonial domination. For example, the notion that culture is a "strategy of survival" (Bhabha, 1994) that undergirds the *hybridity* marginalized groups need to navigate through and across boundaries and borders is evident in the manner in which each participant grounded his cultural, ethnic, and racial identities in who he was as an *African* male living in Bermuda. In his own way, each participant seemed to understand that his sense of self had been influenced to some degree by the onslaught of life—colonialism—in Bermuda. In this respect, these four participants are exemplars of what Bhabha (1994) would call "colonial subjects," which he describes as the "individual or collective psyche of the colonizer or the colonized" (p. 119) that allows for an analysis of who the participants are beyond the political and social realms.

Drawing on the tenets of postcolonial theory, the participants' voices and their self-definitions are most important, since the purpose of this study was to create space for subalterns—in this case, Black Bermudian males—to be heard and hopefully better understood. The act of acknowledging the centrality of their Africanness, or—in the case of some—their cultural association with other Black males across the Diaspora, was a powerful statement that represented an organically potent postcolonial imperative: These men would define themselves for themselves!

Conclusion

In this chapter, I have given specific attention to community-based pedagogical spaces in order to learn how experimentation and experiences in these spaces have impacted the identities that Black Bermudian males form during their journey to manhood. Together, the men who participated in this study affirm the salience of nonschool venues as significant spaces of learning. In the next chapter, I introduce the final three participants within the context of the theme *exposure to life options*. Specifically, I describe some of the intersections between the participants' exposures, their conceptualizations of success, and their life outcomes.

Notes

1. As mentioned in chapter 5, there is a popular song in Bermuda with a similar title.
2. The gombeys are popular Bermudian dance troupes which have origins in African traditions.
3. Between 2009 and 2012, more than 20 Black males were shot and killed in Bermuda. This represented a sharp increase; for example, there were two gun-related murders in 2007 in Bermuda.
4. According to Wikipedia, *Scarface* is an American gangster film originally produced in 1932 and remade in 1983 that chronicles the experiences of a cocaine drug lord. While the main characters—the gangsters—in the 1932 film are White males, the main character in 1983 is a Cuban refugee. The original film is believed to have some connections to the life of Al Capone.

· 7 ·

EXPOSURE TO LIFE OPTIONS

Seeing is Believing

In this chapter, the final three narrative portraits are situated within the third of the four main themes: *exposure to life options*. *What* and *who* participants were able to see or not see, and *what* participants were able to do or not do, greatly impacted the men they have become and their expectations and life outcomes as they transitioned from boyhood to manhood. These dynamics have also impacted the expectations they have met and the outcomes they continue to pursue presently as men. Through the global impact of the media, Black Bermudian males are exposed to typical notions of Western and Black masculinities. These non-Bermudian lenses have the capacity to influence the identity development and definitions of success that Black Bermudian males embrace. By beholding these images, Black Bermudian male identities are exposed to limited constructs of who other Black males are across the Diaspora and, in turn, who they can be as Black males on the island of Bermuda. These intersections reveal potential dangers of a colonial mindset, dominant ideologies importation, and the capacity for non-Bermudian identities to border cross and infringe on the masculinities of Black Bermudian males and their notions of success. In exploring the life options that the participants were exposed to, this chapter also begins to address the third and final research question undertaken in this study: How do Black Bermudian males define success given their life journeys, personal identities, and the influence of community-based pedagogical spaces? I begin by restorying the lives of Brandon, Troy, and Caleb.

Brandon's Journey to Success: Breadth of Exposure

Brandon is an eloquent Black Bermudian male in his late 40s. He is married and the devoted father of two sons and a daughter. Brandon describes his upbringing in his two-parent home as "uncomplicated but complicated." His journey was uncomplicated in that he came from a very supportive family who were intentional about exposing him to various extracurricular activities and mentors, but his journey was complicated by his personal and family identity as a "very dark-skinned Black male" of West Indian[1] heritage. While Brandon's exposure to Black cultures outside of Bermuda broadened his worldview, he also struggled with the intercultural tensions of his border-crossing identity as he sought to *translate* the meaning of his West Indian heritage in Bermudian space. He explains:

> [One of my parents] is actually Jamaican, which gave me a very unique perspective. [And one of my parents] is from Bermuda, and in the 70s there was still an overarching sort of distrust and disrespect for West Indians. I was actually raised as a Jamaican living in Bermuda, which was a very Caribbean value system, but living in the context of Bermuda. So I had this real love/hate relationship for Bermuda, because on the one hand, I couldn't understand as a country where [one of my parents] is from and where I was born, they basically didn't understand who I was as a dark-skinned Black Bermudian male, and [they] judged me based on having a Caribbean parentage, so there was that chip on the shoulder.

As scholars such as Banks (2000) and Glenn (2009) have noted, colorism—the discriminatory practices and prejudices toward particular people or groups because of skin tone—is a common phenomenon that is representative of the intracultural tensions which I discussed in chapter 2.

Grounded in Whiteness as a form of cultural domination and the standard by which beauty and value is judged, one of the consequences of Black oppression for Black identities is the self-hatred that is exemplified by notions like "having good hair" and "not being too dark," to which Brandon refers. In this respect, tightly curled hair is seen as the antithesis of the straight, flowing mane of people of European descent, and dark skin is the polar opposite of the pale skin of Whites. Egged on by the media's privileging of Whiteness, the insidious nature of racism has created a context where Black people exert these prejudices on each other by embracing destructive notions of beauty that marginalize Blackness as ugly. Studies outlining Black children's preferences for White dolls reveal the transcendence of these ideologies to impact the lenses of the young (Powell-Hopson & Hopson, 1988). Thus, it should come as no surprise that prior to the emergence in the media in the 1990s of darker-skinned Black men like the world-famous U.S. actors Wesley Snipes, Denzel Washington, and Morris Chestnut, light-skinned Black males like R&B singer Al B. Sure were the standard for what an attractive Black male looked like. Some of the participants including Brandon shared that growing up in the 1970s, 80s, and early 90s as a dark-skinned Black male had consequences for identity development. Brandon continued:

> I was very dark-skinned growing up in a culture where at the time, dark-skinned Black males were considered the sort of antitype of what male looks were. So you had to endure the names of "Black spook," "Black ace of spades," [and] "Midnight." You grew up with a complex about being dark-skinned. I remember being at [elementary] school and having to endure an unusual amount of teasing about being Jamaican because most people did not care to know that [one of my parents] was Bermudian and I was Bermudian and also dark-skinned. And in my later life, I didn't realize what impact that had on my self-esteem until I became a lot older, in terms of a lot of choices I made and how I viewed myself, just from being teased from [when I was] young.

Brandon's exposure to Black intracultural prejudice—which cannot be disassociated from the tentacles of racism and the privileging of Whiteness as the standard of excellence and beauty—created tensions and insecurities for him as a young man. Trying to forge an identity at a time in his life journey when he did not yet have the tools to understand and navigate how race and racism assaults the construction of a healthy self-image, particularly for dark-skinned Black males, was painful. At the same time, Brandon's family background and personal identity exposed him early to the reality that his Blackness transcended the shores of Bermuda. His family was intentional about exposing him to his West Indian heritage. In fact, he states: "I was actually raised as a Jamaican living in Bermuda, which was a very Caribbean value system." As a boy growing up in the 1970s and 80s, Brandon could feel the anti–West Indian sentiments in Bermuda. Though amiable ties have been forged between many Bermudians and West Indians living in Bermuda, there are still Bermudians who harbor negative sentiments and use labels like "jump-up"[2] to describe West Indians like Jamaicans.

Brandon admitted that it wasn't until he became an adult that he realized how his identity, self-esteem, and life decisions were impacted by the teasing and tensions of trying to develop a sense of self amidst the toxicity of anti–West Indian, anti–dark-skinned ideologies. He asserts:

> It was a weird existence, because on one hand I had a phenomenally strong value system because of my faith and my peer group, but I had this unusual distrust for members of my community … who looked just like me, because of the duplicitous nature of how they treated me growing up.

Looking back on his transition to adolescence and adulthood, Brandon now states: "I was attracted to girls in a way that I felt they validated who I was because of my insecurities." This mindset was a major factor in the development of a high school relationship. In an effort to escape social worlds where both he and his girlfriend felt "misunderstood," he can now see that they "became a lot closer than people should be at 16 or 17." This relationship would lead to the birth of his first child, which I discuss later.

Though Brandon struggled to develop a positive personal identity during adolescence because of his dark complexion, his exposure to peer groups and acquaintances from diverse backgrounds was a positive experience that bolstered his social development. Being raised on the border of two very different neighborhoods—a poor Black neighborhood and an affluent White one—Brandon believes he was exposed to the "best of both worlds." As an adult, he is now able to relate to people from various communities and backgrounds in Bermuda because he was raised in an environment where he border crossed to divergent communities. He states:

> On one hand was the private school White boys, and Black kids on the other side of the neighborhood. I was able to negotiate both worlds with such ease. Even to this day I have friends from the proverbial both sides of the tracks, and it broadened my scope on Bermuda so much. My neighborhood was really strange like that. … One day I would be playing with somebody [from the 'hood]; the next day I would be with the guys from Ivy Secondary out playing basketball. What it did was it gave me a love for Bermuda.

Brandon was also involved in many community-based spaces as he journeyed from boyhood to manhood, including churches and, to a lesser extent, sports clubs. Through activities and mentors in these spaces he was exposed to notions of success in various contexts. In fact, he believes his parents were "before their time" in the sense that they exposed him to many extracurricular activities to keep him out of trouble. He explains:

> My mother recognized that one of the critical tools to keeping us off the streets was a very keen sense of faith, I mean, my mother and my father, but my mother was much

more vocal with it. ... So we got involved in the church ... If a program happened [at church], we were in it, and looking back on it now, it became a saving grace as well. ... Their philosophy was, if we keep them occupied, there is less time to get involved in things that are negative. So we did piano lessons, trombone lessons, Tae Kwon Do, we went sailing and swimming. So we were so tired at the end of the day, there was very little time to get involved in crap because we were just really mortgaged out in activities. There were a few really strong role models at my church and my school that shaped my opinions. I was blessed with very strong role models.

Brandon had a unique schooling experience, having initially attended Hope Academy for high school and then transferring to a predominantly Black school. His exposure to the environment at Hope Academy adds further perspective to the narratives of Dexter and Allan, who, like Brandon, attended Hope Academy.

I went to [Hope Academy and] found out I got people's respect by fighting. So, my siblings and I were very good at sports, but we were also better fighters than anything ... so that became our tool of choice, which was, you know, if you say something against me to hurt me, I'm going to show you my displeasure by planting my fist in your face. So for a very long time, that's what I did if you called me a name or did anything. ... What I remember about [Hope Academy] was very little male structure. I had a lot of female teachers. It was overwhelmingly masculine, in terms of all young guys coming from all around the island, but there was very little development in terms of who and what we were, and that's probably when I drifted into the darkest patch of being a young man, because there was a lack of guidance ... it was almost like *Lord of the Flies*, literally. Every day ... your goal was to survive that day by any means necessary, and it was a really rough social experience.

At Hope, success was survival. Transitioning to a predominantly Black high school exposed Brandon to broader definitions of success which positively influenced his social and academic experience, though he initially chose to fly under the radar academically. He identifies the critical influence of one Black Bermudian male teacher who understood "that there was nobody in our environment that was trained or culturally or spiritually in tune enough" to bring out our potential, "so ... he started to take a critical interest [in us], modeled excellence in how he dressed, [challenged our] attitude and aptitude, and brought certain values out of the guys." This young, dark-skinned, good-looking Bermudian male teacher served as a role model for Brandon and his classmates. The students thrived under the influence of a fellow Bermudian male who saw their "potential," and whose identity, intellect, and personal interest in them challenged the dominant discourses of their other worlds. Brandon's academic ability was exposed when his excellent performance on the ACT examination brought attention to the fact that he was actually capable of far more than was being expected of him. Toward the end of high school, he began to embrace the fact that he could achieve. The border crossing that was taking place ideologically was buttressed by his literal border crossing during his senior year.

Attending a predominantly Black high school exposed Brandon to the expectation of college attendance. Through a class trip to college campuses in the U.S. during his senior year, including a visit to an HBCU, the ideology of Brandon's high school was reinforced: Attending college was a matter of *where*, not *if*. He transitioned to an HBCU in the U.S., and this space exposed him to a nucleus of high performing, spiritually grounded Black males who challenged him to do his best, and helped shape his ideas of success. Brandon recalls his undergraduate experience with enthusiasm and is grateful for the social, spiritual, and academic "rubrics" that he was exposed to. In fact, Brandon believes that his HBCU experience helped him to successfully transition to manhood and traverse one of his most difficult personal challenges: becoming a teenage father. His narrative is worthy of extended consideration. He states:

> To make a long story short, I had a son [and] that changed the trajectory of my life. I became a pariah because I [was] 18 with a child. So my paradigm changed from being the wonder boy to being a guy that "Oh you're just like the other guys." I had to then change my whole frame of reference ... [and] based on my moral fiber, my son became everything. I threw myself into [raising] him, and he became my reason for living. And I used that experience to motivate me to excel in school.

The experience of becoming a parent as a teenager forced Brandon to re-evaluate his sense of self—an identity that now included the role and responsibility of fatherhood. Brandon's data suggest that the crucible of his new role as a father forced him to actively engage the process of border crossing from boyhood to manhood. In this vein, Brandon is clear that becoming a man is a process, and suggesting that a boy becomes a man on a particular day "cheapens manhood in the process." He continues:

> Being a male is a matter of birth. Being a man is the sum total of experiences and responsibilities. There is no one day that you become a man. There is a point when you take responsibility for your actions and you understand your core purpose in the world and the people you are responsible for feel safe. There is no time [I became a man], but I know the period. The period was when I became autonomous. Even though I had a child, I still depended on somebody [i.e., his parents' financial support

in college] for my existence. But I started to make my own money, which gave me autonomy in terms of decision-making processes, when at the end of the day I woke up and if I did not produce, my family did not eat. And the decisions that I made shaped the decisions of a generation, which is my children. I say [it's] "a process," but ever since I became 18, I think I was being groomed for manhood.

Brandon's exposure to various life options, mentors, and periods of adversity were all elements of the "groom[ing]" process that helped him to transcend the borders of boyhood to embrace manhood. His discussion about autonomy is significant for the journeys of Black Bermudian males. As Caleb's profile reveals later in this chapter, many Black Bermudian males live at home due to limited housing space; thus, autonomy can be hard to come by for many Black Bermudian males. This reality underscores the value of Black Bermudian male exposure to college experiences outside of Bermuda, where they are forced to cut the umbilical cords of living at the family homestead and enjoying mama's cooking. This is an important border-crossing imperative for Black Bermudian males.

In Brandon's journey, not only did he redefine himself, but his narrative suggests that his life has also been one of self-redemption. Brandon has developed into a family man and leader who defines his success through his impact on his community and his role as "a priest, provider, protector, and friend." For Brandon, being "a priest" means fulfilling the role as a spiritual leader in his family and community. Being a "provider" means taking care of the physical and emotional needs of his family and community. Being a "protector" means ensuring the safety and security of his family and community. Finally, being a "friend" reflects a recent awakening he had after visiting one of Bermuda's prisons to encourage the inmates. The visit helped him realize that being "a friend" is to be available, compassionate, and relevant to his family and community. For Brandon, these are the fundamental tenets of his life—a life that he describes as "successful" because he has been able to "set reasonable goals" and because he can "share it [his success]" with people who "enjoy" and "appreciate" his success. He asserts, "Success is setting achievable goals that you can measure and you can also attain." Brandon's conceptualizations of masculinity and success as being grounded in familial and community accountability are the antitheses of the destructive Western masculine identities noted by scholars like Kimmel (2006a, 2006b) and Connell (2005). Notably, Brandon's HBCU experiences and exposure were significant in the development of his ideologies about masculinity and success. Brandon continues:

I would not have probably survived at another institution, not because I was not academic, but I needed the rubrics around me that made me see education as more than a tool to make money. [My college] gave me a skill set to make myself a servant in life. ... My peer group was academically inclined, they were all ladies' men, but they were focused on Christ and focused on education. The peer pressure was "Hey, pull your grades up," and the peer pressure was to succeed. So, being competitive by nature, I wanted to be in a peer group of people that were achieving. So positive peer pressure actually worked, and it actually pulled me through, because the cats [guys] I was associated with were hardcore. Most of them, even today, are captains of industry, doctors, lawyers, and entrepreneurs, but at college they set the bar high for me. I came back [home] and got very *stuck in* [involved] at my church, and very *stuck in* my community.

Brandon's narrative offers valuable insights into ways that broad exposure to positive peer pressure and healthy spaces (for example, border crossing to the United States to attend an HBCU) can help nurture Black men into identities that challenge traditional, damaging notions of masculinity, such as the notion that Black males are anti-intellectual brutes who do not take care of their kids. In Brandon's case, and of importance to this study, he defines success as "setting achievable goals that you can measure and you can also attain." He has attained his goals—the most important of which is being present and active as a father and husband, which intersect with his commitment to serving his community and living out his faith in practical ways. In addition to his full-time employment as a high-ranking civil servant, Brandon is an educator who volunteers his time to various community organizations. Brandon's profile is a compelling reminder that given the right exposures, Black Bermudian males are fully capable of turning trials into footstools of triumph.

Troy's Journey: Lack of Exposure and Overexposure

Troy is a Black Bermudian male in his early 30s who characterizes his life journey with the ambiguous phrase, "[it] wasn't hard and it wasn't easy." Notably, many of his life experiences and perspectives seem to reflect some level of tension or contradiction: Troy describes himself as a successful "businessman," though he admits he has "never worked [a traditional job] from, like, 18 years old"; he sees "street life" as "fun," and "the game" as an appropriate means to an end as long as you "don't get caught"; and he claims that "Whatever I'm doing is for my children—they know at the end of the day, if good or bad happens that daddy still done it for us." Troy also admits that it is a challenge to see and spend time with all eight of his children while also dealing with his seven "baby mammas." While some may question some of Troy's views, no one can question his productivity, ambition, and optimism. Troy does own a business and vehicles, though they appear to have been funded by illegal drug activity. But that's not how Troy would tell the story. In fact, if challenged about the course of his life, he would be quick to point out that most systems are "scams," those running the institutions are "corrupt," and his "progress" should not be dismissed or diminished. He states: "Illegally or legally, it don't matter what you've done in life to be successful. At the end of the day, most people have done it illegally." Ultimately, Troy sees his journey as a legitimate "success story," and the crowning moment of his career would be to get off the street corner by the time he is 40 years old and slide out of the game without ever being caught. That is one of his goals. As a keen observer of what he sees as corruption in national and international media and governments, Troy is truly a student of life—though, admittedly, street life is his area of specialization.

Troy's exposure to street life and street education started early. In fact, the streets and its "mentors" in his neighborhood were more influential than any other space or individual that he was exposed to during his journey to manhood. In truth, unlike some of the other participants in this study, Troy wasn't exposed to many positive male mentors. He instead grew up with his mother, stepfather, and sister, with whom he had good relationships. He had significant relationships with his grandmother, aunties, and cousins; still, he did not know any of his grandfathers, and his uncles were actually the ones who attracted him to street life through their example and lifestyles. In this light, his sentiment that "Women show guys everything in life a guy needs to know … a real man would tell you that a woman shows you everything you're really supposed to know in life" is understandable though no less controversial. Based on his limited exposure to his biological father, and contrary to the views of the other participants in this study, Troy does not believe that a man is essential to rearing a boy to manhood.

Notably, Troy's biological father lived in his neighborhood as well. But with the exception of the occasional waves as he drove by on his way to work, and one trip to the United States when Troy was a boy, Troy did not have a relationship with his biological father. He explains: "I used to see him every morning. [W]hen I used to walk out to the bus stop [for school], he used to come driving across." Still, consistent with Troy's life philosophy that you must always be "moving forward," he says he holds no grudges against his father, nor does he feel he missed out on anything by not having a significant relationship with him before he passed away. He states:

> The little time I did get to spend with him, I guess he was alright. … I really don't even worry about him like that though, because I'm already good in life. … I could

understand if I wasn't good, and he ... made me think that's [his absence] why I ain't good, but I don't worry about those things in life.

In the absence of strong role models typically perceived as positive, Troy was exposed to the example and encouragement of street "mentors" who ended up being the most significant men in his life—men who he holds in high regard. He asserts:

> [I] got to see guys from the street that are making it and not making it. ... I was an observer, so I would see [the] *game* [and think] "I want to be like this here when I get older. I don't want to [do that]." I listen[ed] to little advices with guys, like you don't want to be sitting of the street 40 years old selling drugs. ... [T]he guy that put me in the game, I even tell him, like I give him respect, because in actual fact, now I take care of him. He's like my son, and he's older than me. So right now it's basically like returning the favor, like a cycle. ... I literally take care of him today. ... I watch guys in my age bracket. We all started out the same time doing what we doing. We all had a plan in life.

Troy's family-like network of neighborhood associates reflects an amalgamation of the extended kin paradigm often attributed to Black families and informal educative/mentoring relationships, further underscoring that relevance of community-based education for Black Bermudian males. Though many would describe the nature of his education problematic and his career illegal, there is no denying the transference of knowledge—the border crossing—of ideologies, values, and practices.

Besides the neighborhood, which Troy describes as "everything to me," he does not note any other community-based pedagogical spaces as being significant in his life. For instance, attending Sunday school was an activity that fizzled out as he transitioned into adolescence, the sports club was a place to just "socialize" since he stopped focusing on sports once his eyes were opened to "the game," and the barbershop was a locale to "just go ... get a haircut and leave," in part because he was always on the move and "doing things in life." The contrast between Brandon and Troy's experiences and exposure are striking. While Brandon was exposed to numerous extracurricular activities and life options through the mentors he encountered in various community spaces, Troy was underexposed to positive spaces and life options, and overexposed to illegal activities and the trappings of the 'hood.

Troy's schooling experience mirrored his disengagement from other community spaces, excluding the neighborhood. In essence, schooling was not memorable for Troy. Whereas participants like Jeremiah, Giovanni, and

Brandon centralized the schoolhouse in their narratives, Troy was far more succinct in summing up the essence of his schooling experience. He states: "Coming up, [I] went school. Didn't finish high school—got kicked out of high school, and from there, started doing whatever I done to make money." After further prompting, Troy acknowledged that he remembers getting a 2/3 on the transfer exam and that he was expelled in his fourth year (10th grade) of high school after being "accused of inappropriately touching a girl." The abrupt end to his schooling experience encouraged him to go "full ahead" with his business plans outside of school, where he was making far more money than other young people were getting from their parents' allowance. He claims that he was not exposed to or encouraged to explore other options to gain his high school diploma, and he really was not interested anyway when he could stay home as a 15 year old and do what he wanted to do.

Today, Troy's perspective on schooling is somewhat ambivalent. In one breath, he is an advocate of schooling for his children, though many would question the quality of his academic support of his children; in another breath, he denounces the value of schooling in his life because he has made it without it, and because he—quite fairly—questions whether tertiary levels of education guarantee employment or fiscal advancement, especially when his country, as he sees it, has a penchant for hiring foreigners over Bermudians. He states: "Seriously, that's why I tell you that I don't go to school, because at the end of the day I'm going to sit down and analyze everything out. I'm going to look at things from all different aspects, especially from the street life." His analysis reveals that school was unnecessary for him and a waste of money for anyone who—after spending thousands of dollars in college—returns to Bermuda to make less money than him, and still cannot be "a boss."

The manner in which he describes his siblings' college and career decisions is quite telling about perceptions of success and the pathways to it. Much like Kofi's narrative in chapter 5, Troy's description further underscores the reality that the expectations, experiences, and exposures encountered by girls and boys raised in the same household can be totally different. Troy states:

> My sister turned out to be brilliant. … She must be, what do call you them, an auditor? … for one of these insurance companies or something. But, yeah, she does good in life. But she does it in a different way. … [S]he probably didn't even go through hard times, like, you know, same way as me. … My brother went away to school. I even wondered why he went away to school. I'm thinking, "Okay, you're out of school, you could get money where we are …" [In] other places around the world you gotta bust your ass to get money, not here [in Bermuda]. And that's the realistic of it.

... Like, on a regular day you can come outside and make $1,000, you know, $2,000 on a regular day. I'm talking about the small guys, so imagine the big guys ... that have never been caught. Somebody that probably makes $100,000 ... or $200,000 in a day.

Troy feels that he has crossed over to the realm of the successful, and he has few regrets about choosing street life as his path. After all, it was the path that seemed most accessible based on his overexposure to it and his lack of exposure to other life options. In this light, it is significant to remember that neighborhoods have cultures that reflect ideologies absorbed from near and far. When Bhahba's (1994) notion that culture is a "strategy of survival" is coupled with the reality that Troy was raised under the significant influence of his neighborhood culture, his decision to embrace the education and profession promoted through his exposures becomes more understandable. Without significant opportunities to border cross and see other life options being lived by people he respected, Troy was, in a sense, being true to the identity he had been *educated* to embrace, and survival strategies he had been exposed to and *cultured* in. All things considered, he feels good about his businesses, his status as "a boss," and his capacity to fulfill his duty as a man who is taking care of his responsibilities. He explains:

Like, I'll be just taking a shower and I'll just say it to myself, "I'm proud of myself," because who ever would have thought that I would have had what I've got now ... not coming up with a father ... [against] the odds that people probably wouldn't even think that you could [overcome] ... it's all a success story at the end of it.

Still, contradictions abound in his life and in the identities he embodies. For instance, Troy is not eager to expose his children to the path he has taken to success, even though he admits that they are probably being exposed to the lifestyle anyway. In spite of his affirmation of his line of work and the product he distributes—since he questions the criminalization of marijuana—he still tries to steer youth away from street life and does not glorify the accoutrements he has acquired to young people. These are all noble, though somewhat contradictory, gestures.

Equally interesting is his admission that if he could do it all over he would take school more seriously, and that he wants his children to take advantage of schooling and college, even though these avenues are not for him since he is so far along in his career. Much like Allan in chapter 5, he also believes that the media has intentionally created the gang issue in Bermuda for capitalistic gain, and the labels of "wall-sitter" and "gang member" have been thrust upon him and his peers whether they wanted these labels or not. He has personally observed the spike in newspaper sales on days when stories on gang violence and murder are plastered on the front. The manifestations of gang violence today, he believes, are no more than self-fulfilling prophecies of doom rooted in the destructive identities that have been scripted onto the Black male psyche by the media and those in power. He explains:

> Listen, I analyze it. ... If you didn't call these guys a gang, they wouldn't be a gang. They ain't no gang, they're only a group of guys that sit around. But now, yeah, okay, now they're gangs ... because you put in the newspaper, "Oh, the gang." [So some guys then say,] "Okay, yeah, I'm from a gang. ..." And they even got these foreign cops coming here [to Bermuda] and making them [Bermudians] think they're in a gang, because where they [the cops] came from, these guys [in other countries] are already thinking they're a gang, so now you're going to bring this [to Bermuda]. You hear me? They've done this to themselves. Honestly, I blame this on themselves. There's nobody else to blame. You've never heard of gangs in your life. Hear me? Never. That's how you get a trend, when somebody keeps saying something or doing something, that's how you get a trend. You don't get a trend if somebody don't do it, or somebody don't say it, yeah? ... [T]he young, stupid ones ... [now] think they're a gang.

Troy has been personally affected by these labels, much like—in his words—a child who has been "called a fool for 20 years ... will think they're a fool." He continues:

> Remember, when I was coming [growing] up it was "wall sitters." Hear me, "wall sitters" [was the label used] in the newspaper. I thought I was a "wall sitter" ... the other year they were "a crew." The other day they were "a group." What really is it? You go into—okay, let's go say the "freemasons"—what do you call them? What do you call "the police"? You should call them a gang, don't they always sit off together! So what's the difference?

Troy's questioning is profound, and his frustration—as a Black male who has sought to forge an identity and acquire success using the tools and exposure at his disposal—is telling: Many Black males are not who we/they think they are, or who they want to be. Further demonstrating the tensions between the identities some Black males embrace and the dreams they harbor, he claims that he really wants to help his community and would love to be a motivational speaker to youth. He states:

> If anything, I would like to be a mentor—like a motivational speaker, because remember, I'm good in life. I've been through what guys want to go through or what people

are going through, I've watched addicts. I've seen all the different walks in life. My talk would literally be about not wanting to be on the streets, like, wanting to make a better choice in life—not glorifying it.

Perhaps Troy's message is exactly what some Black Bermudian students need to hear. Either way, he is connected to the public education system as a parent of eight children, and an informal community mentor to the young men he directly communicates with in the neighborhood and those who learn lessons—much like he did growing up—by observing and being exposed to his "success" and the identities of others like him. While Troy's profile reveals that being overexposed to limiting identities and life options has negative consequences, Caleb's narrative highlights the reality that delayed exposure to positive identities and life options can also be detrimental to Black Bermudian male identities.

Caleb's Journey: Delayed Exposure

Caleb is a Black Bermudian male in his early 30s who has never been married and does not have any children. He is a lover of life who is known by many as a "pretty boy" and a joker. Like other participants in this study have mentioned, Caleb enjoys working with his hands, and he describes himself as "hard working." He was taught to "work hard, work hard, work hard" by his grandfather, who, along with his grandmother and his aunt, raised him when he was a boy. He has fond childhood memories of sitting in his grandfather's garden as he farmed his crops, and believes this exposure is what solidified his work ethic and desire to "use his hands." But in many other areas of his life journey—a journey he says "had its ups and downs"—Caleb's exposure to life options and a significant relationship with his father was delayed in comparison to the narratives of some of other participants in this study.

Caleb is proud to be Bermudian, though he struggles to articulate characteristics that make Bermudian culture distinctive from those of other jurisdictions. He feels that Bermudian national pride pales in comparison to the national pride he sees displayed by Jamaicans and citizens of other nations, especially when he watches television. In fact, he states: "I don't think we have a culture. No, I don't see nothing." Additionally, he suggests perhaps it is cultural that "most Bermudian men normally don't leave the home until they're like 30 years old," which is reflective of the theme of delayed exposure. Some Black Bermudian males experience delayed exposure to independence and autonomous living arrangements due to limited housing options in Bermuda, the high price of rents, and the reality that some Bermudian males—as other participants have noted—are mama's boys. Underscoring these ideas and some of the potential differences between Bermudian male and female identities, Caleb asserts that "most Bermudian women will branch out [become autonomous and move away from home] early." He also acknowledges the fact that he lives at the family homestead in a small attached apartment that does not have a kitchen, and eats meals prepared by other extended family members at the main house.

Caleb is a mechanic working towards becoming a facility manager. He believes his career choice is consistent with the type of occupations many Black Bermudian males gravitate toward, because of delayed exposure to other options and their ability to provide a sufficient wage to live comfortably and be financially successful. In fact, he says "the average Black Bermudian man is a hard, blue-collar worker. ... You don't see too much of us getting past blue collar, because it's a mentality they just installed in our head. Well, we allowed it to be installed in our head." The "they" that Caleb is referring to are teachers and administrators in school, and the "mentality" that he references is one of subservience, docility, and a preference for remaining "behind the scenes." He believes these characteristics have been ingrained in Black Bermudian males and reinforced on job sites where they are not pushed, or where they are passed over by foreigners. I take up a more in-depth discussion of the intersections between his professional exposure and his identity, his exposure to foreign workers, and his schooling experiences later in his profile. For now, I focus on the delayed exposure he experienced in his relationships with his biological parents.

Caleb experienced disengagement from both of his parents at different times during his journey to manhood, which profoundly impacted his personal identity. He describes his early childhood relationships with his parents this way: "My mother ran away to school. My daddy was supposed to take care of us, but it's hard for a father [to parent alone]—he used to take us every weekend. You know, me and my sister, we grew up there." Although it is common for mothers to be expected to raise children in the absence of a father figure, by noting the fact that "it's hard for a father," Caleb seems to reflect the dominant, mother-centered expectation that single parenting is easier for a woman. Caleb's data reveals that his tolerance for his mother's periods of absence seems to be a bit lower. Notably, at 9 years old, he distinctly remembers his mother re-entering his life. He explains:

> I remember it strong because my momma had first come back; she hadn't been back
> for about a year or so. Or I don't even know if she had been back or she just was

around, and I started to see my mom more. So I just asked, can we come live with you? So we left my auntie—that was a little, you know, they [his auntie and his mother] were arguing about it, but that's what I wanted, just to see my momma. And those were some good years [living with his mother]. I won't lie; the early part of it with my mother was real nice.

This exposure to his mother—though delayed—was very meaningful as he sought to forge an identity, but it would not last very long. Things would shift again when he was 13 years old. He states: "My mom met this man and she married him. I won't lie to you, everything just seemed like it went downhill after that. You know, I started getting into trouble more—not for real serious [offences], but little troubles."

Not only did his mother's marriage cause another disconnect in Caleb's relationship with her, but he was also exposed to family infighting as a result of the tensions between his mother and his biological dad's family. In a delayed but still impactful experience, Caleb began to have greater contact with the neighborhood and the influences of "the boys," as an escape from the tension at home. He states: "I just started to see my grandma and mother fight, and it was just a lot of turmoil in my life. And then at 15 I started hanging [out] down the hill more, hanging on the hill with the boys." Like other participants mentioned in chapter 5, Caleb spent many hours playing sports at various sports clubs, and he was also exposed to some negative elements through unsupervised experimentation in his neighborhood. For example, he says he tried marijuana and got caught up in the drinking and partying culture, but as he matured he knew "the bling-bling world" was not where he wanted to spend his life.

What Caleb did not learn until later in life was that he could actually enjoy school and learning. This delayed appreciation for the learning experience is a recurring theme in the narratives of most of the participants, in part because most of them had delayed exposure to subjects they were interested in and teachers who they felt believed in them. This was Caleb's experience as well. In fact, because he liked to "play" around in school, like Dexter in chapter 4, he remembers being told on numerous occasions by teachers, "You ain't going to amount to nothing. … You ain't got nothing. You ain't going to do nothing." After earning a 3/7 on the transfer exam and spending his first years of high school at a nonacademic school, he was sent to a U.S. boarding school. As with Brandon, this move and choice by Caleb's family exposed him to a structure and overseas school environment that, though delayed, ended up being a life-changing, border-crossing experience for Caleb.

Caleb believes that he would have had a far better schooling experience and even pursued a college degree had he been exposed to the boarding school and the option of college earlier. He believes his early exposure or lack of exposure to a broader set of life options helped solidify his blue-collar ambitions. He explains:

> I just wanted to work. I always wanted to be a mechanic or a top-grade tradesman. ... I wanted to be a carpenter like my father. When I went to boarding school, that just changed my whole world. ... In '95 we were taught as young guys [in Bermuda]: "Just come out and work." College? We didn't ever know nothing about college. ... [I]t wasn't until I went to boarding school, and they said to me, "Hey, [in order] for you to graduate, you've got to be accepted into a college." So then I was like, "Damn, what's this college thing?" And then you got to learn more about trades, how you could take a trade thing to the next level and all that type of stuff. So it wasn't until then I realized life was more than just coming out and working.

Not only does Caleb have a personal appreciation for the importance of young Bermudian males "getting out of Bermuda" to be exposed to other life options, but he now sees the cycle being repeated in the life of his younger brother, who is struggling to figure out what he wants to do in life after two years doing very little at Bermuda College. This notion that Bermudian males need to be exposed to schooling experiences outside of Bermuda has border-crossing implications as well. For example, though Caleb's brother has received notoriety and media attention for his athletic success in local sports, Caleb believes his brother's holistic development is being stunted by his lack of vision beyond the local sports arena. Caleb suggests that border crossing to other jurisdictions is an imperative for Black Bermudian males because of the pervasiveness of "the Bermudian way," which he describes as "lazy." He declares: "Bermuda will suck you into their small-mind mentality ... being here is a fight. It's a fight every day ... against the Bermudian way. ... Bermudians just want everything given to them, for this generation, anyway."

Though Caleb feels that his personal identity development was hindered by the delayed exposure to life options, he is grateful for his delayed exposure to the pervasive and negative images of U.S. cable television that he now sees affecting today's youth in Bermuda and in many other jurisdictions around the world. He believes he was able to forge a Bermudian identity that was less affected by the media in comparison to today's youth, who are inundated with images and identities from around the world. He claims that he has seen a distinct shift in the mentality of Black Bermudian youth from the time he first got cable television as a 12 year old watching Will Smith on *The Fresh Prince of Bel-Air* to the gradual promotion of "thug life" and violence that is now bearing fruit in the identities that Bermudians are embracing. He explains, "The TV, the 2-Pac, Biggie Small stuff started to really creep in, and thug life ... crept in on us. ... You just saw it coming, coming, coming." In the absence of a strong television influence in his life as a teenager, he believes he learned to love himself. He states: "I used to wear my glasses, and girls would say, 'You look like a nerd in your glasses,' [but] I learned from a young age that you have to love yourself, and that's how you grow as a man."

Caleb's delayed exposure in other areas of his life has shifted his perceptions of Black Bermudian male identity. As he has ascended the ladder on his job to a skilled mechanic who now has his own apprentices to lead, he has also been exposed to perspectives that have shifted his outlook on foreign workers and Black Bermudian male workers. He used to think that he was being "screwed upon" by foreign workers, such as those coming from the Caribbean and the Philippines, but he now asserts:

> I enjoy working with a foreign worker more than I enjoy working with a Bermudian guy. And that was hurtful [to admit but] I knew we [he and a foreign worker] could get work done. I wouldn't have to fight with this guy to "make time." I wouldn't have to fight with him on lunch breaks. ... He didn't call in sick. ... It hurts me to see ... [that] we're selling ourselves pretty much. ... [T]he [Bermudian] banks are gone, what else is going to be left? ... What else is going to be left that's Bermudian here?

Caleb believes that foreign workers have a different mentality and stronger hunger for success because they have experienced "more suffering" and "they had to fight for more." He asserts:

> They [foreigners] come here and they see the dollar and they're going to work hard ... because they know what the value of this dollar means back home and where it could take them in their life. ... Bermudians, we talk ghetto. We don't know ghetto though. We don't live ghetto. Look how we live: three-story houses and stuff, okay? We live good. These guys don't live like that, and that's why we don't have that hunger and fight like the rest of them do. That's why they come and take our jobs so easy. Now everybody wants to cry "foreigner, foreigner, foreigner," but you didn't want it last year.

Caleb's references to the dismantling of Bermudian businesses due to the departures of many international insurance businesses and exempt companies, and—by extension—the decline of the construction industry that formerly employed many Black Bermudian males, can also be connected to the notion of border crossing. For example, nationally, the economy of Bermuda has suffered from the decline of the tourism industry—the number of individuals that can afford to *cross over* or visit Bermuda. But personally, Caleb has also had to come to grips with the personal departures in his life in order to develop a more healthy identity. In particular, he has had to deal with the feelings of abandonment in his relationship with his mother. His delayed exposure to a strong relationship with his father and an eye-opening experience that exposed him to some of the realities of life have been instrumental in this process. He explains:

> I got in this big incident—a physical altercation—with this girl one time, and my daddy sat me down and said, "Look, I know what you're going through, but you ain't been *opening your eyes up.*" So he said, "Go to this counseling lady and talk to her for a while." So me and her [the counselor] were talking and she started opening my eyes to a lot of stuff that I was running away from—how I communicate with my father, how I communicate with my mother—and I started to work on them little things and I started to see myself grow and understand more about life and understand what it means to be a man. I thought I knew what it meant, but I wasn't living right. ... That was a significant change in my life. I was 26.

Caleb has seen significant improvements in his lived experience since his delayed exposure to Black male role models, particularly his dad. His words are powerful and summative in this regard. He states:

> I think I always looked up to my father, even though we weren't that close. But when we got closer and we got to sit off and talk and rap—more and more I fell in love with him. ... [S]ometimes when I think about it, it hurts me to know that it took this long, but hey, I'm grateful, and I'm just going to push forward. I just feel that we Black men need more father figures. We need somebody there to be there for us. ... Bermudian men don't take a lead role in nothing. You see a lot of Bermudian women. To me, I just would like to see Bermudian men leading more—more of our faces out there.

Caleb is not the only participant to note a delayed development of a relationship with his father. Like other participants such as Kevin, Giovanni, and Malcolm, Caleb has a better understanding and appreciation for who his father is; equally significantly, like Brandon, Caleb has had a front row seat in the maturation of his father and the positive effects this has had on his life.

Additional Theoretical Connections

Border crossing as a literal and ideological imperative for Black Bermudian males was a key tenet that undergirded my approach to this study. Prior to the study, my belief was that Black Bermudian males were required to border cross in highly nuanced ways because of Bermuda's unique geopolitical positionality and because of the impact and persistence of British colonial rule. I saw post-colonial theory as an analytical, border-crossing approach that could be used to center the voices of the participants as I sought to better understand their personal identities as Black Bermudian males. The narrative portraits in this chapter reveal how the intersections between border crossing and postcolonial theory are specifically relevant to the exposure of Black Bermudian males to various life options.

Harking back to Anzaldúa (2007), who uses the term *intracultural* to describe elements "within the Chicano culture and Mexican culture" and *intercultural* to mean the relations with "other cultures like Black culture, Native American cultures, the white culture and the international cultures in general" (p. 233), data in this chapter showed that these ideas are relevant to the lives of Black Bermudian males. For instance, as a dark-skinned Black Bermudian male, Brandon was exposed to the *intracultural* tensions within Black Bermudian culture, and as the son of one West Indian parent, he faced the *intercultural* tensions between Bermudians and Black people from other islands. It is interesting to note the hierarchical dynamics at work in the perspectives some Bermudians had/have about Black people from other islands, yet there does not seem to be that same tension between Black Bermudians and Black people from the U.S. or the U.K. Perhaps this is a matter of exposure as well, in that Black people from the West Indies were more likely to come to Bermuda to work, whereas Black people from other regions would likely be coming to Bermuda as tourists and citizens of nations that are considered economically prosperous. As citizens of a country that for many years relied on service to tourists, Black Bermudians may have embraced what Brandon calls a "massa done like me a little more than you" mentality in response to Black people from the Caribbean. With this attitude, greater tolerance and respect are given to Blacks who have crossed over from Western territories like the U.S. and U.K. This not only reveals the deeper idiosyncrasies of Black identity but it also has ramifications for subalternity as a shifting positionality because of the intracultural identity wars. Within Bermuda's unique context, the usefulness of Anzaldúa's (2007) border-crossing theorizations is enhanced when partnered with Bhabha's (1994) appreciation of the transnationality of culture:

> Culture as a strategy of survival ... is transnational because contemporary postcolonial discourses are rooted in specific histories of cultural displacement, whether they are the "middle passage" of slavery and indenture, the "voyage out" of the civilizing

mission, [or] the fraught accommodation of Third World migration to the West. (Bhabha, 1994, p. 172)

The "love/hate relationship with Bermuda" that Brandon describes having as a young man is reflective on a micro scale of the intracultural and intercultural tensions created by the "specific histories of cultural displacement," the "voyage[s] out" of Africa (Bhabha, 1994), and the exposure to diverse cultural and geopolitical "consequences" of colonialism and imperialism (Hickling-Hudson, 1998). Equally noteworthy is Brandon's acknowledgment that he developed a love and appreciation for Bermuda while attending an HBCU in the U.S. By being exposed to Black males from across the Diaspora who challenged him to pursue broader conceptualizations of success, he gained a greater appreciation for the intracultural diversity of Black people and a greater sense of his value as a Black Bermudian male. Clearly, participants' exposure or lack of exposure to diverse life options and definitions of success were significant factors in the life outcomes of the men. Each man had a unique journey that affected him in unique ways. Similarly, consistent with the anti-essentialist stand of most postcolonial theorists on the divergent effects of colonialism on various jurisdictions (Spivak, 1999), data suggest that colonialism has not affected Black males within Bermuda in exactly the same way either. One reason for this is the exposure to and impact of the media on a highly technological society like Bermuda.

Caleb is confident that he saw the invasion of U.S. identities "coming" towards Bermuda's borders in the form of the media. His narrative suggests that the transnationality of culture and identities has mushroomed with the continued emergence of the U.S. media in Bermuda during his short lifetime, though he does not use this exact language. It is interesting to note that though Caleb is proud to be a Bermudian, he is not quite sure what this actually means, and he is also critical of Bermuda's lack of national pride, based on his observations of Black Caribbean people in Bermuda and on the television. In this light, Bhahba's (1994) words are informative. He asserts: "Culture is transnational because such special histories of displacement—now accompanied by the territorial ambitions of 'global' media technologies— make the question of how culture signifies, or what is signified by *culture*, a rather complex issue" (p. 172, emphasis in the original). By extension, the global media can also influence how particular cultures are signified and seen via the media. Troy believes that the global media's portrayal of Black males around the world as violent brutes, thugs, and gang members has impacted the identities of Black Bermudian males who have been exposed to these images and ideologies. He also believes that Bermuda's media outlets have been key propagators of the notion of gangs in Bermuda, which has forced identities onto Bermudian males that they would not have embraced except for the influence of the local and global media that consistently portray Black males in this context. The images of the violent Black male serve as virtual "border people" (Anzaldúa, 2007) that, through the pervasiveness of the media, exposed Black males to a narrow life option.

If we look back at two men profiled in this chapter, Brandon and Troy, each one reveals lessons that have ramifications for the theories explored in chapter 2. For example, Brandon was a border crosser. He was exposed to various life options and communities during his developmental years that broadened his understanding of difference and deepened his sense of self. His exposure to an HBCU in the U.S. also broadened his sense of self, deepened his appreciation of his Bermudian heritage, and strengthened his understanding of the intracultural diversity of people of African descent. He has learned how to function in multiple worlds, and he has succeeded at it. Troy, on the other hand, was never exposed to multiple worlds, but that does not mean he has not found ways to cross borders. Rather than crying over realities he felt he could not change, he has mastered the rules of street life in order to aim for the best of what his options have to offer. He refused to be marginalized to the limited space of an "oppressor-victim dualism" (Whitehead, 2002), choosing instead to find a way to be a "victor." Troy also refuses to passively accept the labels that he feels the media uses to characterize who he is—in this sense, he rejects the border crossing that can infringe upon the identities of "colonial subjects." He is resistant to the label of gang member, and he believes that his success is as legitimate as the success that is espoused by mainstream systems: He has money, he owns a business, and he is acquiring assets. In essence, he is reflective of the Western masculine ideal of success. Caleb is eager to make up for lost time and missed opportunities in his relationship with his dad and in his personal growth. Though delayed, Caleb's exposure to the joy of a healthy relationship with his father and the joy of learning during his time in community college in the U.S. have significantly impacted his personal identity and outlook on success. He is now setting new goals and crossing new borders. At the time of his last interview, Caleb was completing a managerial program at Bermuda College in order to fulfill his goal of becoming an office manager at his present place of employment.

Conclusion

In total, the data in this chapter reveal how exposure to life options informed who the participants would become as Black men. It is evident that each man embodies the legacies and lessons received in various contexts. While the men in this chapter had little difficulty articulating the unique contours of their life journeys, it was clear that the process of becoming a man was a complex one that continues today. Rather than seeking a static end, the men seem to embrace manhood as a process of continual becoming. Each day presents unique borders to cross, boundaries to traverse, and oppressive elements to resist. This points to the importance of analyzing their journeys in context—a context that can be best appreciated by understanding the complexities of identity construction, masculinities, colonialism, and Bermuda's geopolitical positionality. A conceptual framework like an amalgamation of postcolonial and border theory, which seeks to account for all that Black Bermudian male identity entails, is vital in this work. Using a research design that incorporates qualitative methodology and community-based pedagogical spaces, as I have done in this study, has also been an important means of hearing the voices, hopes, and journeys of the subaltern. In the final chapter, I discuss how Black Bermudian males define success as an *expression of their identities*, offer key conclusions, and identify relevant implications for school stakeholders.

Notes

1. The terms *West Indian* and *Caribbean* are often used synonymously. Bermuda is not a part of the Caribbean, though there are cultural and geopolitical connections between Bermuda and Caribbean nations.
2. The origin of this pejorative label is not clear. Some attribute it to the notion that Jamaicans came to Bermuda to "jump up" the economic ladder, while others attribute this label to the lyrics of popular songs in the Caribbean.

· 8 ·

LAYERED IDENTITIES

Bermudian culture and identities are layered. As subcategories of identity, masculinities are as unique as they are complex. The profiles describing the identities and nuanced journeys of the twelve participants in this study suggest that Black Bermudian masculinities are no exception. As the title of this book asserts, each participant is a border-crossing *brotha* in his own way. The maturation process from birth to boyhood to manhood is a border-crossing experience that each participant engaged in during his journey. By utilizing an amalgamation of border-crossing theory and postcolonial theory, this study offers new lenses and language for understanding the multiple layers and tensions that impact how Black males are educated and socialized in various learning spaces, across geopolitical paradigms and sociocultural borders. Moreover, if Dantley's (2005) assertion is true that "what happens in the schoolhouse is inextricably linked to what is going on in the local and wider community" (p. 653), then this study is significant for all school stakeholders because it uses the lenses of border-crossing and postcolonial theories to refract and re-examine the roles of significant educative *spaces* in the lives of Black males in Bermuda. Specifically, I set out to learn how Black Bermudian males form personal identities as they journey from boyhood to manhood, how the identities that Black Bermudian males form during their journeys to manhood are influenced by community-based pedagogical spaces (i.e., those outside of the schoolhouse), and how Black Bermudian males define success given their life journeys, personal identities, and the influence of community-based pedagogical spaces.

Participant data offered an array of complex, contextual variables that informed their expectations of manhood, their experiences/experimentation in community-based pedagogical spaces, their exposure to life options, and their expression of the identities they embody and embrace. Data affirmed that participants' *expectations*, *experiences/experimentation*, *exposure*, and *expression* were interrelated and interconnected variables that each man encountered and embraced in different ways and in different spaces. Their initial experiences and experimentation were usually initiated by and/or within families, and then experiences were encountered and/or extended through exposure to spaces outside of the home. The data reveal that there is a wide range of expectations that Black Bermudian males encounter during their journeys to manhood, extending from high expectations to low expectations to—in some cases—few expectations. The expectations to which participants were exposed helped influenced their definitions of success, which became an expression of their identities once they began to embody and embrace these definitions.

This study is significant for educators who are seeking to understand and disrupt the disturbing educational and social trends that impact Black males, because it interrogates Black masculinities, even as it explores paradigms and challenges borders that frame Black masculinities: namely, definitions of success, constructions of identity across generations and geographical borders, and the roles of community-based pedagogical spaces. From this study, I believe vital insights have emerged that will promote and facilitate stronger partnerships that can benefit Black men who have felt systemically marginalized in Bermuda. Providing an outlet for the sharing of voices and experiences of Black Bermudian males in this book is a vitally important step that can lead to greater understandings of Black masculinity, Black male identities, and the experiences that frame and lead to particular conceptualizations of Black male success.

In the remainder of this chapter, I will revisit my conceptual framework and expand the theories discussed in chapter 2 to offer additional conclusions about the journeys and identities of Black Bermudian males. Based on the data and insights presented in chapters 5 through 7, I will posit conclusions that directly address my research questions. I will also describe the salience of community-based pedagogical spaces, while asserting theoretical and educational implications for research, theory, and practice.

Journeying to Personal Identities: A Border-Crossing Imperative

To varying degrees, the narratives of the participants indicate that they are Black Bermudian men questioning the "masterscript" of colonial identities and ideologies. This includes questioning Eurocentric history lessons that threatened to whitewash their sense of self in schools, and problematizing Western mindsets that seek to impose the label of Black Bermudian male as sufficiently representative of all that they are. The participants not only named how their identities transcend the borders of Bermuda but also demonstrated how their exposure to various expectations and experiences helped them to form and express personal identities along the way. In this respect, the participants' journeys reflected the "hybridity" Bhabha (1994) declares is necessary in order to appreciate how their identities as Black males have had to shift over time and space. In so doing, participants also revealed strategies of personal and cultural resistance and exemplified elements of what Hicks (1991) calls the "border subject" and "border culture" (p. xvi). These are manifestations of the transformational power of border positionalities and "polarities" to rupture dominant positionalities and deconstruct vestiges of the colonial/postcolonial, center/periphery binarisms (Hicks, 1991, p. xvi). For example, Allan's narrative shows that some Black males express their personal and cultural resistance through their disinterest in school. Allan felt that his school was "a straight-up zoo" and he was not learning about events that were relevant to who he felt he was a Black male in Bermuda. Rather than remaining a *subject* of the school system, he chose to disengage. He would later fall in love with history on his own terms as an adult, once he read history books on Africa for himself and discovered that his people were far more than displaced slaves. It was at this point that he began to do his own "homework" (Spivak, 1990) and actively embraced the process of self-discovery and self-definition. As a cultural and analytical lens, "hybridity" was also an imperative I utilized as a researcher doing "homework" (Spivak, 1990) to better understand the borders the Black Bermudian male participants navigated and the masculinities they embraced, embodied, and resisted along the road to manhood.

Resisting and Complicating Typical Notions of Black Masculinity

Data from this study suggest that Black Bermudian masculinity may embrace *atypical* notions of Black masculinity. Scholars like Kimmel (2006a, 2006b) and Mutua (2006) highlight the centrality of domination to typical masculine conceptualizations. While data reveal instances where concepts related to domination are evident, such as Malcolm's discussion of how competition was an important part in his journey, overall, the narratives suggest that participants in this study embrace egalitarian ideals. In many ways, the participants were living their own "progressive Black masculinities" (Mutua, 2006) by resisting stereotypes and labels that many participants saw as *foreign* to who they were and who they wanted to be as men. Notably, a number of participants used words like "passive," "laid-back," and "docile" to describe Black Bermudian males, which are labels that are inconsistent with typical Western notions of masculinity discussed in chapter 2. Similarly, while instances of violence did emerge in some participants' narratives, the men in this study detailed that violence was usually a desperate means of protecting someone they loved—family or friends—or a means of protecting themselves from being teased or embarrassed in school. All of the participants were gentle and warm individuals who sought to care for their families by any means necessary with the skill sets they had developed. In the cases of two particular participants, Kevin and Allan, attempting to take care of their families was the context that led to jail time and the vilification of their identities in the media. Still, rather than becoming bitter, both of these men found ways to reinvent themselves and learn from their mistakes in order to forge healthier identities and lives for themselves and their families; this was not just an example of their willingness to border cross back into mainstream society, it also exemplified their commitment to pursuing personal success. In fact, all of the participants attached their personal success to their capacity to take care of their families, as husbands, partners, sons, and fathers.

Still, there is more to consider. In addition to the amiable identities that the participants embody, data also suggest that complexities abound as to how and if Black Bermudian males fully express who they are and how they feel during their journeys to manhood. A number of participants described their journeys and lives in Bermuda through language that suggests that there is more to consider behind the masks and "performances" of Black Bermudian male identities (Butler, 1993). Moreover, data revealed that the participants are/were all required to cross borders in their minds as they seek/sought to make sense of the "dichotomous" and "duplicitous" nature of life in colonial Bermuda as a Black male. Each man undertook and described this challenge in his own way: For example, Jeremiah's inexplicable redundancy after he had "done things the right way"—the colonial way—(i.e., earning schoolhouse degrees, passing certification examinations, and demonstrating loyalty to his White firm) forced him to acknowledge the hostility to Blackness that exists in corporate Bermuda. Though Jeremiah would claim to have little in common with Troy's "grassroots" experiences as a father of eight who has "never worked" in *traditional* settings, Jeremiah's journey has now led him to question the system in much the same way as Troy. Troy's declaration that his life journey "wasn't hard and it wasn't easy" resonates with the complex journeys and identities articulated by other participants: For example, Brandon said his journey to manhood was "uncomplicated but complicated," Kevin noted the "dichotomous" nature of his adolescent experiences, and Shaka described Black Bermudians as a people who are "suffering and smiling." To ignore, in Brandon's words, "the duplicitous natures" revealed in the participants' language and experiences is to ignore the centrality of ideological border crossing for Black Bermudian males—individuals for whom navigating between postcolonial dreams and colonial realities is a necessity. More than this, to uncritically suggest that passivity and friendliness adequately or completely express the identities of Black Bermudian males in this study is to oversimplify and essentialize Black Bermudian men.

Harking back to earlier discussions in this study of how colonialism has impacted jurisdictions differently, it is significant to consider how the history of slavery in Bermuda and the service-oriented industry of tourism may have contributed to Bermudian masculine tendencies. Because of Bermuda's small geographical size, there were few large plantations for slaves to work in Bermuda. Instead, during the 1700s Black male slaves worked in the shipbuilding industry as deckhands on the boats of White overseers (Bernhard, 1999). This made for a unique and unusually accommodating master-slave dynamic. A more hostile arrangement would not have been in the best interests of White seamen—slave masters—who, often outnumbered by Black deckhands, would have wanted to minimize the likelihood of mutiny. Though enslaved, Black Bermudian males are said to have had privileges that were not given to slaves across the Diaspora (Bernhard, 1999); this was done to protect White interests in Bermuda rather than to benefit Black Bermudians. In a letter written in 1722, Governor Hope notes "no slaves in the West Indies are us'd so well as the Negro's are here [in Bermuda]. ... These Negroes are all sensible of the Happy Situation they are in" (Bernhard, 1999, p. 189). These historical dynamics add context to the intracultural tensions that Brandon describes as the "subconscious ideology that somehow, some way we [Bermudians] were a little better" than other Black people. More than this, these historical dynamics offer critical context for better understanding contemporary Black Bermudian masculinities. Brandon declares:

> Culturally there is an ingrained passivity that comes with us being able to have a little more because of our social advancement. ... But in that passivity there has been aggression. Also our industry is based for the last 200 years ... on tourism. That was a "smile and grin" culture. So our dollar was attached to making other people feel comfortable. So if somebody worked in a hotel industry [or] drove a taxi ... guess what [we] did: We put on a smile: "Hey sir, how are you doing." And we had this shtick that was tied to "people in Bermuda are so friendly." But this same guy would go home and be nasty to his wife, nasty to his girlfriend, and have two families [e.g., a wife and kids, as well as a mistress or kids who others may or may not know about].

Brandon's comments in this regard are paramount, because he highlights the complex performance of "passive-aggressive" Black Bermudian masculinity while also suggesting how these dynamics intersect with Black Bermudian males as husbands and fathers. But perhaps there are also generational implications to consider as well, such as the contemporary uprising of violence, aggression, gangs, and frustration amongst Black Bermudian males in this generation. In particular, there appears to be a contemporary generation of Black Bermudian males who do not desire to wear Bermuda shorts or smile and wave like *Johnny Barnes*[1] while their economic and educational opportunities are marginalized. Additionally, it must also be noted that notions of a "better-off slave" that Brandon appropriately highlights are problematic and oppressive ideologies that have infringed upon Black masculinities, instigated intracultural tensions, and complicated understandings of Black identities.

The Identities of Black Bermudian Fathers

Much has been written about the supposed failures of Black fathers. As discussed in chapter 2, documents such as the Moynihan Report and others have exacerbated the challenges within Black families to suggest that Black men cannot be good fathers. Data in this study suggest that understanding the roles and relationships between Black fathers and their families is far more complex than generalizations and stereotypes can account for. One of the complexities is the generational dynamics that impact the decisions and perspectives of Black males. Thus, prior to discussing key insights about the participants as fathers, it is helpful to better understand who they are as sons who emerged from various familial arrangements. Specifically, of the twelve participants in this study, seven were raised in two-parent homes with either biological, adoptive, or stepparents (Jeremiah, Dexter, Giovanni, Malcolm, Allan, Brandon, and Troy); one was raised by one parent and the strong influence of grandparents and/or aunts (Caleb); one was raised in a single-parent home where he lived with his mother but there was active involvement from his father (Shaka); and three were raised in single-parent homes with little to no influence from their fathers (Kevin, Kofi, and Devon).

Harking back to the work of Hunter et al. (2006), what is noteworthy about participants in my study is that they sought to avoid their fathers' mistakes, irrespective of whether they came from a single-parent home or not. In some cases, such as Allan's relationship with his dad, fathers were transparent about their fallibility in order to encourage their sons to learn from their successes and failures. In many other cases, sons had to figure this out on their own, which may have contributed to the delayed development of strong father-son relationships. For example, Kevin found that in his efforts to avoid being like his father, who he scarcely knew in boyhood and grew to despise in adolescence, he "ended up repeating a lot of his mistakes." Like Kofi, who noted a similar experience, Kevin also highlighted the strength of his relationship with his dad now that they are both men. Other participants like Giovanni and Malcolm struggled to understand the expectations of their fathers during their early development, but now appreciate the guidance they received. Overall, for all of the participants except Jeremiah, who seemed to have a consistently positive outlook on his father's expectations, the Black Bermudian males in this study experienced times when they were emotionally, ideologically, or physically disconnected from their fathers and the masculinities they saw being modeled. There were various reasons and contexts for these disconnects, but as boys and young men, few participants were able to give voice to the disconnects or to fully understand the reasons for them. In some cases, these understandings came later, as participants transitioned to manhood and were exposed to the demands of being a man, which helped them process childhood dynamics. In Brandon's case, he had to make demands of his father. He explains:

> My father was a quintessential Bermudian male, which was, I bring the money, I smack you upside the head if you do wrong, but the communication connection was not there. ... So, even with a father in the home, you tend to sometimes, still navigate the journey by yourself.

Brandon's relationship with his father was transformed when his father became a Christian, and when "some family realities" led him and his brother to "become much more vocal with what we wanted and needed from him." Brandon's experiences with his own father have significantly impacted his approach to parenting and his commitment to being a "priest, provider, protector, and friend." Across generations, Brandon sought to cross relational borders for the sake of his own identity as a man who recognizes that his past does impact how he sees himself and how he relates to the next generation.

Contrary to dominant ideologies that question the intentions and capacity of Black males to be good fathers, the data in this study consistently revealed that the participants value their roles as fathers and father figures. It is significant to note that four of the participants have also embraced the roles of adoptive fathers or stepfathers to the children of their wives or partners. Again, this challenges the dominant discourses on Black males. Many men in this study demonstrate their willingness and capacity to embrace another man's biological child as his own—in this respect, these participants again reveal another instance of border crossing.

After transitioning to manhood, some participants were able to develop strong relationships with their fathers after taking the time to dialogue with them and broach difficult topics that may have caused disconnects in the past. Other participants chose to take a different path in dealing with the disconnects with their fathers. In Devon and Troy's cases, due to the experiences in their neighborhood and their lack of exposure to strong father-son relationships, they both accepted low expectations for their fathers and embraced a survival strategy of learning by *trial and error*. It seems, particularly from Troy's narrative, that some Black males short-circuit "picket-fence dreams" (Datcher, 2002, p. 3) of what life could have been like if daddy had "showed up," as a means of psychological self-preservation. They often embrace mantras that reflect the low expectations of their fathers but a high commitment to their own survival. Still, these men desire to be good fathers, even when individuals in society do not see them in this light. Troy notes, "Being good to my children is a big issue in my life. Not just my children, I don't care, like, anybody's children." While many would assert that he is irresponsible because he has eight children by seven different women and he has supported himself through illegal activities, Troy is adamant that all that he does is in order to build a foundation for his children. Irrespective of one's views on Troy's decisions and fathering, of consequence to educators is the fact that he is the parent of eight children who will matriculate through the public school system. The views and experiences of Black Bermudian fathers must be further studied in order to better understand the contexts and complexities that undergird the identities of Bermudian children as they seek to function and flourish in school and nonschool venues.

Nothing Like Mama's Love

Most participants in this study noted that they had very close relationships with their mothers. Giovanni described his mother as "his heart," while other participants used similar warm descriptors. Similarly, participants like Kofi and Kevin noted their admiration for their mothers, who often had to compensate for the absence of their fathers during their adolescent years. Caleb is the only participant who clearly suggested that there had been a disconnect between him and his mother. Caleb's mother left him in Bermuda when she moved to the U.S., and she later remarried, which further undermined their relationship. Underscoring maternal influences, both Caleb and Giovanni noted the impact of grandmothers and aunts, while Kofi highlighted the significant influence of community mothers like Sister Place at church. In all, data suggest that Black Bermudian males not only love their mothers, they also seem to have had closer relationships with their mothers than they did with their fathers during their journeys to manhood. Even in family arrangements where both parents were present and active during boyhood and adolescence, such as the homes of Giovanni and Malcolm, participants noted their affinities with and preferences for their mothers. Contrary to the delayed development of father-son relationships in the journeys of most of the males in this study, participants seemed to have a stronger appreciation and clearer understanding of their mothers all along the way.

Pathways to Identities and Life Outcomes

Though this study focused on the role of community-based pedagogical spaces, the schoolhouse frequently emerged in the data as a space where expectations were conferred and reinforced through participant exposure to various educational pathways. Data suggest that Bermuda's transfer exam was highly influential in sorting and stratifying those who would be exposed to prestigious academic public schools and those who would not. Still, based on participants' boyhood experiences and in-school/out-of-school educational exposures, data also suggest that the stratification had often begun in the minds of the participants long before sitting the exam—the academic expectations of parents and others in community-based spaces, such as the neighborhood, created a context where the transfer exam became a *expectation*-fulfilling prophecy in many instances. In most cases, participants noted that they tested into the school that they expected to attend based on their exposure to multiple influences already mentioned.

For both participants who experienced academic success and those who struggled academically, the data reveal that the participants' personal identities were challenged in schoolhouse spaces: Some Black Bermudian males in this study chose to persist with the identities that had been developed at home, while others chose to perpetrate identities that were validated in or necessitated by school cultures. What often unfolded was a deliberate and sometimes desperate dance—a "performance" (Butler, 1993, 1999)—of particular masculine identities.

Conflating with or competing against the expectations and experiences of the schoolhouse were the expectations and environments of the participants' families. Some participants noted consistencies between the expectations set in their homes and the identities that were privileged in various spaces and popularized by peers. The repetition of similar messages served to deepen the impressions of particular expectations, irrespective of the quality. Participants who found symmetry between the expectations valued in their homes and the expectations valued in one or more space(s) were inclined to embrace the expectations being espoused and reinforced. For example, across the chapters of this book, participants like Jeremiah, Giovanni, Shaka, and Brandon noted the influence of their parents in establishing positive expectations that were reinforced in prestigious academic schools and/or community spaces like the church. Conversely, the expectations set for participants like Dexter, Troy, and Devon could be described as consistently low in multiple spaces. In the cases of Kevin, Malcolm, Kofi, Caleb, and Allan, there were conflicting or inconsistent expectations in their journeys that impacted their life decisions and outcomes.

Good, bad, or in-between, the home was the first and most impactful space in the participants' early journeys and expectations of self and others. The quality of expectations and supervision in the home space was directly related to the exposure or lack of exposure to various community-based spaces and the positive and/or negative experiences/experiments found therein. More simply, exposure led to experiences/experimentation. Reciprocally, experiences/experimentation also led to exposure. These dynamics often occurred in community-based pedagogical spaces where Black males were often able to express the identities they embraced.

Salience of Community-Based Pedagogical Spaces

The schoolhouse was not the most impactful learning space for participants in this study. In fact, schooling, for most participants, was not a good experience. Some participants cited the influence of a particular teacher. In most instances, this influential teacher was a Black male. Still, the majority of their most significant lessons were learned outside the schoolhouse. In the following subsections, I offer conclusions related to the specific spaces investigated in this study.

The Neighborhood Space

The neighborhood was one space that was salient for ten of the twelve participants. For Jeremiah and Giovanni, the two participants for whom the neighborhood was not very significant, living in a middle- or upper-class neighborhood was significant in their lack of engagement in that space. Notably, Jeremiah and Giovanni lived within walking distance of areas where other Black males congregated, but both of these participants were discouraged from crossing over to these environments. Jeremiah asserts that "we couldn't be sitting on a wall," before declaring that "[my] father would break me so fast, [and] slap me so hard [if he saw me sitting on a wall] that ... it just never *crossed* [my] mind." Similarly, Giovanni was too busy doing chores and homework to have time to engage in many activities in the neighborhood. He would sometimes play and swim with his biracial neighbor who had a pool, and, further underscoring the relevancy of space to socioeconomics, Giovanni's house was large enough that he could play ping-pong in his foyer. Thus, he never felt the need to cross over to a nearby neighborhood that had a bad reputation, and he was never encouraged to do so by his "daddy."

Consistent with Sudarkasa (2007) and McAdoo's (2007) discussion of Black neighborhoods in the U.S., many participants noted that their Black neighborhoods in Bermuda were characterized by close interfamily relationships and tight living quarters. As Devon aptly stated, "Bermuda is like a neighborhood." Additionally, social space was important in more congested areas (Stack, 1974), to the extent that border crossing to neighbors' yards and church parking lots was par for the course for most participants. As participants crossed into neighborhood spaces, adults in these spaces often crossed over to the role of surrogate parents. At times, these influences were positive, such as responsible church members who took neighborhood boys to VBS;

other times, these influences were not. The profiles of Kofi, Shaka, Devon, and Troy exemplified these realities clearly. Plus, data suggest that the less space there was in the house, the more important community spaces became in the journeys of the participants.

Furthermore, relational space was also relevant. The larger the relational gap between a son and his parents, the more significant other community spaces became. Based on the data of participants who were exposed to experiences and experimentation in their neighborhood, it was the intentional intervention of adults and exposure to other life options that prevented them from totally succumbing to the negative influences. I found that the two participants for whom the neighborhood was the primary community-based space struggled to cross educational and professional borders beyond those necessary to survive and flourish in the neighborhood.

Church Matters, But Do We Have Black Churches in Bermuda?

Data indicate that the church as a community-based pedagogical space had a very significant influence in the identity-forming processes of five of the twelve participants. Four other participants noted that the church was somewhat significant during their journeys, and three participants referenced that the church was not very significant as they transitioned from boyhood to manhood. Notably, all of the participants mentioned that they attended a church at some point during their journeys, but their level of engagement and connection to this space was directly related to their family's connection to this space. Some participants noted that they were *sent* to Sunday school by their parents when they were boys, but as they got older they made the choice to no longer attend.

Participants who are active members of the church today tended to be individuals who were involved in the auxiliary activities of the church during boyhood and adolescence. Irrespective of the level of church engagement today, data reveal that the church had an enduring impact on the ideologies of many of the participants. Some noted that they developed a moral compass through the Bible lessons they were exposed to, while participants like Devon chose to "forgive and forget" rather than seek revenge on the person who hit him in the face with a bottle. Exemplifying the impact of their boyhood church encounters on their thinking, a number of the men noted how they felt/feel the need to re-engage with the church in adulthood, which underscores the influence of their early encounters with the church on their sense of purpose and success. Kevin is one such participant. Now an active member of his church, Kevin discussed the detrimental impact of experiencing the "dichotomy of two religions" during adolescence, showing that churches can influence the *headspace* of Black males. While it has been established in this book that religion and spirituality are not necessarily synonymous (Dantley, 2005), Kevin's insights highlight the reality that Black male identities are influenced by the ideological and doctrinal borders they must cross as they encounter various faith systems. Understanding how Black Bermudian males develop personal identities must also account for how their understandings of their spirituality have been influenced by the expectations of various religious traditions, which can create dichotomous thinking when inconsistencies and/or instability are added to the mix. Moreover, nearly all of the participants referenced their spiritual identities within the context of a religious tradition.

Based on the data, the existence and meaning of the Black church in Bermuda remains unclear. When questioned about the significance of "the Black church" in their journeys to manhood, more than a few participants seemed to struggle to account for what this label means in a Bermudian context. Demonstrating their own capacity to engage in border-crossing theorizations, some participants also questioned whether other Black people across the Diaspora even know what they mean by "the Black church," beyond the presence of Black people, particular music styles, and "the Baptist hoop." Certainly, all of the participants had been exposed to churches where the majority of the people were Black, but some participants wrestled with how and if their church experiences and spiritual identities were authentically Black. For example, Brandon notes:

> So the question is, did I grow up in a Black church? And the answer is, I grew up in a church with Black people. Did we take into consideration the nuances of a person of color? Absolutely not. ... Even [at my] Black college ... the [pastor] would get up in church and say, "Refrain from any boisterous public displays of emotion." In other words, "Don't clap, don't scream in church; it's not of the Lord." [I]n Bermuda, all our frames of reference of worship are African American. But that's not who we are. And do we have a centralized African theme? And even in Africa, they are more Eurocentric in their worship in the context of Christianity than we are.

Brandon's questioning is reflective of the postcolonial imperative to challenge dominant masterscripts. Drawing on his broad exposure as a well-traveled alumnus of an HBCU, Brandon again demonstrates that he is a border crosser. But he is not alone. Kofi and Shaka ask similar questions. Kofi declares:

> [I am] trying to think in terms of before slavery and how we [Black people] existed then, and how that impacts the way we are now. ... I'm saying, "Okay, I consider myself a Christian man, [but] where did the Christianity come from? And for what reason? [W]hat was the religion before Christianity, or what religions were they using in ancient Africa?" And it makes me look at some uncomfortable questions for myself.

Brandon and Kofi, like other males in this study, are thinking beyond the confines of the constricted identities that have been enforced upon them and their people. Through these border-crossing, postcolonial introspections, they are authentically considering how religion and spirituality have been *translated* in Bermudian contexts. By challenging the pervasive influence of colonialism on Black peoples' ways of knowing themselves as spiritual beings, Brandon and Kofi also highlight the interconnectedness and global infringements on Blackness for people of African descent. In the language of Spivak et al. (1996), these participants are seeking to account for the "epistemic violence" of colonialism on "the Black church" across the Diaspora. Plus, Brandon's comments reveal that though some Black males may attend Black churches, these may not necessarily be spaces where Black males can "just flow." Data suggest that there are conservative, Eurocentric paradigms that limit authentic Black male expression in some church spaces and reinforce typical norms that men are uncommunicative and unemotional. Perhaps this is why there are so many "mother-centered" Black church families. Future research is needed to further explore if and how Black males who participate and openly express themselves in church may be seen as "effeminate" and "unmanly" according to Western masculine norms (Connell, 2005; Gause, 2008). These realities certainly have implications for the identities that Black males form as they seek to understand who they are as Black men and spiritual beings negotiating church spaces.

The Sports Club Space

The relevance of the sports club to the participants in this book could be characterized as *hit or miss*. Six of the twelve men in this study reported that the sports club had a significant impact on their identities during their journey to manhood, while five participants noted that the sports club had very little to no impact on their journeys. One participant described the sports club as having some impact. Irrespective of the personal relevancy of the sports club to the participants, there was a clear consensus on the salience of this space for Black Bermudian males. Some participants, such as Jeremiah, never connected with the sports club because their parents did not feel that the environment was healthy; others, like Troy and Devon, noted that there was no significant sports club presence in their neighborhood, and their athletic interests diminished significantly as they became more engrossed in "the game." Also, a number of participants were highly critical of the underutilization of the sports club, noting that this popular space has also become, in the words of Brandon, a "graveyard" for Black Bermudian males. Brandon offers poignant comments that have border-crossing implications. He states:

> Social clubs in Bermuda are the most underutilized resource in this country, and I think they have done the greatest disservice to our community of any space on this island. ... They are comfortable in making the money from the bar. They [sports clubs] have a graveyard of young men who came through their program who are now living under their potential. A good friend of mine [said] the first time he was ever approached with drugs and alcohol was when he was playing football [at a sports club]. I've had mothers actually take their children out of the footballing programs ... because they said their [children are] getting football, but they are getting overexposed.

Brandon is critical of leaders and affiliates of sports clubs who have failed to "evolve" in their thinking and planning so that these vital institutions mature into more productive spaces. Effectively, he is suggesting that the sports club and its associates have failed to border cross in order to provide stronger platforms for Black male success and development. Like other participants such as Kofi and Giovanni, Brandon sees tremendous potential in the sports club because it is a valued space and conduit for Black Bermudian males. He explains:

> The football club ... particularly [for] men of color, probably [has] the greatest impact on our young men. ... It's probably the most organic space that we have. ... It is where most of the Black young men probably spend, outside of church and school, the largest portion of their development years. If we don't force them [the sports clubs] to be more, we're doomed. Because these guys [men at the sports clubs] have got our young boys, particularly at-risk ones.

The participants' insights are significant for understanding how Black Bermudian male identities are influenced in the sports clubs. The data suggest that the sports club offers Black Bermudian males the opportunity to develop athletically and socialize with other Bermudian males, but there are many negative elements in these spaces that are highly detrimental to their healthy development from boyhood to manhood. Like the neighborhood, one's capacity to negotiate the negative influences in the sports club is directly related to the influence of parents, guardians, and school and nonschool educators who instill positive notions of identity into Black males.

Barbershop Border Crossing

Like the sports club, the salience of the barbershop for the participants in this study was evenly split. Five participants noted that the barbershop was very significant in their journeys to manhood, while five participants asserted that the barbershop was not significant at all. Two participants referenced that the barbershop was somewhat significant in their journeys. Like the sports club, data suggest that the barbershop is an optional and organic space where Black men can be in the company of other Black men and engage in meaningful interactions. Information is shared between fellow patrons and barbers, and identities—both physical and ideological—are fashioned: At a base level, Black males attend the barbershop to have their *physical* appearance enhanced through a haircut. The importance of this experience cannot be understated for Black male identities, especially when one considers the insecurities that many Black men harbor about their appearance. For example, as a dark-skinned Black boy, Brandon's personal identity was impacted by teasing about his appearance; as a Black man who is now confident in his appearance, Brandon appreciates the role of the Black barbershop in helping him develop a positive sense of self. It is interesting to note that Brandon has a standing, weekly appointment at the barbershop.

There are specific spatial relationships associated with the barbershop that deserve further attention as it relates to border crossing and identity. Notably, the barbershop is a space where Black males have input on the curriculum during each visit: They can choose to talk or they can choose to be quiet. They can raise a particular topic or they can engage in self-directed learning by reading a newspaper, watching television, or reflecting on *bulletin board* material that can be found in many Black barbershops. In Ricky's barbershop, *bulletin board* material consist of paintings of Black heroes from across the African Diaspora, newspaper cut-outs of significant events in Black Bermudian history, and pictures of Bermudian football and cricket teams. These images are pedagogically powerful since they consistently reassert the important counternarrative that Black people, and Black Bermudian men in particular, are valuable. Unlike in the schoolhouse, there are no grades on the quality of a Black male's participation in the barbershop; in fact, the pressure is on the pedagogue—the barber—to perform and deliver. The barbershop embraces a patron-centered approach, so that the conversations organically shift depending on who is in the shop at any given time. As facilitators of the educative environment, it is not uncommon for barbers to shift the accompanying music or change the channel of the television in order to provide the right context for the clientele and the conversations. Educators in the schoolhouse could learn from these practices.

Additionally, data from the participants affirm that the core curriculum of the barbershop experience is the haircut: In fact, that is all the barbershop experience is from the perspective of participants like Devon and Troy. For them, the barbershop is not a place to engage in conversation; the haircut is the adhesive that keeps the space relevant to them. Devon and Troy's positions and voices are valuable to understanding the vital intersection of self-determination and agency for Black males in this space. This alone is an important aspect of identity and masculinity, especially for Black males who often feel forced to participate in other institutions.

Still, as I reflected on postcolonial and border theory coupled with the data of all of participants and my visits to the barbershop during the study, I am reminded that when Black Bermudian males enter the doors of the barbershop, they cross over from the pressures of Bermuda's colonial, capitalistic, Eurocentric environment to a realm where Black males are in charge and a platform is readily in place for their opinions to be heard if they choose to engage. In this respect, the Black barbershop in Bermuda is a postcolonial space where males can escape the wider community and find sanctuary. This is border crossing. But there is more.

We must never forget that Black Bermudian males usually enter the barbershop in need of a haircut; this means Black males enter the barbershop not looking their best, physically. The barber's chair serves as a transformational space. Entering the barbershop is one border crossed; transitioning to the barber's chair is another border-crossing experience. The haircut is a collaborative project grounded in the patron's desired hairstyle, the barber's expertise, and the patron's trust that the barber will responsibly wield a razorblade around his face and neck. This is a powerful border-crossing exchange that two Black males engage in toward the fulfillment of a joint vision—the haircut.

Consistent with Bhabha's (1994) notion of *hybridity*, the role of the bar-bershop in the participants' journeys to manhood varied based on the person-alities and positionalities of the men. Some participants spoke of their loyalty to particular barbershops, while others articulated their willingness to bor-der cross to any barbershop that provided the service—a good haircut—they desired. As the participants in this study journeyed to manhood, data suggest that the barbershop space is a source of differentiated learning; participants had varying experiences and gleaned varying lessons related to their needs and identities as boys/men.

The Educative Impact of Other Spaces

Though I set out to specifically learn more about how four particular commu-nity-based spaces impact the identities that Black Bermudian males form, the salience of other spaces emerged in the data—which is consistent with an oral history study. Notably, the prison and the *gombeys* were significantly impactful in the identities of some participants. Both of these spaces are understud-ied in Bermuda. Two participants highlighted how their time in prison was instrumental in their capacities to border cross to more productive identities and lives. One of these participants is now a teacher of *gombeys*. Another participant noted that he would allow his son to participate in the *gombeys*, and he was interested to know how *gombey dancing* could be used to enhance pedagogical practices in mathematics and other subjects for Black Bermudian boys. This is a recommendation worthy of future research and consideration.

Additionally, the water/ocean was another a relevant space noted by a number of participants who mentioned family picnics at the beach and time spent engaging in water activities. For example, Allan notes that he spent a lot of time fishing, which is a common pastime for many Bermudian males who, based on the data, seem to find solace and sanctuary in the uninhibited space of the ocean. In many respects, *jumping overboard* or temporarily leaving the 21-square-mile mainland to enjoy fishing or boating in the vast Atlantic Ocean that surrounds Bermuda is a powerful border-crossing experience that many Black Bermudian males value. As boys, Bermudian males must over-come the fear of *the deep* in order to learn to swim, fish, and participant in the vibrant summer water traditions; as men, Bermudian males often escape the rules, confines, and pressures of their lived experiences (e.g., corporate Bermuda, wives, narrow roads, and tight living quarters) by spending time on the water. Other participants, like Kofi, shared that they had the common

Bermudian male experience of using the ocean as an impromptu escape route from the pursuit of police, dogs, and other forms of danger.

Don't Worry, Be Happy?

Data in this study show that how Black Bermudian males define success is a reflection and expression of their personal identities, as shaped by their life journeys and the influence of community-based pedagogical spaces. Participants defined success in various ways, but many men in this study described success as "being happy."[2] Contrary to typical notions of Western masculinity, most participants rejected the notion that money and ownership of material possessions were markers of success in and of themselves. Instead, most participants saw financial security and material possessions as important for providing a foundation for their children.

Other definitions of success offered by participants included "making progress," "setting and accomplishing reasonable goals," "being at peace," "taking care of what you've got," and "maximizing the opportunities one has been given." Allan suggests that success is "balance and facing reality. We need money, we need to be financially stable, but you also need spiritual balance because there are a lot of peer pressures out there. Good family, good character—a balance of all those things." It is significant to note that Troy was the most affirmative of the participants in stating that having material possessions is a significant marker of success. His mindset in this respect reflected many of the typical Western notions of success, though he seemed to wrestle, at times, with the contradictions between his lifestyle and his values. There were moments during the interview when he convincingly affirmed the legitimacy of his "success" by citing the corruption of larger systems and individuals in power, but his affirmations were also undermined by his own admissions that he would like to ensure a different existence for his eight children, and evolve from street life to a career as a motivational speaker to youth. Further underscoring the tensions between his identity and his "success," Troy notes that his message would be to avoid the lifestyle that he presently lives. Troy exemplifies the "duplicitous nature" of a Black Bermudian male who must ideologically border cross between conflicting values and latent aspirations for a different life experience. In this respect, Troy reveals not only the tensions of competing identities but also how *hybridity* is a daily, ideological imperative for *border-crossing brothas:* Black Bermudian males who seek solace and success amidst colonial infringements that continue to assault their identities, ideologies, and institutions.

Like Troy, Kevin admitted that he formerly saw success as having material possessions, which was significant in his decision to engage in the failed drug deal that resulted in prison time. He no longer sees success in this way, but his narrative, coupled with Troy's view on success, reveals the problems that can arise when Black males embrace the narrow identities associated with materialism and quick money often attributed to Black males in other jurisdictions. Additionally, if success is described by many participants as "being happy," then it is important to consider what participants noted as dynamics that make them happy. In all, data reveal that across the sample, the men saw success and happiness as being related to family (which includes being good fathers), financial security (in order to secure the future of their families), friendship/fun, fulfillment of their potential, and faith. Certainly, the configurations of these ideas were complex and contested in the lives of each man in the study.

Implications for Practice and Research

From my study of Black Bermudian males' life journeys, I conclude that it is important for all educational stakeholders (students, teachers, administrators, community members, policy makers, and researchers) to understand that while the schoolhouse has its place, the education of Black people has also occurred and will continue to occur outside of schools. I believe there is potential for greater utilization of community-based pedagogical spaces to enhance the academic and life experiences of all students, and students of African descent in particular. At a time when policy makers are trying to address the overrepresentation of Black males in the penal system, and scholar-practitioners are trying to close the achievement gap in schools between White students and students of color, this study offers an important reminder of the significance of alternative avenues in the educative experience. In this respect, my study challenges the orthodoxy that reforming schools alone will lead to greater academic success (Cuban, 2010).

Implications for Practice: Educating Black Bermudian Males

Reformation is also needed in the expectations, experiences, and exposures made available to Black Bermudian males. School and nonschool practitioners must be re-educated to consider the complexity, humanity, and struggles of Black Bermudian males as they form personal identities during their journeys

from birth to boyhood to manhood. Black males are never just boys in isolation. Their identities are amalgamated manifestations of personal, family,
cultural, national, and geopolitical histories that impact the lenses through
which they see the world, themselves, and their futures. These lenses, which
are colored by colonialist calculations and racist diatribes, also impact how
the world sees and labels them. Practitioners must reconsider the proscrip-
tions and perceptions that cloud our visions of who Black Bermudian males
are and who we believe they can be. This is an imperative for all educators,
including Black Bermudian educators, because of the tendency to underesti-
mate how colonialism and oppression infects how we view those with whom
we share similarities. This is a point on which I have been particularly cogni-
zant while engaging in mesearch in Bermuda.

Contrary to the way Black Bermudian males are seen and pathologized
in institutions like schools and the media, data in this study affirm that Black
Bermudian males are thoughtful, hopeful, malleable, capable, and resilient.
Participants' narratives remind us that these words are not applicable only to
Black Bermudian boys; they are also equally applicable to Black Bermudian
men who have been vilified as violent and unredeemable. Black male participants who spent long days and thoughtful nights in forgotten jail cells testified
that transformation is always possible. Still, we must never be satisfied when
a Black male has to lose his physical freedom to experience mental emancipation. The conditions that led to Kevin and Allan's transformations must be
fostered in school and community-based spaces so that Black Bermudian males
can maximize their potential and successfully attain their childhood dreams.

The narratives of men in this study offer lessons that may well lead to better practices in engaging Black boys in schools and other educational spaces.
Data indicate the need for educators to create and utilize spaces where Black
males can "just flow." This is the allure of many community-based pedagogical
spaces: For example, the masquerade dance of the *gombeys*, a "tricky move" on
the soccer field or basketball court, and the free-flowing frolicking in neighborhoods all attest that improvisation and creativity are not just accepted in
community spaces, they are celebrated. Schoolhouse norms and expectations
are usually the converse of these dynamics. Thus, it is no surprise that students
often love learning but hate school.

Data further suggest that Black Bermudian males may benefit from periods
of restraint, where the elimination of distractions allows time for personal
reflection and focused effort on desired tasks. For far too many Black males, the
prison is one of the few spaces where they encounter this restraint. Educators

must create and utilize healthy spaces where Black males can express their identities while border crossing between "just flow[ing]" and *just chillin*. Similarly, we must begin to utilize spaces where Black males already *are* and where they already have trusting relationships and meaningful attachments. These are all border-crossing imperatives that offer lessons about Black masculinities and the influence of community-based spaces on the types of learning and relationships that can exist and flourish in schools.

Implications for Practice: Community-Based Pedagogical Spaces

By exploring the educative power of community-based pedagogical spaces, this study challenges educational stakeholders to consider broader conceptualizations of what it means to educate and where education takes place. More than this, this study also challenges school practitioners to explore how their leadership practices can be enhanced by observing and learning from the formal and informal pedagogical strategies employed in spaces outside of schools. In this respect, students are not the only ones who are required to border cross into the ideologies, norms, or grounds of the schoolhouse. Educational leaders, along with their staff members, must be proactive in visiting, embracing, and creating partnerships with the communities and nonschool educative spaces that surround and impact their schools and students (Wilson, Ek, & Douglas, 2014). These dynamics and practices are even more important for students whose home culture is divergent from the ideologies privileged in schools; these considerations are particularly vital for Black males, whether they are in Bermuda, Britain, Brooklyn, or any other part of the Black Diaspora.

My study is significant as a building block for future educative approaches that respect and incorporate the pedagogical potency of non-school–based educational venues. For instance, scholars such as Franklin (1985), Seiler (2001), Mills (2005), and Hart and Bowen (2004) have considered the barbershop as a culturally relevant setting in the Black community for the study of topics ranging from Black male socialization practices to the dissemination of prostate cancer research. But little consideration has been given to partnerships that would foster pedagogical and institutional exchange and engagement between the barbershop and the K–12 schoolhouse (Douglas & Gause, 2009). The barbershop and sports clubs could in fact be possible sites for educational interventions, such as literacy initiatives, intended to help Black male youth in their educational journeys (Douglas & Gause, 2009).

Implications for Research

This study is the beginning of a larger project on the identities, success, and education of Black Bermudian males and fathers. As such, opportunities abound for future research. Many participants in this study noted a shortage of information on educational and life options as they matriculated through school. Similarly, participant narratives revealed the power of educational and institutional pipelines that funnel Black Bermudian males toward particular pathways, ideologies, and identities. Longitudinal studies are needed that explore models of/for Black Bermudian male success and the creation of pipelines to broader educational opportunities and postsecondary success for Bermudians; this should include but not be limited to college completion inside and outside of Bermuda.

Furthermore, ethnographic studies are needed that more closely assess how Black Bermudian masculinities are navigated and performed in particular spaces. Participants' narratives affirm that much is still to be learned about the four community-based pedagogical spaces I sought to explore in this study and the spaces that organically emerged from the narratives of the participants themselves. Comparative studies in the U.S. and across the Diaspora are also needed.

Postcolonial Cravings

Thinking, living, and learning "beyond" colonialism constitute a vision that emerges from an amalgamation of postcolonial and border theory. In spite of Bermuda's colonial past and present, the participants' narratives reveal that Black Bermudian males desire to live in postcolonial spaces. This can be seen in the healthy irreverence participants have for ideologies and identities that have been thrust upon Black Bermudian masculinities from non-Bermudian, non-African sources. The lived realities of many Black Bermudian males have sufficiently troubled the souls of the Bermudian populace. Bermudians and those who have an interest in Bermuda are looking for answers. Now is the time to think beyond colonialism and the *importer's mentality* that would suggest that the answers to Bermuda's problems lie outside our borders. Answers lie within Bermuda's shores and within overlooked spaces. As they pertain to the specific issues Black Bermudian males face, answers lie within Black Bermudian males and our capacity to challenge and transcend ideologies that suggest we have nothing to export. A border-crossing, postcolonial mentality for Black Bermudian males means we must draw on the cultural capital of our expectations, experiences, experimentation, and exposures—in sum, our education—to express to the world that we have much to offer: our minds, our gifts, our passions, our ideas, our identities, and our solutions.

Community-based spaces are paramount to these processes and the re-engineering of our thinking about our identities and education as Black Bermudian males. Complexities certainly abound in trying to understand the implications of this study's findings regarding community-based pedagogical spaces. There are still many borders to be crossed and dots to be connected, both ideologically and institutionally. Distrust and fear are particularly challenging obstacles. Some educational and community stakeholders may fear the lack of traditional structures and controls in these spaces. Some Bermudians may be uncomfortable with a postcolonial mentality that suggests we have the capacity to engineer our own culturally relevant solutions. After all, it is likely that many Bermudians have embraced the "happy situation" of our colonial arrangement and mindsets. Others may express concern that utilizing community venues more intentionally will lead to the inevitable alteration or sanitization of inherently messy, organic spaces.

Still, what is unacceptable is to fail to act. Educational stakeholders must reflect on and account for the unique contours of Bermuda masculinity and the influence of nonschooling venues—especially if discourses around equity, culturally relevant pedagogy, and closing achievement gaps are genuine. The participant narratives attest that Black Bermudian males are more than capable of border crossing to postcolonial identities, and the historical data outlined in this book remind us that community-based pedagogical spaces have consistently buttressed the advances of people of African descent. To ignore the impact of these spaces is to ignore key cogs in the history, development, and sustenance of Black identities and Black cultures, and to ignore sites where education—irrespective of one's perception of its *quality*—takes place.

Black people in the U.S., Bermuda, and other regions—from affluent tourist destinations to forgotten urban districts in a city *near you*—face many challenges. The disturbing statistics on Black male academic achievement and life outcomes across the Diaspora suggest that the causes and potential solutions to these realities are both systematic and systemic. Learning spaces outside of schools where children spend substantial amounts of time, whether in Bermuda or Baltimore, must play some role in addressing these global forms of oppression. Additionally, more nuanced evaluations of the meaning and makeup of Black male identities must be considered if we are to account for the unique geopolitical contexts that mold and mutate particular identities. More than this, better understandings of Black masculinities are vital so that Black males are encouraged to (re-)engineer solutions and pathways for ourselves and our communities (Matthews & Williams, 2007).

The lived experiences of the men in my oral history study suggest that much work still needs to be done to address the disproportionalities and disconnects that inhibit Black males from crossing literal and figurative borders. New pathways must be created. Destructive pipelines must be dismantled and (re)configured so that the successes and failures of previous generations can become platforms for wiser decisions for future generations. Although most of the participants would describe themselves as successful, many of them have had to experience the bitter with the sweet in learning by *trial and error*. Prison and other perilous circumstances have served as both tools of education and inhibitors to the fulfillment of big dreams. What has emerged from my study is the reality that community-based pedagogical spaces alone are not the panacea. In fact, the data reveals that there is no one space that meets the needs of every individual. Participation in community spaces is quite organic and fluid, as Black males go in and out of institutions and organizations.

The implications of these realities are significant. I am reminded that addressing one organization or entity will not allow us to address the needs of every child. Just as we must individualize instruction, an understanding of individual needs and identities must undergird our approaches to evaluating how spaces can be effectively utilized to bolster education in schoolhouse and other mainstream institutional settings. Additionally, greater consideration must be given to the panoply of stages associated with the journey to manhood and the pursuit of success. Border crossing encompasses a range of processes and experiences that, at times, embody notions of deprivation, survival, and thriving.

Notes

1. Johnny Barnes is a Black Bermudian male icon who, for over three decades, smiled and waved to passers-by and motorists as they traveled into the capital city of Hamilton. His stature as a symbol of Bermudian hospitality and friendliness has been affirmed by a statue being made in his honor and the use of his likeness on official tourism documents.
2. Notably, this language echoes Governor Hope's description of Bermudian slaves' "happy situation" in the 1700s.

· 9 ·

MOVING FORWARD

Freesearch, Freeach, Freedership

I'd like to conclude this book by returning to where I started, with the *me*search–*re*search–*we*search paradigm, in order to offer tools that can be used to activate these approaches in your own praxis—particularly for teachers and leaders inside and outside of traditional classrooms. Certainly, this paradigm is not static, but ever developing as I actively engage my work as a border-crossing brotha scholar.

Teaching and leading at the University of Missouri in the months during the campus uprisings in the fall of 2015 is important and intricate work. I have served as a border crosser and bridge builder at a crucial time in the university's history. Being in this space has allowed me to operationalize aspects of the *me*search-*re*search-*we*search paradigm: I was engaging in a NCAA-funded research study of our Black male student-athletes at Mizzou in 2015; many of the student leaders of the campus uprisings are students in my department, and some are mentees of mine; I have also served as a consultant to system- and campus-level administrators as we all sought to navigate race, place, and complex space on this campus and in the city of Columbia, Missouri. For me, tension has begotten innovation.

It was the tension in the opening class of my recent educational leadership course that helped crystallize the final pieces of my emerging framework.

I had the privilege of teaching ten dynamic graduate students, seven of whom were from different countries outside the U.S, and three of whom were American students who all identified as White. The international students were from Ghana, Iran, Turkmenistan, South Korea, Colombia, China, and Turkey. I had never taught a class this diverse in terms of country of origin. Ironically, there were no students in the class who identified as African American, which I noted as we discussed our plans for the semester and our responsibility to critically consider what it means to be a developing educational leader on our campus during these times. The first class was rich and invigorating. I shared the *me*search–*re*search–*we*search paradigm and my desire to use it in leading them on a journey of leadership exploration and development. The students loved the approach. After the class, however, I was questioned by two students who asked about the rationale for centering issues of race and racism during our course. One of the two noted that he had gone as far as to review the syllabi of other universities to see if other professors were utilizing a similar approach. I was taken aback by what I perceived as arrogance, but not fully surprised. I asked him if he had ever questioned his White male professors when their syllabi exclude the voices of people of color or women. He hadn't.

I struggled to sleep that night. I wrestled with my post-class conversation and the overall affirming engagement of most of the class. I thought about our campus, the experiences and activism of many of our Black students, and the recent resignation of campus- and system-level administrators. I was troubled that students who had hopes of leading schools and institutions in these turbulent times were skeptical about the relevance of our approach and conversations. But then it hit me: Whiteness was the standard; Whiteness was their norm; Whiteness was their expectation. I recalled how an Asian student in my class chose to go by a generic White name, "John," rather than his wonderful Asian name. I remembered that a South American student in my class acknowledged that as she prepared for an English proficiency exam, she had watched hundreds of episodes of *Friends* rather than, say, *The Fresh Prince of Bel-Air*. For the international students—many of whom were from colonized or formerly colonized nations—it was a struggle to understand the significance of racism and its implications for their future leadership or teaching. The relevance of race, place, and space in a U.S. context was lost on most of them—in part, because most of the non-U.S. students had never thought about or discussed their own race until coming to the U.S. and, really, until the conversations in my class. Moreover, they had been conditioned to assimilate into a dominant White construct, and these ideologies made it difficult for them to empathize or galvanize around anti-oppressive efforts or approaches related to these issues. Yet, we persisted as a class, and our efforts were liberating for many of them.

In our class, *me*search meant that we considered the borders (literal, figurative, etc.) we were required to cross (or not). Our starting point was that "your story matters and your survival matters." We reflected on the people who have helped us survive, strive, and thrive across borders. I encouraged the students to thank those who had helped them (e.g., by sending an email, a card, etc.) and to make a list of students for whom they could do the same. Students were challenged to consider: Why did you choose the noble profession of teaching? What are your fears related to this border-crossing work? How can you activate your story to connect with and inspire your students? How would your life be different or similar if you were raised in neighborhoods and schools like those that nurtured Michael Brown or Freddie Gray? Students were required to take some time to journal in response to the questions above, in addition to writing a racial autobiography. My commitment to *me*search required that I challenged my students to first look at themselves and the resources right in front of/within them that they might be overlooking.

Educators who want to effectively utilize *re*search must critically consider the nature of the questions being asked and the lenses being used in the research. This is an important aspect of cultural and media literacy. This requires educators to ask critical questions: Is the information or research under consideration utilizing an antideficit lens/approach to Black males or Black families/communities? Does the research approach or conclusion seem to suggest that Black males and Black communities are deficient? How does mainstream media socially construct particular populations? Does the research demonstrate a critical consideration of systems of oppression, marginalized voices, and issues of access as it relates to full participation in political processes in a democratic society?

This work of border-crossing scholar activism is a process that requires a commitment to the journey of learning. It is vital that we are balanced, pragmatic, and hopeful in this work. To this end, *we*search requires that we continue to study and help our students to understand the systematic nature of oppression. I've found the film *Race—The Power of an Illusion* to be an important and helpful resource in this work. Students are exposed to the idea that race is not real, and yet it has real implications for how we live our lives and see each other. In particular, part 3 of the film, *The House We Live In*, is a staple in my work to help students understand the systematic nature of oppression. Students learn how the housing markets for many Black families and neighborhoods in the U.S. were intentionally sabotaged by racist policies (e.g., redlining and blockbusting), and how these edicts institutionalized the mechanisms that maintain wealth gaps between Black and White families today. I typically partner the showing of this film with a Monopoly activity I gleaned from an article by Jost, Whitfield, and Jost, "When the Rules Are Fair, but the Game Isn't" (2005). Students are prompted to play Monopoly with modified rules, including a staggered start that creates opportunity disparities and ultimately determines who the winners and losers are, who gets to buy Boardwalk, and who ends up spending multiple rounds in jail! Even students who are resistant and question the significance of racism today usually find this activity to be eye-opening and powerful.

Utilize Online Resources and Technology

Resources like the #charlestonsyllabus and #fergusonsyllabus are excellent for this work. I seek to nurture the gift of inquiry in my students by responsibly exposing them to online resources they can access beyond my classroom. It is not my responsibility to know all the answers. In fact, one of the most liberating and important declarations an educator can make is: I may not know all of the answers to all your questions, but I have a good idea where to find the answers we do not know, and a willingness to engage the process of research and inquiry *with you* to find them.

Challenge Narrow System-Thinking, Create Systems of Healing

I share lots of stories with my students. One story I typically share is about the opportunity I had to attend the doctoral graduation of a friend and colleague who also happens to be one of the top innovators and leaders in the world in his field. During the course of his doctoral program and even during his graduation weekend, I encountered colleagues of his/ours who critiqued his decision to write books prior to finishing his dissertation. Besides the fact that he has written best-selling books that are actually reaching the community he serves, the problematic reality of their critiques was that my friend has developed a national and international movement that is changing the lives of demographic groups (e.g., urban youth and Black families), which many traditional academicians merely *write about* in journals—journals that are typically read only by other academics. While many scholars go into debt to earn an advanced degree, my friend has managed to experience financial freedom while presenting his messages in culturally relevant, accessible packages that are healing the nations. He has finished his dissertation, but—unlike the average graduate—he didn't have to rely on the system that just schooled him to now employ him. He created a system of healing by combining *research* and *mesearch*. As I encourage my students to engage in *wesearch*, I also encourage them to be on the lookout for folks who may not understand their desire to challenge and change systems. Staff rooms and committee meetings are often full of these individuals. Staying encouraged and finding allies is vital to this work.

Ultimately, as a border-crossing brotha scholar who has studied and reflected on how my identity as a Black Bermudian/African American man has been impacted by systems of oppression, I have been able to account for the epistemic violence of my lived experience, to the extent that I now utilize my positionality, including my British-sounding, Bermudian accent, to challenge these very systems. The result of this ongoing work and the tension of engaging with resistant students has been the realization that the product of doing *mesearch–research–wesearch* is what I call *freesearch*—the capacity to critically and authentically leverage the story of "me," the stories of "we," and the findings of others. The work of border-crossing activist scholars is *freesearch*, and this work impacts our classrooms and boardrooms. *Freesearchers* don't just teach, we *freeach*; *freesearchers* don't just engage in leadership, we engage in *freedership*—we seek to liberate (see Appendix C). I've learned that there is power in accounting for and building on our stories; our families; our communities/counties/cities; and our countries of origin. I want to leave you with the hope and possibility that exists when you have engaged in the requisite *mesearch*, *research*, and *wesearch* … that's when you are truly free to learn, teach, and lead authentically and transformatively amidst the complexities of the spaces and places we occupy as racialized beings.

THE ROAD TAKEN

A Tribute to a Brilliant Blue Collar Worker

Ty-Ron M. O. Douglas

This poem was written after I observed that a front page newspaper story about a Black Bermudian male was printed on the same day his sibling's funeral notice (Brother Blue Collar Worker or "BCW") finally showed up on the back pages of the newspaper. This tribute is to *Everyman*, especially those who stories, dreams, and brilliance have been silenced by lonely tombstones and faded flowers; and to our master tradesmen who, as teenage boys, often had to surrender academic aspirations and childhood fun in order to become the primary "bread winners" for your mothers and funders of your siblings' education ... Thank you. May we hear your pain, accept our complicity, celebrate your wisdom, and commit to creating processes and systems that can heal and honor your legacies ...

Sad commentary on the lives of two brothers—two black men,
One whose name has gone down in Bermudian infamy
And another who, like many others, was lowered into a grave in obscurity.
Both broken. Sad day today.

Brother Blue Collar acquired the Bermudian dream of a house but never made a home.
Never found his Eve. Never had his kid.
Just how they scripted it.

Group home. Devon Lane. Hard worker. No father listed on his obituary.
A white man he never knew, he claimed.
That's why his hair was so straight, he would remind those he knew.
So much unsaid. So much pain he carried. But he worked hard, voted, paid his taxes, right?!
Just how they scripted it … no pension to pay a dead blue collar worker.

But he was so much more than a blue collar worker.
He cared about people … his homeless brother whom he fed at City Hall,
Bermudian athletes who he adored like international icons,
Hungry pigeons he shared his store-bought meals with,
and you and me—his people.

You should know his homeless brother was also a brilliant former utility company employee, he claimed, who also once owned a piece of the rock.
This brother of his would never accept Brother Blue Collar Worker's invitation to live with him. He didn't forget those who were kind to him.
I remember seeing him at a prominent black leader's funeral, respectfully standing over the grave to express gratitude for defending his brother, the other family member in the paper today; the one who has been controversially—and perhaps unjustifiably—vilified.

Abuse at a foster home. Unchristlike Christians.
Coercion into the baptismal pool … actually they dunked him in the ocean.
Forgotten once his name was added to the church books and the crusade quota had been met.
Do Better Church, it was. Not *Lead with Love Fellowship* as the paper wrongly noted or someone incorrectly communicated.
Lover of sports. Harmless. Bullied.
Controversial official. Die hard fan. Riding to work in fear.
The recipient of many *f-offs*.
Living a life of fear. The punch line of too many jokes.
Bermudians like to drink. Cover up … for his pain—and ours too!
Admirer of 'local' celebrities … former athletes who he looked up to as they made fun of him. Broken. Anonymous. Seeking love, fulfilling lust.
Did she help him or leave him alone to die?
Hard way to go, Brother BCW.
Sadly, just another joke for the boys to crack about him in his absence … his permanent absence 6 feet under as relatives and mistresses argue over his estate, recheck his will, and sell the piece of the rock he thought was his.

I wonder if anyone else noticed the connection between the two dead black brothers on the front and back pages of the newspaper.
The road taken.

I wonder if he was saved. Sigh.

Blessed to have met you, Brother BCW.

Glad I obeyed God on the morning He told me to take a ride on South Shore the day we met.

I was tired of seeing you abused, bro. Heard one too many fans and players curse you off.

Glad I got to share the Father's love. Sorry I couldn't do more.

Not sure you got it, but at least you knew I cared.

God, I hope you're saved!

If you didn't make it, you will have at least one person who will be looking out at you through the walls of the New Jerusalem with tears to be wiped away.

Two roads diverged on the road of life and I'm glad I didn't have yours because I can't promise that my path would have been any different.

Not just "BCW," Blue Collar Worker, or some crude nickname hurled off of drunken lips.

His name was Brother Blue Collar Worker, Dr. Blue Collar Worker even! ...

And he was my brilliant brother,

Your amazing uncle, the barbershop politician,

Today's student, tomorrow's leader,

A gombey chaser, our misunderstood father,

The grump on the couch, a generation's grandfather,

Her godpa, his cousin,

The practical jokester, someone's baby boy. ...

He loved us and we should have loved him better.

He deserved more. I miss him.

Whose justice was really denied and who was the real third man?

Looked for his funeral notice for over 4 weeks. Did many others care?

Puts my day into perspective ... water damage to our home.

Frustrated. Overwhelmed with projects.

Time to grow up and get up! No more moping around. I have it easy.

Can you relate?

I love you. You matter.

AUGUSTUS FUNERAL HOME regrets to announce the death of Mr. Bermudian Blue Collar Worker. A home-going service for Mr. Bermudian Blue Collar Worker son of late Mrs. "I Did the Best I Could," brother to Hope, Courage (Adversity), Faith and the late Resilience, Persistence and Triumph in his 65th year of 7 Hidden Gem Lane, Apt. # 4 Pink Sand Parish will be held at *Do Better Church* in Pink Sand Parish TODAY, May 24th, 2014 at 3:00 pm. Interment will follow at *Stop the Secrets* Cemetery. Flowers may be sent. THERE WILL BE NO VIEWING. Also surviving are: nephews: Cycle Breaker, Victor (Joy), Legacy (Believe); nieces: Jewel, Promise, Chosen (King), other nieces and nephews too numerous to mention; special friends: I Can, I Will, We Must; Sports Clubs & Country Clubs International; and the Blue and White Collar Workers Association. Bright colors may be worn. He was a success. His life was not in vain.

APPENDIX A

PARTICIPANT INTERVIEW PROTOCOL

Examining Bermudian Masculinity, Education, and Identity
Dr. Ty-Ron Douglas
Participant Interview Protocol

Date: _____

Name & Age: _____

Gender: _____

Race/Ethnicity: _____

This interview is part of a study that investigates the lives of Bermudian males across generational, socioeconomic, sociopolitical, religious, and ethnic lines to gain a perspective on their educational and life experiences. This project may serve as a pilot study for future dissertation work, although data collected in this study will be processed, analyzed, and used for potential publication. I am going to ask you some questions related to this topic.

You do not have to answer any of the questions I ask if you do not want to. You can choose to exit the interview at any time you wish, with no personal consequences to you. You can also ask me any questions you like about the interview or the research study.

Any questions before we begin?

I. Personal and National Identity

1. How would you define/describe your identity? (Who are you?)
2. What does it mean to be a Bermudian? How would describe/define Bermudian identity?
3. How would you define/describe Bermudian culture?
4. What impact does your nationality and/or ethnicity have on how you see yourself?
5. What impact do you think your nationality and/or ethnicity have on how others see you?
6. How would you describe the neighborhood in which you grew up?
7. How do you believe your neighborhood influence who you are?

II. Masculinity

8. What does it mean to be a man/male?
9. What does it mean to be a Black man in Bermuda (*a Black Bermudian man*)?
10. How do outside forces (TV, family, school, church, sports clubs, etc.) inform how you see yourself or your role as a man?
11. Do you have a mentor/hero(es)/heroines? If so, who would you describe as your mentor/hero(es)/heroine(s) and why?
12. How do you define success and do you feel that you are successful?
13. What does it mean to be a father/daddy?
14. What are your thoughts on violence?
15. How do you explain the recent increase in gang violence amongst Bermudian males?

III. Schooling/Education

16. How would you describe your schooling experience: *great, good, average, not good, awful*? What did/do you like most/least about school? Please explain.
17. Did you aspire to reach any personal/career/professional/ambition(s) and goals? If so, what were they? If not, why not?

18. Have you reached your goals? Do you believe you will reach them? Why or why not?

19. Did/do you plan to attend college/technical school? Why or why not?

20. Do you feel that school prepared/is preparing you for life and/or your goals and ambitions? Please explain.

21. How would you describe your educational path? What have been the forces/experiences that have shaped your educational path (e.g., particular schools, people, organizations, examinations)?

22. Did the *transfer/11+ exam* impact your educational path/life? If so, how

23. Are/were you supported and encouraged to do your best in school? If so, by whom?

24. Are there (community, social, religious) institutions or organizations outside of the school that influenced who you are today? If so, what are they and how did/do they influence your life?

25. What does the Black church mean to you?

26. What role, if any, did the Black church play in your journey from boyhood to manhood?

27. What does the Black barbershop mean to you?

28. What role, if any, did the Black barbershop play in your journey from boyhood to manhood?

29. What does the sports club mean to you?

30. What role, if any, did the sports club play in your journey from boyhood to manhood?

31. What does the neighborhood mean to you?

32. What role, if any, did your neighborhood play in your journey from boyhood to manhood?

IV. Family

33. What role did/does your family play in the male/man you are today?

34. Who was the leader in your home?

35. Describe your relationship with your father/daddy.

36. Do/did you have significant relationships with your grandfather and/or uncles?

37. Do you have children? If so, how would you describe your relationship with them and their mother?

38. What are your thoughts on Bermudian women?

39. How would you describe your relationship with your mother?
40. Do/did you have significant relationships with your grandmother and/or aunties?
41. Who do you talk if you have a problem or need support?

V. Political & Social Views

42. How do you feel about the fact that a Black woman is the leader of your country?
43. How did/do you feel about the election of Barack Obama as the first Black president of the United States?
44. Do you feel connected in any way to the United States, the United Kingdom, and/or the Caribbean? If so, please explain
45. As a Black male, do you feel that your views and voice are heard and respected in your community/country?
46. Are you proud to be a Bermudian? Why or why not? Please explain.
47. Do you have any questions for me about this interview or the research study?

Thanks. If at any time during this research study you want to withdraw from it, you have the right to do so with no personal consequences to you.

APPENDIX B

METHODOLOGY

Overall Research Goals

To conduct this study, I used qualitative research methods to extract rich and detailed data in context. Participant interviews and participant observations were the chief methods of data collection. In particular, I implemented an oral history research design to learn about the life experiences of twelve Black Bermudian males.

Research Questions

Three research questions guided my study of Black Bermudian masculinity, including:

Question 1. How do Black Bermudian males form personal identities as they journey from boyhood to manhood?
Question 2. How are the identities that Black Bermudian males form during their journeys to manhood influenced by community-based pedagogical spaces (i.e., those outside of the schoolhouse)?

Question 3. How do Black Bermudian males define success, given their life journeys, personal identities, and the influence of community-based pedagogical spaces?

These questions were chosen based on the themes that emerged from the results of my pilot study, my review of the relevant literature on the various topics encapsulated in this study, and my personal experiences as a Black Bermudian male and educator.

Oral History

I utilized oral history research in this study because, like Thompson (1978), expressed in *The Voice of the Past: Oral History*, I believe "[o]ral history gives history back to the people in their own words. And in giving a past, it also helps them towards a future of their own making" (p. 226). I conducted narrative interviews to construct oral histories. I conducted two rounds of individual interviews. In the first round of interviews, I asked the grand narrative question, *Tell me your journey from birth to boyhood to manhood*, to learn about the life experiences of my participants (Casey, 1993). I selected narrative research because I believe it is congruent with the strong oral culture in Bermuda (Douglas & Peck, 2013; Zuill, 1999). Through this approach, I sought to subvert the traditional power structure and social relations of the researcher/researchee relationship: Specifically, the storyteller became the expert. This was particularly significant for me as a Black Bermudian man interviewing other Black Bermudian men. Rather than allowing my own experiences and perspectives to color the subjects to be discussed, I sought to combat my own biases by allowing my participants to set the agenda through their narratives.

Overview of Data Collection Procedures and Methods

Sampling of Participants

I sought to better understand the various components of Black Bermudian masculinity through the utilization of "network sampling" and "homogeneous sampling" (Wolff, 1999) of Black Bermudian males drawn from one of four community-based pedagogical spaces: the Black church, the Black barbershop, the sports club, and the neighborhood. I sought participants who actively participate in one of the four spaces under investigation. The notion of *active participation* encompassed Black males who were regular and consistent members, attendees, and/or participants in these educative spaces. For example, in the church context, participants were individuals who attended and participated in weekly or biweekly church activities. In both the Black barbershop and the sports club, participants were customers or members who patronized the barbershop or sports club *no less than* twice per month (approximately every other week). Because neighborhood contexts and *neighborhood participation* are a little less structured than attendance at the physical locales of the other three spaces, I initially drew from one of my childhood neighborhoods and then drew on my connections in other neighborhoods and networks to identify and invite participates who were regular members of particular communities.

Interviews

I interviewed each participant twice. In addition to the open-ended first interview, the second round of interviews used a semistructured interview protocol, based on my initial analysis of the data from the participants' responses to the grand narrative question: "Tell me your journey from birth to boyhood to manhood." Interviews were conducted in the homes of the research participants or in other locations mutually agreed by the researcher and the researchee. For example, some interviews were conducted in parks, church parking lots, and employment offices. I collected 38 hours of data, with interview lengths varying from 1 hour to 3 hours. Specifically, twelve participants were drawn from each of the four community-based sites. In this light, I was sensitive to matters of confidentiality as I planned and conducted the interviews. Pseudonyms were used to assist in this process.

Observations

Black males who are active participants in the four community-based spaces were the focus of the study. As such, I informally observed the participants in the community-based pedagogical spaces as context for the oral histories they constructed and shared during our interviews or interactions. Initial *space observations* were for the researcher to simply "hang out" in the community-based space in order to learn, adjust, and become acclimatized to the environment. Observation field notes were recorded in a journal soon after I left the site.

Data Analysis

The data from the first round of interviews was audio taped, transcribed, analyzed, and coded through attentiveness to the participant's selectivity, slippage, repetition, and "the pattern[s] of their own priorities" (Casey, 1993, p. 19). Participants' narratives were assessed based on the topics, ideas, people, recollections, and stories that were privileged during the interviews. I was also attentive to the dynamics that were omitted by the participants or those experiences that *slipped* into participants' narratives (e.g., contradictions in the narrative accounts or cursory references to particular people or ideas). The findings from the first round of interviews were used to help select additional questions and contexts for the interview protocol that were used in the second round of interviews. During the second round of interviews with the participants, I used a semistructured interview approach based on an interview protocol, as well as field observations of the participants in community-based pedagogical spaces (Glesne, 2006). Thematic analysis as outlined by Glesne (2006) was used to analyze the second round of data. The steps of the thematic analysis process was (1) collect data; (2) code and categorize the data; (3) search and synthesize for patterns; (4) and interpret the data. Using this method, themes emerged from participants' responses to the questions. In pursuit of validity in this study, I allowed for and examined "competing explanations and discrepant data" so that my study affirmed the knowledge, perspectives, and experiences of the Black males who participated, rather than being a "self-fulfilling prophecy" of my own biases (Maxwell, 2005, p. 126).

"I Am Because We Are": Researcher Subjectivity Connects with Research Subjects

Based on the data and feedback from many of the participants in this study, my subjectivity and identity as a Black Bermudian male was central to their willingness to participate and honestly share their stories. I found that the participants were appreciative of the opportunity to have their voices heard and their experiences validated by a "son of the soil" (a Black Bermudian man) who also respected their roles as educators and the non-school–based pedagogical

spaces in which many of them function. It was clear that my participants'
validation was not based on any patronizing hierarchies between them and
me, but on a shared understanding of *Ubuntu*: "I am because we are" (as cited
in Ladson-Billings, 2000). On the rare occasion, I had to remind my participants that their stories, education, and identities were valuable and valid. For
example, upon being invited to join the research study, one older gentleman
replied: "I am not one of those educated fellas." I saw these encounters as even
more important than the actual interviews: These were opportunities to *speak
truth to power* by dismantling the myth that I was somehow more intelligent or
more educated than him. Not only did this gentleman *own a piece of the rock* (a
Bermudian colloquialism for a Bermuda home/property), he actually built his
home himself. He was never validated by traditional schooling, but his life's
work as a committed husband, father, employee within the tourism industry,
and self-taught mason spoke louder than a college degree ever could. Moreover, as I interviewed and observed Black males, I believe my study continued
to respect the wisdom, knowledge, and difference that undergirds *our being* as
Black Bermudian males.

A CONCEPTUAL MODEL OF FREESEARCH, FREEACH, AND FREEDERSHIP

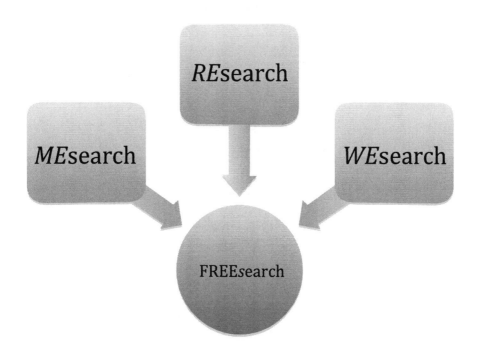

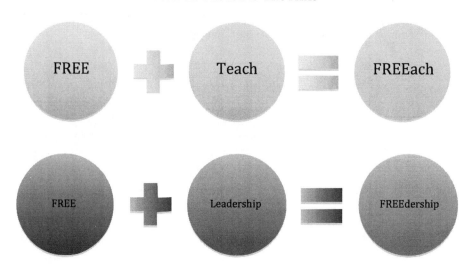

APPENDIX D

30 KEYS/CS TO CRACKING COMMUNITY CODES AND CLASSROOMS

By Dr. Ty-Ron Douglas

1. Care and Compassion (live and lead with it)
2. Communication (initiate and sustain it)
3. Collaboration (build it)
4. Change (be open to it)
5. Challenge (face it)
6. Core Values and Key Stakeholders (learn it/them)
7. Conceptual Framework (conceive it)
8. Cultural Relevancy (demand it)
9. Complexity (lean into it)
10. Community and Collegiality (help build it)
11. Cast Vision (then catch it)
12. Create … and then Create anticipation (believe in it)
13. Constructive Feedback (solicit it)
14. Critique (expect and balance it)
15. Civic organizations and centers (engage it/them)
16. Conflict (don't be afraid of it)
17. Connect (diversify it)

18. The Currency of Capitalism (unpack it)
19. Context (understand and account for it)
20. Church and Other Faith-based Spaces (collaborate with it/them)
21. Colonialism (think beyond it)
22. Competence (don't enter the space without it)
23. Character (don't leave home without it)
24. Caution (employ it)
25. Culture (respect it)
26. Conscience (use it)
27. Conceit (no place for it)
28. Consciousness (there's levels of it)
29. Courage (draw on it)
30. Call Out Injustice (just do it!)

BIBLIOGRAPHY

Anderson, J. D. (1988). *Education of Blacks in the South: 1860–1935*. Chapel Hill: University of North Carolina Press.

Anzaldúa, G. (2007). *Borderlands la frontera: The new mestiza* (3rd ed.). San Francisco, CA: Aunt Lute Books.

Bahr, R. (1976). *The virility factor: Masculinity through testosterone, the male sex hormone*. New York: G. P. Putnam's Sons.

Balswick, J. (1988). *The inexpressive male*. Lexington, MA: Lexington Books.

Banks, T. L. (2000). Colorism: A darker shade of pale. *UCLA Law Review 47*, 1705–1746.

Bell, S. E., & Bell, W. E. (Eds.). (1946). *The standard guide to Bermuda: Beautiful Bermuda*. New York and Hamilton, Bermuda: Beautiful Bermuda Publishing.

Bermuda Department of Statistics. (2000). *Report on the 2000 census of population and housing*. Hamilton, Bermuda: Bermuda Press.

Bermuda Department of Statistics. (2004). *Bermuda's social dynamics—Bermuda's academic standing: Are you qualified?* Hamilton, Bermuda: Bermuda Press.

Bermuda Department of Statistics. (2006). *Characteristics of Bermuda's families*. Hamilton, Bermuda: Bermuda Press.

Bermuda Department of Statistics. (2010). *Report on the 2010 census of population and housing*. Hamilton, Bermuda: Bermuda Press.

Bermuda Ministry of Education. (1993). *Restructuring implementation plan*, Hamilton, Bermuda: Author.

Bermuda Ministry of Education. (2009). *Bermuda schools, 2009* [Data file]. Retrieved from http://www.moed.bm/default.aspx

Bernhard, V. (1999). *Slaves and slaveholders in Bermuda: 1616–1782*. Columbia: University of Missouri Press.

Bettie, J. (2003). *Women without class: Girls, race, and identity*. Berkeley: University of California Press.

Beynon, J. (2002). *Masculinities and culture*. Buckingham, UK: Open University Press.

Bhabha, H. (1994). *The location of culture*. London: Routledge.

Billingsley, A. (1968). *Black families in White America*. Englewood Cliffs, NJ: Prentice Hall.

Billingsley, A. (1992). *Climbing Jacob's ladder: The enduring legacy of African American families*. New York: Simon & Schuster.

Billingsley, A., & Caldwell, C. H. (1991). The church, the family, and the school in the African American community. *The Journal of Negro Education, 60*(3), 427–440.

Bonilla-Silva, E. (2006). *Racism without racists: Color-blind racism and the persistence of racial inequality in the United States* (2nd ed.). Lanham, MD: Rowman & Littlefield.

Boogie Down Productions. (1990). *Edutainment* [CD]. New York: Jive.

Bowker, L. H. (1998). *Masculinities and violence*. Thousand Oaks, CA: Sage.

Brenner, M. E. (2006). Interviewing in educational research. In J. L. Green, G. Camilli, & P. B. Elmore (Eds.), *Handbook of complementary methods in education research* (pp. 357–370). Mahwah, NJ: Lawrence Erlbaum.

Brittan, A. (1989). *Masculinity and power*. Oxford, UK: Blackwell.

Burchall, L. (2007). *Fine as wine: From coloured boy to Bermudian man*. Chapel Hill, NC: Professional Press.

Butler, D. (1987). *Dr. E. F. Gordon: Hero of Bermuda's working class*. Bermuda: The Writer's Machine.

Butler, J. (1993). *Bodies that matter: On the discursive limits of "sex."* New York: Routledge.

Butler, J. (1999). *Gender trouble: Feminism and the subversion of identity*. New York: Routledge.

Carruthers, J. H. (1994). Black intellectuals and the crisis in Black education. In M. Shujaa (Ed.), *Too much schooling, too little education: A paradox of Black life in White societies* (pp. 37–55). Trenton, NJ: Africa World Press.

Carson, C. (1995). *In struggle: SNCC and the Black awakening of the 1960's*. Cambridge, MA: Harvard University Press.

Casey, K. (1993). *I answer with my life*. New York: Routledge.

Children's Defense Fund. (2007). America's cradle to prison pipeline: Summary report. Washington, DC: Author.

Christopher, J. T. (2009). *A random walk through the forest: Reflections on the history of education in Bermuda from the middle of the 20th century*. Winnipeg, Manitoba: Hignell's Book Printing.

Connell, R. W. (1987). *Gender and power*. Cambridge, UK: Polity Press.

Connell, R. W. (1995). *Masculinities*. Cambridge, UK: Polity Press.

Connelly, F. M., & Clandinin, D. J. (2006). Narrative inquiry. In J. L. Green, G. Camili, & P. Elmore (Eds.), *Handbook for complementary methods in education research* (pp. 477–487). Mahwah, NJ: Lawrence Erlbaum.

Cornelius, J. (1983). "We slipped and learned to read": Slave accounts of the literacy process, 1830–1865. *Phylon, 44*(3), 171–186.

Cox, R. (2009). *Evolution of the soul: The transformative connection between cultural consciousness, spirituality, and self-empowerment for African American community college adult learners.* Unpublished doctoral dissertation, the University of North Carolina at Greensboro, Greensboro, NC.

Cremin, L. A. (1970). *American education: The colonial experience, 1607–1783.* New York: Harper & Row.

Cremin, L. A. (1980). *American education: The national experience, 1783–1876.* New York: Harper & Row.

Cremin, L. A. (1988). *American education: The metropolitan experience, 1876–1980.* New York: Harper & Row.

Crooker, R. A., & Gritzner, C. F. (2002). *Bermuda.* New York: Chelsea House.

Cuban, L. (2010). *As good as it gets: What school reform brought to Austin.* Cambridge, MA: Harvard University Press.

Dantley, M. E. (2005). African American spirituality and Cornel West's notions of prophetic pragmatism: Restructuring educational leadership in American urban schools. *Educational Administration Quarterly, 41,* 651–674.

Datcher, M. (2002). *Raising fences: A Black man's love story.* New York: Putnam.

Davis, A. Y. (1981). *Women, race, and class.* New York: Vintage Books.

Delpit, L. (1995). *Other people's children: Cultural conflict in the classroom.* New York: The New Press.

Delpit, L. (1998). The silenced dialogue: Power and pedagogy in educating other people's children. *Harvard Educational Review, 58*(3), 280–298.

Derrida, J. (1978). Cogito and the history of madness. In *Writing and difference* (A. Bass, Trans.). London and New York: Routledge.

Dodson, J. E. (2007). Conceptualizations and research of African American family life in the United States. In H. P. McAdoo (Ed.), *Black families* (4th ed., pp. 51–68). Thousand Oaks, CA: Sage.

Donne, J. (1624). Meditation 17. In M. H. Abrams (Ed.), *The Norton anthology of English literature* (6th ed., p. 1123). New York: W. W. Norton.

Douglas, T. M. O. (2012). Resisting idol worship at HBCUs: The malignity of materialism, Western masculinity, and spiritual malefaction. *The Urban Review, 44*(3): 378–400.

Douglas, T. M. O. (2013). Confessions of a border crossing brotha-scholar: Teaching race with all of me. In D. J. Davis & P. Boyer (Eds.), *Social justice and racism in the college classroom: Perspectives from different voices* (pp. 55–67). Bingley, U.K.: Emerald Publishing Group Ltd.

Douglas, T. M. O. (2014). Conflicting messages, complex leadership: A critical examination of the influence of sports clubs and neighborhoods in leading Black Bermudian males. *Planning & Changing, 45*(3/4): 311–338.

Douglas, T. M. O. (2016). Black fathers as curriculum: Adopting sons, advancing progressive-regressive black masculinity. In L. Bass (Ed.), *Black mask-ulinity: A framework for black masculine caring* (pp. 93–107). New York, NY: Peter Lang Publishing.

Douglas, T. M. O., & Gause, C. P. (2009). Beacons of light in oceans of darkness: Exploring black Bermudian masculinity. *Learning for Democracy, 3*(2).

Douglas, T. M. O., & Peck, C. M. (2013). Education by any means necessary: Peoples of African descent and community-based pedagogical spaces. *Educational Studies, 49*(1), 67–91.

Douglas, T. M. O., & Witherspoon-Arnold, N. (2016). Exposure in and out of school: A black Bermudian male's successful educational journey. Journal manuscript. *Teachers College Record. 118*(6).

Drake, S. C., & Cayton, H. (1945). *Black metropolis: A study of Negro life in a northern city*. New York: Harcourt, Brace & Company.

Du Bois, W. E. B. (1973). *The education of Black people: Ten critiques, 1906–1960* (2nd ed.). New York: Monthly Review Press. (Original work published 1898)

Edley, N., & Wetherell, M. S. (1996). *Men in perspective: Practice, power and identity*. Hemel Hempstead, UK: Harvester Wheatsheaf.

Emdin, C. (2016). *For White folks who teach in the hood … and all the rest y'all too: Reality pedagogy and urban education*. Boston: Beacon Press.

Fanon, F. (1967). *Black skin, white masks*. New York: Grove Press.

Ferguson, A. A. (2000). *Bad boys: Public schools in the making of Black masculinity*. Ann Arbor: University of Michigan.

Fitzgerald, R., Finch, S., & Nove, A. (2000). *Caribbean young men's experiences of education and employment*. Research report 186. London: DFEE.

Flake, S. G. (1998). *The skin I'm in*. New York, N.Y.: Jump at the Sun.

Foucault, M. (1978). *The history of sexuality* (R. Hurley, Trans.). New York: Pantheon Books.

Franklin, C. W., II. (1985). The Black male urban barbershop as a sex-role socialization setting. *Sex Roles, 12*(9/10), 965–979.

Franklin, J. H. (2007). African American families: A historical note. In H. P. McAdoo (Ed.), *Black families* (4th ed., pp. 3–6). Thousand Oaks, CA: Sage.

Franzway, S., Court, D., & Connell, R. W. (1989). *Staking a claim: Feminism, bureaucracy and the state*. Sydney: Allen & Unwin.

Frazier, E. F. (1973). The failure of the Negro intellectual. In J. A. Ladner (Ed.), *The death of White sociology* (pp. 58–60). New York: Random House.

Frazier, E. F. (1974). *The Negro church in America*. New York: Schocken Books.

Freire, P. (1970). *Pedagogy of the oppressed*. New York: Seabury Press.

Gause, C. P. (2008). *Integration matters: Navigating identity, culture, and resistance*. New York: Peter Lang.

Gillborn, D., & Gipps, C. (1996). *Recent research on the achievements of ethnic minority pupils*. London: HMSO.

Giroux, H. A. (2005). *Border crossings* (2nd ed.). New York: Routledge.

Glenn, E. N. (Ed.). (2009). *Shades of difference: Why skin color matters*. Stanford, CA: Stanford University Press.

Glesne, C. (2006). *Becoming qualitative researchers: An introduction* (3rd ed.). Boston: Pearson.

Goffman, E. (1959). *The presentation of self in everyday life*. New York: Anchor/Doubleday.

Goffman, E. (1963). *Stigma: Notes on the management of spoiled identity*. Englewood Cliffs, NJ: Prentice Hall.

Grant, J., & Tancred, P. (1992). A feminist perspective on state bureaucracy. In A. J. Mills & P. Tancred (Eds.), *Gendering organizational analysis* (pp. 112–128). Newbury Park, CA: Sage.

Gray, C. S., & Sloan, G. (1999). *Geopolitics, geography, and strategy*. Oxon, UK: Frank Cass Publishers.

Gresson, A. D., III. (2008). *Race and education primer*. New York: Peter Lang.

Hale, J. E. (2001). *Learning while Black: Creating educational excellence for African American children*. Baltimore: Johns Hopkins University Press.

Hall, S. (1993). New ethnicities. In J. Donald & A. Rattansi (Eds.), *Race, culture and difference* (pp. 252–259). London: Sage and Open University.

Hall, S. (1996). When was 'the post-colonial'? Thinking at the limit. In I. Chambers & L. Curti (Eds.), *The post-colonial question: Common skies, divided horizons* (pp. 242–260). London: Routledge.

Hall, S. (2003). Cultural identity and the diaspora. In E. J. Braziel & A. Mannur (Eds.), *Theorizing diaspora* (pp. 233–246). Malden, MA: Blackwell Publishing.

Hall, S. (2005). Old and new identities. In P. S. Rothenberg (Ed.), *Beyond borders: In thinking critically about global issues* (pp. 167–173). New York: Worth Publishers.

Harper, S. (2006). *Black male students at public flagship universities in the U.S.: Status, trends, and implications for policy and practice*. Washington, DC: Joint Center for Political and Economic Studies.

Harper, S. R. (2012). *Black male student success in higher education: A report from the National Black Male College Achievement Study*. Philadelphia: University of Pennsylvania, Center for the Study of Race and Equity in Education.

Harris-Lacewell M., & Mills, Q. T. (2004). Truth and soul: Black talk in the barbershop. In M. Harris-Lacewell, *Barbershops, bibles, and BET*. Princeton, NJ: Princeton University Press.

Hart, A., & Bowen, D. J. (2004). The feasibility of partnering with African-American barbershops to provide prostate cancer education. *Ethnicity & Disease, 14*, 269–273.

Hatty, S. E. (2000). *Masculinities, violence, and culture*. Thousand Oaks, CA: Sage.

Haywood, C., & Mac an Ghaill, M. (1996). Schooling masculinities. In M. Mac an Ghaill (Ed.), *Understanding masculinities*, pp. 50–60. Buckingham, UK: Open University Press.

Hearn, J., & Collinson, D. L. (1994). Theorizing unities and differences between men and between masculinities. In H. Brod & M. Kaufman (Eds.), *Theorizing masculinities* (pp. 97–118). Thousand Oaks, CA: Sage.

Hickling-Hudson, A. (1998). When Marxist and postmodern theories won't do: The potential of postcolonial theory for educational analysis. *Discourse: Studies in the Cultural Politics of Education, 19*(3), 327–339.

Hicks, D. E. (1991). *Border writing: The multidimensional text*. Minneapolis: University of Minnesota Press.

Hill, R. (1971). *The strengths of Black families*. New York: Emerson Hall.

Hodgson, E. N. (1997). *Second-class citizens, first-class men* (3rd ed.). Canada: The Writer's Machine.

Hodgson, E. N. (2008). *The experience of racism in Bermuda and in its wider context*. Bermuda: Bermuda Press.

Holliday, L. (1978). *The violent sex: Male psychology and the evolution of consciousness*. Guerneville, CA: Bluestocking Books.

hooks, b. (1994). *Teaching to transgress: Education as the practice of freedom*. New York: Routledge.

hooks, b. (2004a). *The will to change: Men, masculinity, and love*. New York: Atria Books.

hooks, b. (2004b). *We real cool: Black men and masculinity*. New York: Routledge.

Howard, T. C. (2000). Reconceptualizing multicultural education: Design principles for educating African American males. In M. C. Brown, II & J. E. Davis (Eds.), *Black sons to mothers: Compliments, critiques, and challenges for cultural workers in education* (pp. 155–172). New York: Peter Lang.

Howard, T. C. (2010). *Why race and culture matter in schools: Closing the achievement gap in America's classrooms*. New York: Teachers College Press.

Howard, T. C. (2014). *Black male(d): Peril and promise in the education of African American males*. New York: Teachers College Press.

Hunter, A. G., Friend, C. A., Murphy, S. Y., Rollins, A., Williams-Wheeler, M., & Laughinghouse, J. (2006). Loss, survival, and redemption: African American male youths' reflections on life without fathers, manhood, and coming of age. *Youth & Society, 37*, 423–452.

Iverson, S. V. (2007). Camouflaging power and privilege: A critical race analysis of university diversity policies. *Educational Administration Quarterly, 43*(5), 586–611.

Johnson, A. (2006). *Privilege, power, and difference*. New York: McGraw-Hill.

Johnson, C. S. (1934). *Shadow of the plantation*. Chicago: University of Chicago Press.

Jost, M., Whitfield, E. L., & Jost, M. (2005). When the rules are fair, but the game isn't. *Multicultural Education, 13*(1), 14.

Justus, J. B. (1978). Ethnology: Black clubs in Bermuda: Ethnography of a play world. *American Anthropologist, 80*(2), 434.

Karenga, M., & Karenga, T. (2007). The Nguzo Saba and the Black family: Principles and practices of well-being and flourishing. In H. P. McAdoo (Ed.), *Black families* (4th ed., pp. 7–28). Thousand Oaks, CA: Sage.

Kaufman, M. (1994). Men's contradictory experiences of power. In H. Brod & M. Kaufman (Eds.), *Theorizing masculinities*. London: Sage.

Keating, A. (Ed.). (2009). *The Gloria Anzaldúa reader*. Durham, NC: Duke University Press.

Kennedy, V. (2000). *Edward Said: A critical introduction*. Malden, MA: Blackwell Publishers.

Kimmel, M. S. (1987). Rethinking masculinity: New directions in research. In M. S. Kimmel (Ed.), *Changing men: New directions in research on men and masculinity* (pp. 9–24). Newbury Park, CA: Sage.

Kimmel, M. S. (1994). Masculinity as homophobia: Fear, shame, and silence in the construction of gender identity. In H. Brod & M. Kaufman (Eds.), *Theorizing masculinities* (pp. 119–141). Thousand Oaks, CA: Sage.

Kimmel, M. S. (2006a). *Manhood in America: A cultural history*. New York: The Free Press.

Kimmel, M. S. (2006b). What about the boys? In H. S. Shapiro, K. Lathan, & S. N. Ross (Eds.), *The institution of education* (5th ed., pp. 281–285). Boston: Pearson Custom Publishing.

Kivel, P. (1992). *Men's work: How to stop the violence that tears our lives apart*. New York: Ballantine Books.

Ladson-Billings, G. (2000). Racialized discourses and ethnic epistemologies. In N. K. Denzin & Y. S. Lincoln (Eds.), *Handbook of qualitative research* (2nd ed., pp. 257–277). Thousand Oaks, CA: Sage.

Leonardo, Z. (2004). The color of supremacy: Beyond the discourse of 'white privilege.' *Educational Philosophy and Theory, 36*(2), 137–152.

Lewis, H. (1957). *Black ways of Kent*. New York: Van Rees Press.

Lincoln, C. E., & Mamiya, L. H. (1990). *The Black church in the African American experience*. Durham, NC: Duke University Press.

Lipsitz, G. (1994). *Dangerous crossroads: Popular music, postmodernism, and the poetics of place*. New York: Verso.

Love, B. L. (2012). *Hip hop's li'l sistas speak: Negotiating hip hop identities and politics in the new south*. New York: Peter Lang.

Lovell, J., Jr. (1939). The social implications of the Negro spiritual. *Journal of Negro Education*, 8(4), 634–643.

Mac an Ghaill, M. (1996). *Understanding masculinities*. Buckingham, UK: Open University Press.

Manning, F. E. (1973). *Black clubs in Bermuda: Ethnography of a play world*. Ithaca, NY: Cornell University Press.

Manuel, P. L., Bilby, K., & Largey, M. (2006). *Caribbean currents: Caribbean music from rumba to reggae*. Philadelphia: Temple University Press.

Martin, P. P., & McAdoo, H. P. (2007). Theological orientation of African American churches and parents. In H. P. McAdoo (Ed.), *Black families* (4th ed., pp. 51–68). Thousand Oaks, CA: Sage.

Matthews, L. E. (2003). Babies overboard! The complexities of incorporating culturally relevant teaching into mathematics instruction. *Educational Studies in Mathematics*, 53(1), 61–82.

Matthews, L. E., & Williams, B. A. (2007). Beyond 'commentaries of despair': Reengineering pathways to design in the schooling of Black men. *The Negro Educational Review*, 58(3–4), 187–199.

Maxwell, J. A. (2005). *Qualitative research design: An interactive approach* (2nd ed.). Thousand Oaks, CA: Sage.

McAdoo, H. P. (Ed.). (2007). *Black families*. Thousand Oaks, CA: Sage.

Mills, Q. T. (2005). "I've got something to say": The public square, public discourse, and the barbershop. *Radical History Review*, 93, 192–199.

Mills, Q. T. (2006). Color-line barbers and the emergence of a Black counterpublic: A social and political history of Black barbers and barbershops, 1850–1970. Unpublished doctoral dissertation, University of Chicago, Chicago, IL.

Mincy, R. B., Jethwani-Keyser, M., & Haldane, E. (2009). *A study of employment, earnings, and educational gaps between young Black Bermudian males and their same-age peers*. New York: Columbia University School of Social Work, Center for Research on Fathers, Children and Family Well-Being.

Monroe, C. R. (2005). Understanding the discipline gap through a cultural lens: Implications for the education of African American students. *Intercultural Education*, 16(4), 317–330.

Morrell, E., & Duncan-Andrade, J. M. R. (2002). Promoting academic literacy with urban youth through engaging hip-hop culture. *The English Journal*, 91(6), 88–92.

Morris, J. E. (2009). *Troubling the waters*. New York: Teachers College Press.

Moynihan, D. P. (1965). *The Negro family: The case for national action*. Washington, DC: Department of Labor.

Mutua, A. D. (Ed.). (2006). *Theorizing progressive Black masculinities*. New York: Routledge.

National Assessment of Educational Progress. (2007). *Reading report card for the nation and states*. Washington, DC: Office of Educational Research and Improvement, U.S. Department of Education.

Nobles, W. W. (2007). African American family life: An instrument of culture. In H. P. McAdoo (Ed.), *Black families* (4th ed., pp. 51–68). Thousand Oaks, CA: Sage.

Ogbu, J. (2007). African American education: A cultural-ecological perspective. In H. P. McAdoo (Ed.), *Black families* (4th ed., pp. 79–94). Sage, CA: Thousand Oaks.

Osterud, O. (1988). The uses and abuses of geopolitics. *Journal of Peace Education, 25*(2), 191–199.

Packwood, C. O. (1975). *Chained on the rock*. Bermuda: The Island Press.

Peck, C. (2001). *Educate to liberate: The Black Panther Party and political education*. Unpublished doctoral dissertation, Stanford University, Stanford, CA.

Perkins, W. E. (2000). Matriarchy, Malcolm X, and masculinity: A historical essay. In M. C. Brown & J. E. Davis (Eds.), *Black sons to mothers: Compliments, critiques, and challenges for cultural workers in education* (pp. 15–34). New York: Peter Lang.

Perlstein, D. (1990). Teaching freedom: SNCC and the creation of the Mississippi Freedom Schools. *History of Education Quarterly 30*, 297–324.

Perlstein, D. (2002). Minds stayed on freedom: Politics and pedagogy in the African American freedom struggle. *American Educational Research Journal, 39*(2), 249–277.

Powell, C. T. (1991). Rap music: An education with a beat from the street. *Journal of Negro Education, 60*(3), 245–259.

Powell-Hopson, D., & Hopson, D. S. (1988). Implications of doll color preferences among Black preschool children and White preschool children. *Journal of Black Psychology, 14*(2), 57–63.

Raynor, T. (2009). Changes in traffic laws to be implemented. *The Royal Gazette*, February 10.

Rhamie, J. (2003). *A study of the educational experiences of African Caribbeans in the UK*. Unpublished doctoral thesis, Institute of Education University of London, Psychology and Special Needs.

Rizvi, F. (2009). Postcolonialism and globalization in education. In R. S. Coloma (Ed.), *Postcolonial challenges in education* (pp. 46–54). New York: Peter Lang.

Said, E. (1994). *Culture and imperialism*. New York: Vintage Books.

Schwalbe, M. (2005). *The sociologically examined life: Pieces of the conversation*. Boston: McGraw-Hill.

Segal, L. (1990). *Slow motion: Changing masculinities, changing men*. London: Virago Press.

Seiler, G. (2001). Reversing the "standard" direction: Science emerging from the lives of African American students. *Journal of Research in Science Teaching, 38*(9), 1000–1014.

Shujaa, M. J. (1994). Education and schooling: You can have one without the other. In M. J. Shujaa (Ed.), *Too much schooling, too little education: A paradox of Black life in White societies* (pp. 13–36). Trenton, NJ: African World Press.

Spivak, G. C. (1987). *In other worlds: Essays in cultural politics*. New York: Methuen.

Spivak, G. C. (1988). Subaltern studies: Deconstructing historiography. In R. Guha & G. C. Spivak (Eds.), *Selected subaltern studies* (pp. 4–32). New York: Oxford University Press.

Spivak, G. C. (1990). *The post-colonial critic: Interviews, strategies, dialogues*. New York: Routledge.

Spivak, G. C. (1999). *A critique of postcolonial reason: Toward a history of the vanishing present.* Cambridge, MA: Harvard University Press.

Spivak, G. C., Landry, D., & Maclean, G. (Eds.). (1996). *The Spivak reader.* New York: Routledge.

Spring, J. (2005). *The American school: 1642–2004.* New York: McGraw-Hill.

Stack, C. B. (1974). *All our kin: Strategies for survival in a Black community.* New York: Harper & Row.

Stokes, O. P. (1972). The Black perspective: Christian education in today's church. In R. Earl Riggins, Jr. (Ed.), *To you who teach in the Black church.* Nashville, TN: National Baptist Convention Publishing Board.

Straus, M. A., Gelles, R. J., & Steinmetz, S. K. (1980). *Behind closed doors: Violence in the American family.* New York: Anchor Press/Doubleday.

Sudarkasa, N. (2007). Interpreting the African heritage in African American family organization. In H. P. McAdoo (Ed.), *Black families* (4th ed., pp. 51–68). Thousand Oaks, CA: Sage.

Swan, Q. (2009). *Black power in Bermuda: The struggle for decolonization.* New York: Palgrave Macmillan.

Thompson, P. (1978). *The voice of the past: Oral history.* Oxford, UK: Oxford University Press.

Threadgold, T., & Cranny-Francis, A. (1990). *Feminine, masculine, and representation.* London: Allen & Unwin.

Tillman, L. (2006). Research and writing from an African American perspective: Reflective notes on three research studies. *International Journal of Qualitative Studies in Education, 19*(3), 265–287.

Turner, S. L., & Bagley, C. A. (2000). The role of the Black church and religion. In N. J. Burgess & E. Brown (Eds.), *African American woman: An ecological perspective* (pp. 115–134). New York: Falmer Press.

Villaverde, L. E. (2008). *Feminist theories and education primer.* New York: Peter Lang.

Villenas, S., & Deyhle, D. (1999). Critical race theory and ethnographies challenging the stereotypes: Latino families, schooling, resilience and resistance. *Curriculum Inquiry, 29*(4), 413–445.

Washington, B. T. (1901). *Up from slavery.* New York: Doubleday.

Watters, P. (1964, December 20). Their text is a civil rights primer. *The New York Times Sunday Magazine,* 10–11.

Webber, T. L. (1978). *Deep like the rivers.* New York: W. W. Norton.

West, C. (1993). *Race matters.* Boston: Beacon Press.

Whitehead, S. M. (2002). *Men and masculinities: Key themes and new directions.* Cambridge, UK: Polity Press. Wilder, S. W. (2013). *Ebony and ivory: Race, slavery, and the troubled history of American universities.* New York: Bloomsbury Press.

Williams, H. A. (2005). *Self-taught: African American education in slavery and freedom.* Chapel Hill: University of North Carolina Press.

Wilson, C. M., Douglas, T. M. O., & Nganga, C. (2013). Starting with African American success: A strengths-based approach to transformative educational leadership. In L. C. Tillman & J. J. Scheurich (Eds.), *Handbook of research on educational leadership for diversity and equity.* (pp. 111–133). New York, N.Y.: Routledge/Taylor & Francis.

Wilson, C. M., Ek, L., & Douglas, T. M. O. (2014). Immigrant youth navigating educational borderlands: Implications for progressive politics and pedagogies of difference. *The Urban Review, 46*(1), 1–24.

Wolff, R. F. (1999). A phenomenological study of in-church and televised worship. *Journal for the Scientific Study of Religion, 38*(20), 219–235.

Woodson, C. G. (1911). *Education of the Negro prior to 1861*. New York: Knickerbocker Press.

Woodson, C. G. (1932). Is the education Negro a liability? *Chicago Defender,* May 21.

Woodson, C. G. (1933). *The Mis-education of the Negro*. Trenton, NJ: Africa World Press.

Wrench, J., & Hassan, E. (1996). *Ambition and marginalisation: A qualitative study of underachieving young men of Afro-Caribbean origin*. DFEE Research Series No. 31. London: DFEE.

Wright, H. K. (2003). An endarkened feminist epistemology? Identity, difference and politics of representation in educational research. *International Journal of Qualitative Studies in Education, 16*(2), 197–214.

Wright, M. M. (2004). *Becoming Black: Creating identity in the African Diaspora*. Durham, NC: Duke University Press.

Wright, R. (1945). *Black boy: A record of childhood and youth*. Cleveland, OH: World Publishing.

Zuill, W. S. (1999). *The story of Bermuda and her people* (2nd ed.). London: Macmillan.

INDEX

C

ABOUT THE AUTHOR

Dr. Ty-Ron M. O. Douglas is Assistant Professor and PK–12 Program Coordinator in the Department of Educational Leadership and Policy Analysis at the University of Missouri. He earned a Ph.D. in curriculum and teaching with a concentration in cultural studies and a Post-Master's Certificate in school administration. Dr. Douglas' work explores the intersections between identity, community space (e.g. barbershops, sports fields, and churches) and the socio-cultural foundations of leadership and education. He was awarded the 2013–2014 UNCG School of Education's Early Career Award, a 2013 Distinguished Dissertation Award by the American Educational Research Association (AERA), and the 2016 Mizzou College of Education Early Career Outstanding College Teaching Award. Dr. Douglas has delivered keynotes, motivational talks, and lectures in Africa, Europe, Bermuda, Brazil, the Caribbean, and the United States. He has shared the stage with renowned motivational speaker "ET The Hip Hop Preacher" and served as an invited keynote speaker for the NCAA and the 2016 Sport Exchange Summit, drawing on his NCAA grant-funded study report on Black male student-athletes. Dr. Douglas' most recent publications have appeared in outlets such as *Educational Studies*, *The Urban Review*, *Teachers College Record*, and *Race, Ethnicity, and Education*. He is the co-editor and a contributing author of *12*

Shades of Man: Testimonies and Transitions to Manhood, and co-author, with his wife, of *So Amazing … Her Story: Secrets to Finding and Keeping a Great Man.* The co-editor of a 2016 special issue (with Drs. Chezare Warren and Tyrone C. Howard) on the My Brother's Keeper Initiative in *Teachers College Record,* Dr. Douglas is operationalizing his scholarship for maximum community impact.

ROCHELLE BROCK & CYNTHIA DILLARD
Executive Editors

Black Studies and Critical Thinking is an interdisciplinary series which examines the intellectual traditions of and cultural contributions made by people of African descent throughout the world. Whether it is in literature, art, music, science, or academics, these contributions are vast and far-reaching. As we work to stretch the boundaries of knowledge and understanding of issues critical to the Black experience, this series offers a unique opportunity to study the social, economic, and political forces that have shaped the historic experience of Black America, and that continue to determine our future. Black Studies and Critical Thinking is positioned at the forefront of research on the Black experience, and is the source for dynamic, innovative, and creative exploration of the most vital issues facing African Americans. The series invites contributions from all disciplines but is specially suited for cultural studies, anthropology, history, sociology, literature, art, and music.

Subjects of interest include (but are not limited to):

- EDUCATION
- SOCIOLOGY
- HISTORY
- MEDIA/COMMUNICATION
- RELIGION/THEOLOGY
- WOMEN'S STUDIES

- POLICY STUDIES
- ADVERTISING
- AFRICAN AMERICAN STUDIES
- POLITICAL SCIENCE
- LGBT STUDIES

For additional information about this series or for the submission of manuscripts, please contact Dr. Brock (University of North Carolina at Greensboro) at r_brock@uncg.edu or Dr. Dillard (University of Georgia) at cdillard@uga.com.

To order other books in this series, please contact our Customer Service Department:

(800) 770-LANG (within the U.S.)
(212) 647-7706 (outside the U.S.)
(212) 647-7707 FAX

Or browse online by series at www.peterlang.com.